T0150815

The
Break

Born on the Wirral, Steve Cummings was a track rider for Team GB from 2001 to 2007 before racing for top pro teams including Team Sky, BMC and MTN-Qhubeka-Dimension Data. He achieved two of the most spectacular stage race victories in recent Tour de France history: at the mountain-top finish in Mende in 2015 and through the Pyrenees in 2016, as well as taking a stage in the Tour of Spain. He was crowned both British Time Trial and Road-Race National Champion in 2017, the first rider to 'do the double' since Tour de France star David Millar ten years earlier. Recently retired, he is now development director at Ineos Grenadiers.

Alasdair Fotheringham is a British journalist writing mainly on cycling, Spain and Americana music. Based in Spain for the last 30 years, he is a freelance foreign correspondent for *The Times* and *Al Jazeera* and on cycling for the 'I' newspaper and *Cyclingnews*. Apart from covering the Tour de France since 1992, he has written four books, including the first English-language biographies of cycling's greatest ever mountain climber, Federico Martín Bahamontes, aka The Eagle of Toledo, as well as a history of the 1998 Tour de France. Alasdair first met and interviewed Steve during the Spring Classics races of 2007, somewhere in darkest west Flanders.

Steve Cummings

The
Break

Life as a Cycling Maverick

With Alasdair Fotheringham

ALLEN&UNWIN

First published in hardback in Great Britain in 2022 by
Allen & Unwin, an imprint of Atlantic Books Ltd.

This paperback edition published in Great Britain in 2023 by
Allen & Unwin, an imprint of Atlantic Books Ltd.

10 9 8 7 6 5 4 3 2 1

A CIP catalogue record for this book is available from the British Library.

Paperback ISBN: 978 1 83895 393 5
E-book ISBN: 978 1 83895 392 8

Printed and bound by CPI Group (UK) Ltd, Croydon, CR0 4YY

Allen & Unwin
An imprint of Atlantic Books Ltd
Ormond House
26–27 Boswell Street
London
WC1N 3JZ

www.atlantic-books.co.uk

To my Mum, Lesley. I'm eternally grateful for everything. You encouraged us but didn't pressure us. You supported us but didn't let us forget our roots. You dedicated your life to helping us grow. Every day is a blessing thanks to you. I will continue to try and improve day by day. Thank you for all the wonderful memories. See you soon.

Contents

Foreword

Geraint Thomas

When I first met Steve, I was definitely nervous. The first time I'd come across him was reading about him in *Cycling Weekly* when he'd won the Eddie Soens as a junior. That was impressive enough. Then he and Brad Wiggins were about five or six years older than me and what they were doing, road racing and track racing and World Championships and so on, they were the things I wanted to do in my career.

On top of that, when we actually met face to face the first time, I had just moved into the GB senior track team pursuit squad, and even though he was one of the younger blokes in it, Steve was already one of the leaders and driving forces. He was hungry for it – you could just see that in him – and I really admired him and wanted to have the same attitude.

At the same time, I was definitely nervous – not just because of what he'd done as a racer; it was him being a Scouser as well, and you'd hear stories about them too! Seriously, though, when I joined the group, to my relief I found he was very approachable. At the same time, no matter what it was, Steve always had this attitude: 'I'm doing all this to be successful; why aren't you?'

Steve wanted everyone around him to have that same outlook and when they couldn't manage to do that, he struggled with it a bit. In team pursuit you're reliant on the other guys to be as professional and as good as you, and that goes from everybody rolling out on time together on group training rides to being 100 per cent committed to the racing. Yet he was super-determined and wanted to do everything right too, and fortunately I was of a similar mentality so I ended up being quite close to him.

I think where we had our best times together was at Quarrata in 2008 or so, when we were racing for the same team, Barloworld, on the road, but I was focused on the track and the Olympics too. It was all part of a learning process to be a good road racer, but at the same time I was more of a track rider and the road was more of a tool to get fit for that.

There was a good group of us sharing the flat and then meeting with everybody in the piazza in Quarrata for a coffee before training. It was a nice lifestyle, and serious too; if we had to do five hours' training, more often than not we'd do five and a half or six. Then in the second part of my time there, it was harder for me, because I'd been part of the British Cycling Academy and suddenly I found I didn't have the support every day which I'd been used to. I was out there doing it alone. But while I was young and single at that point, Steve was there with Nicky and they really looked after me, cooking me food and so on. In that way, Steve is a very caring guy and having them both around was just what I needed.

In the two years he spent at Sky, the situation was new for them but obviously everybody at the top, be it Dave Brailsford or Rod Ellingworth or Tim Kerrison or Shane Sutton, had Brad as their main concern. I think Steve would probably have felt, 'Hang on, there are another twenty-five guys in the team too.' Everybody got dragged a bit into doing the same as what Brad was doing, and that probably wound Steve up.

The main thing I recollect at Sky was seeing him getting pulled this way and that way, while he's someone who likes to have his plan and go full bore on it. And when that gets chopped and changed five or six times within a few weeks, that's frustrating – and Steve was asking why it was happening.

Fortunately, there was a golden period for him later on, because there were two or three years where everything clicked for him and there was a time you'd go, 'Ah, today's a breakaway day; Steve's going to win.' And he would go and just win, stage after stage and then the Tour of Britain on top of that. It was great to see him get the recognition and success he deserved, because I knew he'd worked so hard and was so determined to get there.

Now having him at Ineos has worked out very well for me, because – like I'm writing here – I've grown up with him as a racer. He's somebody who's been in the peloton with me ever since I started and he's someone I can talk to about anything on my mind, not just the bike racing.

If you wanted me to pinpoint the main reason why Steve succeeded, it's the way he sees bike racing, his willingness to try something new, to do something differently. Those are his strongest characteristics even though I think that might have been a problem too when he was younger. He was maybe overthinking things and working out how to deal with that.

But then when it all clicked for him, he'd learned to use his gifts in the right way. There are so many guys out there who are strong, but Steve didn't just have the legs, he had the brains and the head for it all as well and that was his big advantage. Ever since I first met him, in fact, Steve has always being thinking outside the box.

Preface

The Landmark That Wasn't

I've always liked breaks in bike races. For what they are, visually, for one thing, but also for how they're created. There's something about a rider winning alone and ahead of the main field that always looks good. But it feels good as well. You know it's been born out of strength, for one thing, but there are tactics, foresight, experience and race-reading ability as well. Some more, some less, but they all count, they all contribute, and they all make that kind of winning even more special. At the same time you know a breakaway victory is always a win against the odds, one for the underdog. So it appeals to the romantic in me as well.

To be honest, what I also liked about them was that from a very young age, I was very good at getting into breaks too, either alone or with others. The only problem was I didn't really have the kind of perspective to appreciate how good I was.

For example, for many people, the first time I took a landmark, trademark breakaway solo win was when I raced the Eddie Soens Memorial Race in Liverpool in 1999. It was a handicap race ridden round laps of Aintree racecourse: it was open to all categories, one of the first events of the British cycling season and traditionally one of the biggest as well.

Growing up on the Wirral, there was no escaping that race if you wanted to show how good you were. It didn't matter that I was only seventeen. Or that I had never ridden it before. People in the Merseyside area and down at the Eureka cafe – a local Mecca for cyclists that's sadly closed down now – were always saying, 'Oh, you're doing the Soens?' 'I'm sure you're doing the Soens,' 'You'll be doing the Soens, yeah?' So that was it, then, as soon as I was old enough, it was, 'OK, whatever, I'm doing the Soens.'

The weather on the day was terrible. Five degrees and rain. But there was still a good crowd gathered round the finish, maybe up to a hundred or so. I wasn't nervous beforehand, I was looking forward to it. After all, it was my first race of the year. My dad came and drove me over in the car, but he wasn't normally overly pushy or expectant about races and the Soens that year wasn't an exception. To be honest, I don't think I'd have listened to what he'd have said anyway – truthfully, does anyone ever listen to their dad? He preferred to be practical and put me in touch with good people that he thought might be able to help me. But when I got out on to the course, in any case, it didn't matter who backed me or supported me; I knew I was doing this on my own.

The key move happened when I got into a break of four with my regular training partner, Mark Baker, which was part of the plan we'd created beforehand about dropping all the older guys and getting ahead of the field. But then there was another lad from Preston, Iain Armstrong, who wasn't in on the plan but who was fine with us two because he'd been up there in the same race the previous year and he knew what he was doing.

However, the man who definitely wasn't part of the plan in the break was Phil Bayton, a real star veteran, the 'Staffordshire Engine' as he was known. Being a mouthy, punky sort of rider I kept on saying to him, 'Fucking hell, come through and give us a turn,' – riding on the front of the break or peloton to keep the pace going and allow the other riders to rest a little from their effort in your slip-stream – which was more than a bit disrespectful to one of GB's cycling heroes of the era. But at the time, in my defence, I was so new to the scene I had no idea who he actually was.

Then respect due or no respect due, I dropped them all. I did the last three laps of the Eddie Soens on my own. I don't think I ever really jumped away. I just killed them, one by one. But as I rode towards victory, for lap after lap, rather than savouring this as the glorious start to my budding career as a breakaway specialist, was I thinking, 'This is something special' or 'At your age it doesn't get bigger than this' or even 'Treasure it, mate, well done'?

No. I was thinking about how many Bosswipes I'd be taking home.

Bosswipes were (and are) good for cleaning your bike – they're like industrial baby wipes but stronger – and that year in the Soens, the company that made Bosswipes were spon-soring the primes, the prizes that were on offer for leading the race at different points of the event. And I was quite greedy when we were in our break. I wanted to win all of the primes. No mercy. No gifts.

So after I'd won, I remember feeling rich, because I'd made £100 or £200 or whatever. But I remember feeling particularly pleased that we drove away with my dad's car packed to the ceiling with Bosswipes. Two different types, boxes as big as a breakfast cereal packet, and a huge tub of Bosswipe gel cleaner for your hands, which lasted me for years.

And the win itself? People at the Eureka used to harp on about the Soens for months and how much it mattered like it was the World Cup final or something, but at the time to me it seemed insignificant. Plus I had this thing at the time that if I did something good, I'd put it behind me straight away and move on to the next objective.

The problem was, fundamentally, I don't think I was rounded enough as a person at that time to appreciate what I'd achieved. Which was a pity because my next win on the road, as a professional, took the best part of a decade to happen. And my first Grand Tour stage win took nearly another five years after that.

What those victories have in common, of course, with the one at the Soens is that my wins were nearly all taken from breakaways – often on the so-called 'transition' or 'medium-mountain' stages. These are the days in a race when the battle for the overall win is put on hold because the terrain is challenging, but not quite hard enough for the big names to risk attacking and losing more than they gain in the process. These kinds of stages are the best days for the outsiders in the peloton, to shine in breaks. They're days for the non-conformists and for the dark horses. For the guys, like me, who were pretty good at everything but with no standout talent, and yet who were determined to keep thinking outside the box until we did win. Because we don't – with no disrespect intended – simply settle for working for a team leader as the be-all and end-all of their career, rather we know we can never go for the win in the Tour de France. But we do want our own share of the glory all the same.

At this point I should make it clear that no two breakaway specialists use exactly the same strategies for winning. Some, like one of Germany's former top racers, Jens Voigt, apparently do it almost purely through driving themselves through their pain barriers and hurting themselves: if he was famous for that phrase of his, 'Shut up, legs', surely must have been for a reason.

But I wasn't like that, I wanted to win by maximizing my performance in all areas, not just going into the hurt locker deeper than anyone else. You could say I was trying to race with my brain and not my legs. But to do that, to get from the Soens at Aintree racecourse to becoming one of the international peloton's best-known riders for getting in breakaways (and winning, which is the hard part), took a lot of hard thinking and a lot of trial and error, a lot of finding out what I didn't want too, as well as hard graft. Until – finally – I paved a way forward that brought me success not just occasionally, but in race after race.

And because it wasn't all about pain, the lessons I learned in those twenty years can be applied not only in cycling, but in all walks of life. What I want to show in this book is how being a top breakaway specialist can help normal people succeed. Because it's about making the best of your abilities and how to focus on seizing your opportunity when it comes.

You might even win a few Bosswipes while you're at it too.

Chapter 1

Doughnuts

Maybe it was to do with growing up on the Wirral in a working-class family, or maybe it was my own personality, but one of the key lessons cycling has taught me is that if you look hard enough, the most unexpected raw materials can help you attain your objective. Like, for example, doughnuts.

This happened just before I won the Soens, when I was seventeen, and I had Mark Baker as my regular training partner. Mark was ideal in some ways as he was an extremely good racer in GB's National Road squad. But on the downside, his dad bought him all the flash kit right down to the Oakley glasses and Carnac shoes, the works, and every time he said, 'Steve, why don't you get these new tyres?' I had to admit I felt peer pressure. The thing was I was only earning £8 a week on a paper round, which really wasn't the kind of money that would get me that kind of high-end equipment.

So I put my thinking cap on and hit on the scheme of selling doughnuts at school. And it worked out really well. I'd get a first paper round done super-early, then I'd do a second one,

1

then just before school I'd go to Tesco, where at the time you could buy ten jam doughnuts for a pound. I'd buy fifty doughnuts, sometimes seventy, and by selling them for 20p each I'd make £7 a day. Put together with the money from my two paper rounds, it all went on getting better cycling equipment.

It was never quite enough. If Mark had Oakleys, I'd still have to settle for the Brikos, a cheaper kind. On top of which he'd started racing earlier than me and his bike was lighter than mine. But thanks to Tesco's doughnuts, when we both got away in the Soens in the winning break that year, the playing field was a lot more level.

It was the same kind of DIY initiative that helped me to my breakthrough win at the 'schoolboy' category, aged fifteen, when I won one of that level's biggest one-day races, the GHS 10 Mile individual time trial. I was riding on a bike that had been put together starting from, literally, nothing. Based entirely on parts begged, borrowed and not quite stolen from friends, the construction process consisted of, 'Oh, we've got this bit, let's put this bit on to this,' and 'Then we can add this,' and 'Then we can add this.' The part of the process that nearly defeated us was trying to fit the crank on to the bottom bracket. So we went round to my trainer at the time, Keith Boardman – and that name should ring a bell with most readers, or at least his son Chris should do – and we cut up a Coke can and made a kind of shim around the bottom bracket axle. Then I put the crank on to make the axle wider, and we drove south to wherever the race was held, with me down to compete using a bike which actually moved thanks to a fixed wheel with an old tri spoke that had belonged to Chris at some stage and a rear disc wheel on loan from The

2

Bike Factory. Somehow, utterly improbably, we had created the bike though, and I ended up winning the GHS Schoolboy 10 Mile Time Trial on it too.

Being resourceful with what you had at your disposal was one area I realized I had to get good in if I wanted to be a good cyclist. Another life lesson was learning about how to turn things you didn't like into something beneficial. I hated school, for example, and wasn't a good student, so I'd try to bunk off as many lessons as I could to ride my bike. Particularly religious education.

After I'd won the Schoolboy 10 I think the teachers realized I was doing something relatively productive compared to the rest of the kids playing truant. So I realized that was the perfect moment to have some off-the-record discussions with them, and rather than getting myself thrown out of RE class by making trouble, from then on I knew some teachers would turn a blind eye if I disappeared early on Tuesday afternoons to go ride my bike before it got too dark.

But there's only so much you can do for yourself at that age, of course. I wouldn't have won that Schoolboy 10, for example, if it hadn't been for a kind-hearted big guy we knew locally as Stevie Light. Stevie wasn't a bike rider, but he just liked cycling and he was good enough to drive me and Mark to races. Others I'd like to thank here and now include Alison France, Jack McAllister (more on those two later), Stan Moly, Danny MacD, Tempo, Big Kev, Chubbie, Woodsie, Bobby Mac, Keith and Carol, Mike and Pat... it's a long list! Key to my progress in cycling, though, were my mum and dad, who although there wasn't any history of major sport in the family, both always thought lots of cycling as a hobby.

My dad, Dave, who was a policeman in Liverpool, where they're both from, was a bit nuts about sport himself. He'd run to work and then ride home. My mum, our Les, was really into running too. She did a marathon when she was forty in under four hours and she was holding down a full-time job as an NHS receptionist as well. For me as a kid, football and cycling were the two things I liked the most. But my individualism started coming out pretty early on, and I left off football even though I loved it – and still do – because I sort of felt I was overly reliant on the team and couldn't control the way things played out if it was you and ten other guys on the pitch. For me, that was frustrating. Plus I wasn't good enough.

At the same time, when I was a little kid I was always riding my bike, round and round the block on the housing estate where we lived in Pensby on the Wirral. I must admit, though, that the 1992 Olympics, when Chris Boardman had his breakthrough by winning gold, it went completely over my head. But I liked the freedom cycling gave you regardless, and when I got older, the way it got me to places I'd never been to before like Delamere Forest, the Cheshire Plain, sometimes a bit of North Wales. Then there was the bit of banter with the other guys on the training rides too.

At first, when I was eleven, they wouldn't let me sign up for Birkenhead North End cycling club because they weren't insured for kids. But we got round it through my dad joining. Even before that I'd go out with my dad and my elder brother and his mates out from home in Pensby along the Chester High Road – which you wouldn't dream of doing now as it's way too dangerous – to the Eureka cafe. I remember the first time I did that I probably only rode eight miles in total and

I fell off on the way home and cut my knee because I was so fucked, but I didn't care. I loved what I was doing.

There was a bit of racing right from the start in my club, when we'd meet up on a Thursday at the community centre, have a cup of tea then go on a club run which normally involved either racing for town signs or riding to a climb, which most or all of us would race up as well. But what really got me into competitive cycling were our camping holidays in France when I was a teenager. I remember how everyone on the campsite would be sitting round drinking beers in their tank tops in some dodgy bar and watching the Tour de France. At that age it felt like not only the whole of France was watching, but all the Dutch and Belgian tourists were too – everybody in the rest of Europe in fact. I didn't understand the race, but I wanted to understand why all these people were drawn to it, and that way the Tour and road racing got under my skin.

My dad was really encouraging about it all, given I was so committed. He even helped me avoid certain classes at school to go riding, so if I said to him, 'Dad, I've got Spanish today,' and in fact I'd go out on my bike, he'd turn a blind eye. My mum kind of knew that I was not a good pupil, but as she was always at work throughout the day, it wasn't such a big deal. My dad, though, worked shifts, and sometimes I'd get his shift wrong, come home from school early and he'd be sitting there on the sofa, asking me what I was doing. But it was fine. I'd say I was going out on my bike and he'd say, 'Don't tell your mother,' and we'd leave it at that.

Dad used to take me down to the cycling club as well in the community centre, which was where all my mates and a few other people I'd know would go and drink and smoke weed outside. Being very glad it was usually dark when club night got under way, I'd try to avoid being seen by my mates going in. But I couldn't dodge a few embarrassing moments when the old guys in the club would be slagging off 'those bloody scallies' who had lit fires outside the fire escape door, and I knew exactly who the bloody scallies were.

There weren't many young people at the time doing cycling. Sometimes you'd go down to Pensby Park on a Thursday evening and there'd maybe be only five or six riders actually there for racing. But I had the backing of my parents, there was the crowd at the club and the Eureka cafe that I'd go racing and riding with as well, and people from other clubs like Port Sunlight Wheelers were very supportive too.

Up until I was thirteen or fourteen, I'd been on a mountain bike, working my way through the sizes. One high point of that time was getting a really good one, a Diamondback, which I managed to blag my father into buying for me and I cannot for the life of me remember how I convinced him. But there was one guy, Jack McAllister, who'd only met me once at the club but straight away he lent me his wife's bike to be my first proper road bike, which I used through the winter while I saved up to buy my own. There were a lot of good-hearted people there too, like Jack, who'd take responsibility for me on the training rides because my dad couldn't get out. Or Alison France, who helped with expenses, while somebody else would provide petrol money. I was really fortunate to have these people around me, and at places like the Eureka, I had a place where I fitted in.

This was very different to school where they might have turned a blind eye to my playing truant, but until I won that Schoolboy 10 race I'd have to tell everybody my age I was going to be a boxer to stop the other dropouts asking me why I wasn't smoking dope and drinking like they were.

Then by the time I hit sixteen, I really committed to working with Keith Boardman and I'd go out training three or four times a week, twice at weekends. One day off a week and that was it. I used to listen a lot to Keith – he talked a lot of sense – and you couldn't help but think that he had to be right because of the way Chris had progressed. On top of that he definitely liked a plan and everything had to be objective-driven, so if we were going to do something it had to have a purpose. One slight issue was that Keith was always trying to get me to do more time trialling – Chris's speciality on the road – but even at that age, although I could see how beneficial time trialling was, I wasn't so keen on it. Riding up and down a dual carriageway by myself, as you did so often in time trials back then, didn't appeal to me that much. And some people love the equipment side of it, but to me the idea of being able to make a difference through aerodynamics when I didn't have a big budget didn't appeal either. Finally, at that time, I liked being in company when I rode my bike. So we eventually reached an agreement that every road race I did, I'd do a time trial as well and we went on working together, which was great.

Obviously, being from the Wirral and with Keith as my trainer, I knew Chris at the time too, but I didn't go out riding with him much because he obsessed with getting every tiny detail right and although I completely get that now, at the time, as a teenager, it wasn't much fun. When I did go out training with him, he was scarily serious. You'd tell a joke to break the ice early on and he wouldn't laugh, and then you'd think, 'Fucking hell, we've got four hours riding ahead of us here, Chris.' So although I had and have huge respect for what he'd done, it wasn't a tremendously appealing prospect.

I was always grateful to get a chance to talk to the pros though. I remember after the Soens win, when I got into the GB Junior team, another star of the 1980s and 1990s, Robert Millar (now Philippa York), came out to a training camp we had organized for us in Spain and I had a chat with him during a training ride. It was so rare for us to be able to get to talk to pros at that time that any information at all about what it was like in that world was like gold dust.

Another pro I came across early on was Max Sciandri, who is half-Italian and half-British. Max was going to become a very close friend, but when I first met him, at the Junior World Championships in Verona in 1999 when he was with FDJ, I was just star-struck. We were all sitting round a table having dinner and he'd just come in from racing one of France's biggest races, Paris–Tours. We were nudging each other and saying, 'Oh my God, it's Max Sciandri,' and he came over, sat down and said, 'Hey, how's it going, guys?' I was so nervous I was sweating! But he had a really friendly way of doing things: 'How long did you guys ride today?'; 'Hey, I went and did the climb, it's nice.' Even if I remember at that time his English wasn't great – 'What do you call those little pies again that taste of nothing? Oh, yeah, York-s-hire [pronounced Max-style with three syllables] pies' – it meant the world to me to have just had even a brief contact with him. But I didn't see him for ages after that, until he started working again for British Cycling and helping them place riders, like me, in pro teams.

Apart from riding under Keith's tuition, I was broadening my talents in other ways: I started going up to Kirkby Track League up on the far side of Liverpool and that was a scream. The journey itself was always fun, four of us driving up there as we were crammed into this small van with only two seats. So there'd be two of us in the back along with the bikes, slamming around on the corners of the Mersey Tunnel, which is quite twisty. There were some real characters around like Pete and Lee Matthews, and I loved the racing: we did everything – points, Devils... we had different groups too, A, B and C, depending on how you were performing. Normally, if you were a junior you'd be in with the Bs, but I was good enough for the commissaires to put me in with the As. However, they'd never call you by name. It'd be 'You're in group A, rider,' or 'Watch your line, rider.' Odd, but I didn't mind.

Then if the weather was bad at the weekend, and I couldn't get out on the road, I would head over to Manchester track with Graham Weigh, a big cycling fan who has one of the biggest bike shops in North Wales just over the border from the Wirral, and where I did a bit of work. I'd do the drop-in induction sessions at the Manchester track centre and that was where I got an invite to the National Team Junior training session from Marshall Thomas, the guy running them at the time. That quickly got me an invite to the National Track Championships as a first-year junior, where I did the points race, with Bradley Wiggins as my biggest rival. Apart from being a year older than me, performance-wise Bradley was on another planet. But I qualified for the individual pursuit as well, so I was very quickly moving through the levels.

I'd got one big road win apart from the Soens in the bag too in 1999, when I took the Junior National Road Race. More than the victory in itself, I was proud of how I won, just riding off on my own again, and it made me think about what I could maybe do in the future. But I still couldn't believe that I could make money out of something I enjoyed so much.

Still, I looked at what that junior title meant I could do, which was to put me in the circle of British junior racers who could get away to race abroad. I wanted to move on and see what was next. And while it opened quite a few doors, I was still quite intermittent in terms of results, so I didn't develop a big ego from winning it. In the time trials for one thing, there was always Brad Wiggins who was always three minutes faster than me. That always helped put things in perspective.

Chapter 2
Dilemmas

A round this time my formal education experience was petering out. I'd managed to get out of my school in Pensby – it wasn't exactly full of drug dealers, but the teaching was far from great – and I went to work in a restaurant on the Wirral as a dishwasher. Academically, I was borderline although I did briefly manage to get into a good sixth-form college, at Calday, partly because I'd won the Schoolboy 10 race and they wanted some promising athletes, and partly because Mum had contacts. But although I was doing business studies, sports studies and maths there – and these three subjects I still like – it was a really affluent area and I didn't feel I fitted in. To make matters even worse, I got glandular fever and that set me back almost a year, so I went to work in a restaurant instead all the way through to the spring of 2001.

Ever since 1999 and the wins in the Soens and Nationals, apart from being on the GB Track squad, I'd been part of the GB Junior National Road team too. The only problem at that point was that it was run on a shoestring, and you'd barely get a jersey if you were part of it. You couldn't fault some of the staff though for trying their utmost and keeping our feet on the ground. Mike Taylor, the Junior National coach, was one guy I remember for being great as a trainer. He was a charming, wonderful person but he was fantastically straight-talking too, and after I'd won the Soens he'd take the piss out of me: 'So you think you're a superstar, now?' And I remember him calling another GB trainer 'about as much use as a fucking chocolate fireguard'. Mike had worked with top British cycling names like David Millar, John Herety and Charly Wegelius, and he'd tell funny stories about them, which kept us interested too. As a person he amused me, by doing things like happily swearing away if we were talking in the team, but abruptly stopping whenever anybody's parents turned up.

Blessed with a strong anti-establishment outlook (which I also appreciated), Mike was honest enough to recognize that as we were operating with such a tiny budget, that meant we had to keep our options open. Apart from the restaurant work, my other business in those days was selling cigarettes when we went to France for race trips. So Mike would say on the Channel ferry when he saw me, 'What the fucking hell are you doing buying 1000 cigarettes; are you smoking?' and I'd say, 'No, no, I sell them,' to which he'd say, 'Right, we'll buy some fucking more then – come on.'

Cycling had, indirectly, introduced me to my future wife Nicky too. Her boss at her place of work was in our cycling club and his son was a year younger than me so we all used to go riding a lot. Then I'd go into their shop a lot as well and 'run into' Nicky. She used to swim at county level competitions, so she understood sport, which helped ease things along. At first I'd just joke around, asking when she'd come on a date with me and how 'you should get rid of that boyfriend of yours.' And eventually she did get rid of him and started going out with me.

I wanted to be on my bike and pretty much nothing else, and I'd started working hard in the restaurant, doing more than twenty-five hours a week there as well. I'd start training at 7 a.m. then ride straight to the restaurant, grab lunch and eat while doing the vegetables and then head off to the gym afterwards. It was a great time in some ways as the chef and I got on very well and we'd be listening to rap like 2Pac and the Notorious B.I.G. all day. But as Christmas 2000 approached it got pretty crazy. I was helping the chef doing overtime and ended up doing fourteen-hour shifts, before which I'd been on my bike. So I was quite relieved when I finally quit in March 2001 and concentrated fully on racing instead.

Could I have gone straight on to the road and left the track behind at that point? Possibly, but at the time you didn't have that many British pros out there – Chris had just retired and Sean Yates and Robert Millar had long gone, so there was only David Millar, Roger Hammond and Jeremy Hunt at the top level. It didn't feel like a realistic option. I didn't know the people to contact or the best way to go about it, and probably I just wasn't proactive enough either.

I'd also been drawn into the structure that GB track racing seemed to offer so clearly. I'd got used to that struc-tured approach with Keith, but I'd stopped working with him because he thought he'd done all he could to help me. But things gradually got harder with the track too, because

I never found anyone to take over Keith's role until I came across Simon Jones and Steve Peters, and that gap meant that when I went from Junior to Under-23 in 2000, suddenly I got into a real mess. After years of moving forwards, albeit patchily, I found that I didn't have that sense of direction I so badly needed.

I'd be lying if I wrote that for the first two decades of my life I knew that I was definitely going to be a racing cyclist. But I'd be lying too if I didn't admit I really needed help to work out how much I wanted to buy into track racing and how much I wanted to buy into road racing.

That help didn't really arrive for another four years. So it was just as well I wasn't going off the rails completely. It was more when I hit twenty I had got a bit lost and just did what my mates were doing. My elder brother, who'd left home first, was looking after a pub, which didn't help, as after going out on the bike, I'd go down to the pub myself.

But after the Antwerp World Championships, when GB offered me some regular funding and things got more serious, in the autumn of 2001 I moved on myself. Things were not easy at home at that point, and my two brothers and I were a handful to say the least. This made things hard to say the least for my mum and dad and at times I wanted to be anywhere else but there. I needed to figure out how to get out.

Fortunately, that opportunity came, thanks to the track. I had got as far as the GB senior team pursuit squad that year, when I first started training with them, but up to that point cycling still almost felt like a hobby. Even getting into the seniors hadn't seemed like a massive deal, as somebody had said, 'He's doing all right, let's put him in.' But after I'd been working in a kitchen doing dishes, it was something to enjoy, particularly as the World Class Performance Plan, which later transformed British Cycling, was still in its infancy. It hadn't been that long, in fact, since people were still doing full-time 'day jobs' to be part of the national team. The competition to get into the team was fierce, but there weren't so many people and the level wasn't amazing. Suddenly, though, when Dave Brailsford got a much bigger role in the GB team and Simon Jones took over in the track programme, the whole track programme moved up a gear and, out of nowhere, it became a career option.

There were catches. The management knew I was a bit of a lad so they said the only way they'd give me the funding on the GB track programme was if I moved up to Manchester, which meant I lived with Paul Manning in Stockport for six months. When I was with them I was 100 per cent committed, and Nicky used to drive up to Stockport once or twice a week, and because of her things started to settle down more as well.

I talked it over with Simon Jones and Nicky and we moved back to the Wirral and rented a place in Moreton – though we then saved up a bit of money and that later got us a down payment on a house in a nicer part of the Wirral, in Irby.

I'd also had a brutal wake-up call about the effects of alcohol. Another guy I'd train with, Mark Bell, was really strong as a racer, but at that time he had a drink problem so you'd not see him for a week or a month at a time. During the Commonwealth Games in Manchester in 2002 I went to his flat, and it was in an awful mess. That really planted a seed in my head about drinking and I basically stopped then. It got to the point where I had to stop seeing Mark too.

I didn't want to do that, but he'd got into a vicious circle and I couldn't do anything more for him. Besides, I was heading towards my own personal moment of crisis too.

*

One morning in 2004, British Cycling boss Dave Brailsford summoned me into his office at the Manchester Track Centre, sat me down and gave it to me straight: 'The problem I have with you,' he said, 'is I can't figure you out. When you want you're the best rider out there we've got, but I don't see it enough. I need you to be consistent. I need you to buy in.'

I didn't know what to answer. At that time, my cycling life consisted mainly of racing regularly all year with Britain's senior team pursuit track squad and I had been doing that since 2000. But inside myself, I didn't have any sense of direction, and it didn't help either that when that conversation happened, I had just lost three people I was quite close to in a very short period of time. My grandmother had died and then Dan Baird, a young friend of mine who lived up the road, died, and that was a big shock. Finally, a good friend of my dad's, Doug Phillips, a really special guy who used to go to the track, died too. It was very tough because they all meant a lot to me.

My personal crisis had got to the point where I had been in France on a road race that year – something we did as a way of building up our resistance, or endurance as it's known in cycling, for our track racing – and rather than strengthening my resistance, somewhere in the middle of the event I had broken down and started crying. Basically, I hated it all.

*

How did I get out of this situation and move on? Probably the biggest element to all of my moving ahead was what I learned from Steve Peters, who was working with British Cycling as a psychologist, even though he'd trained as a psychiatrist. Just when I had lost the plot and had had that conversation with Dave Brailsford about buying in, Steve came into the velodrome in Manchester and began sitting me down for chats. And apart from helping me get over the people I'd lost, he also helped me enormously with what was essentially a fear of failure.

Up until then, I'd never really committed to anything on the track, because no matter what, when I say I'll commit to something I'll do it. So when Steve asked what my biggest fear was, I said 'that I wouldn't be able to do it'. But over the course of several sessions, he gently outlined to me that if I didn't try, then I'd never be able to get there. That was like a switch that flicked to 'on'. After that, every time my leg went over the bike I was determined to give it 100 per cent. There was no more fucking around.

In fact, I went to the opposite extreme. I then became so scared of not getting the best out of myself, it was like I was on a mission. Failure is defined as not being able to do something, but after my work with Steve I didn't care if I could do it or not. All I cared about was getting the best out of myself; I had to do that, and if I failed, I failed. But if that was good enough, then great.

Steve worked closely alongside Brailsford, of course, who also kept tabs on me. Dave told me I was to ring him every

Monday morning at 9 a.m. and tell him what was going on, how I was, what I'd been up to. Not just training, everything.

But I didn't actually need to call Dave. From that point on, I drove myself so hard and it was so fucking intense that at times it was ridiculous.

Imagine your degree of commitment to something as a kind of continuum, where one end of it is a completely intense, obsessive attitude, and the other is you're not buying it at all or doing anything – you don't give a fuck. The first key to anything consistent, like Dave wanted me to be, is to find whatever is sustainable, the right balance for varying periods of time, depending on the objective, and in a way that meant I stayed happy. So I would go right to the obsessive end of the continuum, take the fewest of a few steps back and boom! That's what's became sustainable for me.

As I stepped up our game and I became a senior member of the squad, I grew much harsher and demanding with everybody, including myself. I developed the same attitude that the most dedicated racers have, guys like Rohan Dennis, the former World Time Trial Champion. If somebody's not as committed as he is, Rohan gets very upset about every single question, such as the famous occasion when it wasn't clear if the right skinsuit for his TT was available.

I was intense. I used to call my team-mates out. Like Rohan I had legitimate frustrations at times, but they'd overspill and came out in ways that weren't effective at getting results, like questioning their commitment. But it was partly because my communication skills weren't great at the time, and partly that you know young guys come in thinking it's an adventure or a bit of a joke, and I wanted to try to get them to see how much I was relying on them and we, the team, needed them. We'd worked exceptionally hard at getting it right and the squad had got bronze in Sydney's Olympics, and then we got silver in Athens in 2004, but we kept on getting stuck on silver, silver, silver, pretty much always to the Australians. The whole question was, what more did we need to do?

*

On paper, the team pursuit looks pretty straightforward. Four people in each team line up on opposite sides of the track; they race each other for 4 kilometres in a single line, and the first team to get three of its riders to complete the distance is the one that wins. But in fact, it's so simple that no detail can be overlooked, from the speed that you start, to following your team-mate's back wheel at exactly the right distance, through to getting your changeovers and the communication between all four of you to be as smooth and effective as possible. You have to be incredibly concentrated, particularly as it's the fastest endurance event in track racing and you know the smallest error can blow it all apart.

The velodrome itself is key too, because – for example – on every track there's always a slightly different point where it's best to do your changeover, and it is only with time where you feel where it is and can be sure that your changeovers are in tune with the nature of the boards. There are lots of advantages to getting your changeovers right, but one is you're not dropping into the line again in the straightaways. Instead, using the steepest points, you're flung back down where you want to be thanks to gravity and don't have to accelerate to regain contact with the line.

Getting back in is crucial too, and that changes a lot with each track. In Manchester, say, where you're so used to that, it's automatic, and in any case it is a lovely big bowl. But some tracks have such long straightaways, it almost feels like you're going uphill in the middle and your cadence can drop off quite a lot. And the banking is so tight, you get flung round really hard.

A key point of a good change in a team pursuit is what's called 'delivery', which is how you get out of the front of the line and away from the team. In my mind, the last three pedal strokes before you do that are critical and that's when you really have to push away from the team, giving them a positive momentum. But if you're slowing up at the end of your effort, just before you do that push-away, then that has an opposite knock-on effect down the line, and then suddenly all the team is backing up, which is a disaster.

Then when you move out of the line, it is all about being able to produce a smooth arc as you do so. If you go up and down too fast, then you can scrub your speed off, and while doing it smoothly looks like a little bit of showboating – Bradley's very good at it – you do keep that momentum.

There are ways of checking each rider's delivery style: time splits on the turns each rider takes sometimes partly expose that positive or negative effect. Say somebody will do 14.4 seconds but then somebody will do 14.9 seconds, that's a huge difference, because you want an evenly timed split. However, it could perfectly well be that the third guy does an amazing turn of 14.5 seconds and 'redelivers' the team successfully again. But if we wanted to get that right, we found the best way was by putting timing devices at every ten metres around the track and that gave us the full profile of what was happening on each lap for each rider. (For the record the main riders at the time – 2003 or so – were Paul Manning, Chris Newton, Bryan Steel and me because Bradley and Rob Hayles were often off being road pros then, at FDJ and Cofidis.)

It was all painstakingly hard work. But it also shows how incredibly detailed an approach we took to try to improve, and with time we turned the changeovers in particular into an art form. Some things though we deliberately kept very simple, like communication between each rider, just yelling out 'hold' for hold your speed, or 'change' because you could feel the rider ahead was slowing down. Knowing what needed to be straightforward and what needed to be broken down into really detailed parts to make sure each bit worked right is one way of saying that it was all about the bigger picture. And in fact one of the most useful skills I learned through Steve Peters in that era was gaining perspective, as in 'it's only a bike race, no one's going to die.' When you're young, it does feel like life and death, and that's all you want to do, so that was particularly useful!

But Steve also helped with another technique called visualization, about what to do if you start to panic, and splitting the race into sections. My changeovers were already that practised that I could do them without thinking, and with the visualization, whenever I did a good one in training, I'd store it up and think, 'That's how I do it.' At times it felt like there were a million other things to learn to handle, even if it was actually quite simple. You'd feel like you could be able to do another half lap, but then coming towards it, you might start thinking you were tying up. There was having to remember every time that your entire turn doesn't finish when you swing out from the lead position, but when you rejoin the line. Thanks to Steve Peters, getting that sort of perspective and visualization on such techniques was really useful, because while there was a lot of sports science involved, it was always backed up with feelings.

It was never all about us, either. There was also the degree of crowd support: in Los Angeles, the crowds weren't ever good there, while in places like Manchester and Australia in the Commonwealth Games they were great. Then at the Olympics in Athens, where I was part of the squad that took silver in the team pursuit, the velodrome design was really cool, because it was on the edge of the Olympic areas and it was open-sided. So at night in particular and for the finals everybody would come past and look and you felt like the world was watching.

But in terms of visualization that's not such a big deal. You're in the zone, you do your work and you come out. And at that point in my career, having got through my phase of nearly going off the rails then getting ultra-committed, I was definitely fast getting to a point of I've been there, bought the T-shirt, now let's go and do something else.

*

Even in the final moments before a World Championships like Los Angeles in 2005, where we finally got that win we'd been looking for for so long, I didn't have any special structure to my personal countdown before I got on the bike. As a track rider, the thinking was that you had to be really fresh when you started your race, something I'm still not convinced about, but which meant there was a lot of free time. So I basically would go around talking to people. Anybody. I didn't want to sit in my room unless I deliberately wanted to sit there and think hard about the good changes, the good start... again, visualization. But then when that was done, I'd go and find anybody and have a chat and a bit of a laugh; just to keep my mind occupied.

Even when the final warm-up began and the 'rules' were simply visualize and don't fuck around, sometimes I'd relax even a bit more that way and end up talking to soigneurs before we began our ride. It was all a long way from other people who'd absolutely have to do twenty minutes on the rollers in silence as their way of dealing with the pressure. You'd respect that, and you'd know you'd never talk to Bradley, for example, because he wouldn't ever want to chat at all. But my way was five minutes on the rollers, put some chamois cream on if I had to and get a bottle, try to get a bit warm. I wasn't that scientific – I was what I called ballpark scientific, which to me meant use the science, follow the outline of the proposed warm-up and in the last five minutes don't talk to anybody because it's a distraction, but don't get preoccupied, stay very relaxed, and use your feelings as well. Above all, you have to look at it as just another effort, doing what you'd been trained to do. And with that outlook, at the end of the day it was all about going to see what you could do. There might have been a few fist bumps and talking ourselves up in the last minutes. But not much more.

In the final at Los Angeles we took on the Dutch but we'd got history in our favour – we'd always been better than them. We had an opportunity too, if I'm honest, because a lot of the top Australians, like Brad McGee, went off after the 2004 Olympics to concentrate fully on being road pros. So it was either then or never, and we didn't do a great time because the track was slow. While we were good, our victory was probably as much to do with the competition as anything else.

One odd moment of L.A. was when I said Merry Christmas on the winners' interview we did afterwards with the BBC. That was because somebody had asked me before what it felt like waiting for the final and I'd said it was like waiting for Christmas, meaning rather than fearing something you were looking forward to it. And I really was quite happy with my input and happy for Chris and Paul and Rob because they'd been trying to get that result a lot longer than me. But more than anything else I felt relief and just having that feeling was quite sad, particularly compared to how pleased I had felt when Cav and Rob Hayles unexpectedly won the Madison in Los Angeles, or how sorry I'd felt for Geraint, because he'd turned up there desperate to ride his bike, but couldn't race because he had crashed and had to have his spleen removed and was still recovering.

Essentially, I'd got to the point where I was just over it and there were still some very major things that needed to be sorted inside me. So when all the other pursuiters went off to a party afterwards to celebrate, I just went out to the velodrome car park to set up my road bike with Doctor Rog, because I wanted to sort out some shoes and cleats to try to go better as a road racer.

The biggest issue wasn't the cleats though, it was that no matter how much I committed, there was no getting away from the fact that I didn't do track for any particular reason any more, if I'm honest, beyond the financial.

This couldn't be underestimated. Like everybody else, I needed to have a wage of some kind, if only to get out of Moreton, the town on the Wirral where my girlfriend – now wife – Nicky and I were living. Our place there was not very nice – it backed on to some kind of football pitch or park and people tried to break into our house and into my car three times. We didn't have a great deal of money as, unlike most of the other members of the track team, I was paying rent – in our case £600 a month. Throw in petrol and a few bits of insurance and at times we were struggling to pay the bills.

But thanks to my work with Steve Peters I had become obsessed with getting the best out of myself and – ironically enough given he was the GB psychologist – rather than stick at the Team Pursuit, getting the best out of myself meant I had to stop it. I couldn't accept that I was reliant on three other people and four years waiting between one Olympics and the next was too long in my book. So I was increasingly certain that road racing was all I wanted to do.

Finally and thankfully, an answer of sorts presented itself. A second division Belgian team, Landbouwkrediet, reached a deal through my agent at the time, Richard Allchin, where I'd race for them during the road season in 2005, but I was free to do my training and stick with British Cycling's track programme at the same time.

This change of direction was partly because the guy in charge of the team pursuit at the time, Heiko Salzwedel, really believed in getting a massive road base for the endurance track squads. He'd sum up a weekly training programme as '200 kilometres, 220 kilometres, 240 kilometres, rest. 200, 220, 240, rest. 200, 220, 240, rest.' And we'd done a lot of road racing in 2004 in the lower category side of the professional scene, such as the Rás in Ireland, the Circuit des Mines in France and the Cinturón a Mallorca, but it was an expensive strategy. Putting us out with professional teams like Landbouwkrediet meant you didn't need to fund a sports director or support staff and then the rider would come back and do their track training.

So this move wasn't meant to be the start of a shift to road racing as a profession and indeed, after I'd done a year in Landbouwkrediet, the next year Ed Clancy and Paul Manning, two of the other men's team pursuiters, went to the same squad. But for me, the prospect of riding in Belgium for eight months a year meant I'd actually been able to find a way forward to something I wanted to do. It was the beginning of a whole new part of my career. Nicky was really supportive, as were my family. But I barely talked it through with people much, partly because I'm not given to shouting out that much about what I want to do. There was probably some underlying fear of failure in there too. And because so few people had succeeded in making it as pros on the continent, it did seem like a long shot. Unlike the track had always been though, this wasn't just a means to an end. Less than a year after that conversation with Dave Brailsford, I knew for sure which direction I wanted to go.

Chapter 3

Contrasts

After five years in the highly structured world of British track racing, my first steps as a professional road racer in mainland Europe were largely learning to live in a much more unpredictable kind of sporting world – and the opposite extremes of it too. It was a very steep learning curve as well. In just three seasons I went from racing in Landbouwkrediet, a poorly organized, underfunded and singularly unambitious squad, to Discovery Channel, one of the biggest and most powerful teams on the planet.

But it wasn't just the radically different workload, budgets, organization and personal goals I had in each – chasing breakaways in Landbouwkrediet, a team workhorse in Discovery Channel. In an uncertain, morally murky universe like professional cycling, I also came to appreciate how often the best strategy was to take care of yourself.

My self-reliance also increased considerably. For one thing, linguistically, I'd learned to fend for myself in some unexpected ways. Initially, I'd ferried myself back and forth to the UK between races, but Landbouwkrediet needed me closer at hand, given they never knew what races they'd be doing. The solution for this was for one of their sponsors, a Belgian couple I only ever knew as Jef the builder and his wife Marie-Claire, to put me up for the best part of two years. But they didn't speak any English. I didn't speak any Flemish. So we mainly communicated through a series of grunts.

If that sounds off-putting, at least that was a better system than how I communicated with my room-mate at Jef the builder's place. A former Under-23 world champion from Uzbekistan, Sergey Lagutin didn't speak a word of English beyond 'fucking shit' and a couple of phrases he picked up off films. On top of that, Sergey was as miserable as sin and always looked like he badly wanted to kill somebody. So for two years, despite sharing the same team and bedroom, we didn't exchange a single word.

(Funnily enough, after I had left Landbouwkrediet, Sergey moved on to race in the States, learned English and married over there too. When I ran into him one time at a race in Europe somewhere a few years later, he was all chirrupy and talkative, firing off phrases like 'Hey, dude, how's it going?' and 'Way to go.' It felt like a Martian programmed in North American slang had taken over his body.)

Language issues aside, there was a very different approach to racing. Almost as soon as I got there, I quickly appreciated Landbouwkrediet's main mission was not to win anything at all. Their main aim was to get in the breaks before the main action, not to actually go for the victory. If we did that successfully, even if or when we were brought back to the main peloton, we'd done our job. Again, a long way from the GB's near-obsession with winning.

Their laid-back attitude had quickly become apparent at their first training camp in a beach hotel near Livorno in north-western Italy. For some reason I was late getting to the camp, and my room-mate Ludo Dierckxsens was even later because he'd only been signed by the team at the last minute. But far from getting some high-intensity training to make up for lost time, the rides Landbouwkrediet asked us to do were crazy easy. It got to the point where often as I headed to the hotel lift after our morning's training, I would be saying to myself, 'Fucking hell, we're not even touching the pedals. I'm going faster on my own than in the group.'

Ludo and I were so concerned we were under-training that we both opted to stay on for another week after the camp and we went out for high-power rides instead with the top-level Fassa Bortolo squad, who were getting in their early season training in a nearby resort and whose roster featured big name Classics guys like Juan Antonio Flecha, Fabian Cancellara and Filippo Pozzato... we'd sit at the back of their group, trying to keep out of the way and hoping nobody would notice us. Hardly a glamorous way of getting the miles in, but I was fascinated and open to learning how real pros trained. It was also far better than the workouts we'd been getting in the previous week with our own team. I remember Giancarlo Ferretti, the legendary Fassa director, would roll along the side of the group at the end of a training ride and for the final hour he'd bark instructions at them as if it was a rolling race: 'You three, attack'; 'You, pull them back'; 'You, follow the break'; 'Tu, fuga! Tu, alla fuga!' (get in the break, go for it!). It was a super-cool way of training, a race simulation with a big sprint at the end, which I've never seen before or since.

That was a solution of sorts, but once it got into racing itself, there was no getting away from the fact that Landbouwkrediet was like night and day compared to Team GB. I took it as seriously as I could, to the point where I'd do self-reflection forms for each race, an idea I'd first picked up from Chris and Keith Boardman. These are quite formal questionnaires, carefully printed out and taken by me over to Belgium each time I travelled across the Channel, and it'd consist of five questions, starting off with what was the purpose of the team in the race, and how did I fit in with it. Then there'd be how did I fulfil my role, what could I have done better in that role and would an alternative role be more effective and finally what would I do next time.

If you couldn't answer that particular question, which generally I couldn't beyond 'get in breaks', it highlighted how I had an opportunity to formulate my own objectives. More often than not my team-mates would turn up at a stage race, ride around and have a bit of a laugh during the day then take some Stilnox and drink a load of beer in the evening. Then the next day and in the next race they'd do the same thing all over again.

But although I couldn't stop them from doing that, obviously, I refused to spare myself. Based on the self-reflection forms I'd be asking myself stuff like 'What was my particular goal?', 'Did I achieve it?', 'Could I do better?' and so on. It was all really useful stuff that would help me think about things in a bit of a deeper way. And you'd start to pick out stuff like 'I wasn't in a good position,' or 'I wasn't strong enough,' or 'I could have done this or that,' and as a result, even in a team like Landbouwkrediet, you'd start to get better. As a way to keep your head together, if you are in a team of next-to-no-hopers, I can't recommend self-reflection forms strongly enough. You've got your own plans, your own space and you're getting something to take away from even the direst of situations which allows you to improve in the future. Time spent thinking about the race was never time wasted.

*

On the plus side, Landbouwkrediet realized quite quickly that I was one of the stronger riders in the line-up – so I had a lot of freedom of manoeuvre. And they weren't the only team who appreciated that either. In one of the first races I did, the Volta ao Algarve, I was in a break with Benoît Joachim from Discovery Channel and two other guys and rode away from all of them. I remember hearing later through Sean Yates, that Johan Bruyneel, the Discovery director, had got on the phone in his team car to his second-in-command Dirk Demol and asked him, 'Hey, who's this guy? We have to sign him.' In my own team from that point on, although there was always a question of what races Landbouwkrediet could do, and we certainly weren't doing races like the Tour de France, they always let me pretty much choose the ones I preferred. And Discovery's impressions were going to prove very important a couple of years down the line as well.

Another plus side of Landbouwkrediet was that the directors were really nice people, particularly Claude Criquielion, who was a Belgian cycling legend, and Marco Saligari, an Italian and former pro. Marco really tried to make things more professional, but the truth was that the team's real

31

objective was just getting media exposure, and the disorganization and lack of funding that sometimes characterized Landbouwkrediet made itself felt in all sorts of ways.

Even the race food was disastrous – to the point where I'd bring my own all the way from England. If I didn't, either they didn't have any rider food at all for the races, or they'd go to a local bakery just before the start, bring in a load of frozen goodies like Belgian rice cakes rammed full of pastry and butter and fat and then eat that in the race. And as a result of it all still being half-frozen when they began wolfing it down during a race, the riders would sometimes get the shits. So I quickly figured out it wasn't worth the risk.

I was still on a learning curve, that's for sure, but apart from Dierckxsens, whom I admired as a rider and person, I wasn't following my team-mates for advice. In Belgium in the Classics I used to make a point of following, or rather trying to follow, some of the top names in one-day racing, like Peter van Petegem. Peter would often be right at the back of the bunch and then as the crunch moments of the race approached – a tough little climb or a section of cobbles – and the peloton would be fighting like crazy for 10 kilometres, he'd pop up at the front out of nowhere, somehow magically up there in the top three positions. How he did that was something I definitely wanted to learn, plus he had a real sense of perspective too – you could see that he'd be really disconnected in the races that didn't matter, that he was there just to keep ticking over and gain form. But the Classics were another story altogether: that was what mattered the most and he would be utterly committed. Watching and trying to learn from riders like Peter, about when to ease back and save energy and when to commit, both in races and throughout a year, was a strategy that paid dividends for my getting into breaks.

*

There was learning in other ways too. When I went to the Worlds that autumn in Madrid, there was a scandal in the British road team involving Charly Wegelius allegedly being paid to ride for the Italian team. I got on well with Roger Hammond, the British leader for the men's race, and with Bradley, who was there for the time trial, but I was too naive to realize what Charly was allegedly doing and I was too over my limit physically to think about it much either!

As I was still learning the ropes, I didn't get too many top results, with a silver medal in the British National Championships road race one of the few high points in that first year. I was still, though, fighting a battle inside myself between racing on the track and the road, all the way through 2005 and deep into 2006, where we took the gold at the Commonwealth Games. Doing Track World Cups into the season meant it was hard, mentally and physically, to get back on terms with the guys who were purely doing the road. But I was gradually getting less resigned to accepting the situation too – for one thing, I was taking ownership of my own programme and my own training. And I wasn't making it up as I went along, either, I was building on what others taught me or wanted me to do. I remember going into the track and Jonesy would say, 'What are you coming in for today?' and I'd say, 'To use the treadmill,' and he'd say, 'Shall I put it on

380 watts?' and I'd say, 'No, 400.' I always wanted to find the limit and push it, push it, push it. Furthermore, a lot of people saw the winter and the road cycling off season as an opportunity to recharge your batteries, but increasingly I'd see it as a chance to improve. So I'd work very hard during that time, and as a result I'd almost always start the following season well. Key to this is, before you rest up from something, don't just view it as time to switch off completely, give it a structure: recognize you need a break, think about how you're going to rest and plan the break time in detail so that when you come back, you've got your engines going and a reasonable chance of hitting the ground running.

*

Starting in such good form had a lot to do with my first big professional result, when I took second in Italy's toughest early season race, the one-day Trofeo Laigueglia in the north-west of the country. There are often the same three climbs at the end of that race, although they swap the order around, and that year, 2006, before we dropped back down to the coast I remember the last kilometre of the last climb was really hard. As a result, there were only twenty of us left at the top of the climb, including some big names – one of them was already a World and Olympic Champion, Italy's Paolo Bettini, and another guy, Alessandro Ballan, would go on to take the Worlds in 2008. When we dropped back down to the coast from the Ligurian hills towards Laigueglia, I tried a move but it didn't work out, then Ballan and I got away with three other Italians. He sat on my wheel all the way to the sprint, and I couldn't win, but in terms of what it did for my morale and attitude, getting second there represented a massive shift upwards in my targets.

In my first year as pro I had been trying to finish as many races as possible, but I needed to find a niche to create a career, and that result told me that I could find one and helped me see myself in a different perspective. I saw that I could get results for myself; I didn't only need to think about being a domestique. That was particularly true as Ballan went on to do so well in the spring Classics that year – he got third in Roubaix and fifth in Flanders.

At that point both my pulling away from the track and, at the same time, my pulling away from Landbouwkrediet both became clearer objectives. It was ironic because the team pursuit were getting better and better at that time, and I was committing to them much more thanks to my work with the Steve Peters conversations. In the spring of 2006, I went to the Commonwealth Games in Melbourne, and they were tremendously successful. But I felt sad about the time I spent away from road racing because I knew more and more that that was where my heart was. So that was finally why I didn't do any track in 2007 and why it was even harder to come back to it in 2008, because even if physically I was in good enough shape, my going away and then returning made me feel like an outsider.

But the Commonwealth Games, once I'd actually got there, were truly something to enjoy. Nicky was there, and some family we have in Australia drove over to Melbourne from Perth to see me too. Apart from being happy and relieved we won the Team Pursuit, I did the Individual Pursuit as well and got a bronze, although rather than being a particular target, it was more that the place on the team was going vacant. It was the first time in my life I'd done a decent Individual Pursuit and I could maybe have won if we had prepared for it more specifically. By this I mean working on keeping a sustained pace along a particular, pre-established level of effort, which is the key to individual pursuits, whereas in team pursuits you're constantly going above or below that kind of effort.

But we didn't, and I got what I got. Even so, the signs were there, in any case, that I was making some massive strides forward across the board and both I and everybody else were starting to see me as a very different kind of racing animal.

That was why the Commonwealth Games road race was probably the event I took the most from – the English side were outnumbered and I was swamped with fast and/or powerful Australian racers like Mat Hayman, who'd go on to win Paris–Roubaix, and Allan Davis, who'd finish on the podium of Milano–Sanremo the following year. I was hoping for bronze, but tactically I wasn't on it. I should probably have let Davis, who was fastest in a sprint, move ahead and then tried to outpower Hayman, although he was also fast, so I'm not sure if the outcome would have changed. But in either case I was at the sharp end of things from start to finish and both of the Aussies were specifically road riders so I was pretty happy with fourth.

Then it was back to Europe and back to Landbouwkrediet and their frozen race food diet and the main aim of the game for the rest of the 2006 season was working out how to move on from the squad. It helped that Dave Brailsford and the track squad could see that Landbouwkrediet weren't always ideal when it came to top performance in the velodrome either, so they didn't oppose the move. But most importantly, Discovery and Bruyneel hadn't forgotten seeing me in that break in 2005 and again my agent Richard Allchin helped me out there. He was friends with Sean Yates, one of the legends of British cycling who was directing at Discovery by that time, and on top of that Max Sciandri had come on board and he gave Bruyneel a call to help put the case for signing him. I'll never forget him saying, 'Hey, I talked to Bruyneel. He's interested!'

Knowing Max, who is very persuasive, I guess he would have reminded him that I was not expensive, as well as everything else I had going for me. It was very late in the year by the time the deal with Discovery came through, and I was getting seriously concerned at the prospect of having to go on racing with Landbouwkrediet for even one more year. But finally I signed on the way to the airport and to the team's first training camp in California.

*

From the moment Alan Butler, the British mechanic with Discovery, hooked up with me somewhere at a motorway station in the middle of England to hand over a load of equipment prior to the season starting, it was clear to me that Discovery were operating in another league to Landbouwkrediet. In 2005 and 2006 I'd had things that would always cost me in terms of performance – from the unreliable bike to the kind of unclear race programme which was more normal in mainstream professional cycling than it had been at British

Cycling. For someone who likes the season to be structured and to plan when to be good and when to be working towards that, it had never been straightforward.

But Alan gave me everything – bike, kit – I needed in November, way before the season started or before I'd even signed and that, in itself, was a huge difference. Then when we went to the training camp in California I got the same again – bike, kit and so on – because it turned out that in November they'd given me the previous year's equipment. On top of which we got a free laptop and headphones as well. I remember walking into one of the hotel rooms and Lance Armstrong wasn't a rider then with the team but he was there with Sheryl Crow. It all felt a million miles away from driving across half of Europe in a grotty caravan with Landbouwkrediet and evenings of conversational grunting with the team.

So I was really happy to be leaving possibly one of the lowest budget teams in the professional world to go to one of the biggest and best. It felt like I was finally getting some-where in the sport, and with a team like Discovery there was a platform to find out what my true top level was in a squad. All through the winter months I had been training crazy hard, doing five hours a day, then six the next, seven the next and having one day off for weeks and weeks, partly because I was a little bit scared I wouldn't keep up with the rest at the camp over in California. It was certainly a bit intimidating, riding past places you'd only seen on TV like Michael Jackson's Neverland home.

But one day we went up a climb which felt massive at the time, as it was maybe forty minutes long and I managed to stay with one of the star names in the team, George Hincapie. Armstrong was in the team car following us when he stuck his head out of the window and said, 'All right, Steve?' and I nearly fell off my bike because it turned out he knew my name. Armstrong stuck around most of the camp, socializing with guys he knew from earlier in his career like George and Matt White. But when Sean told me that 'Lance, man, he's really happy with you; says you've got a great cadence. That was a good start, yes, going to the front like that with George, yes,' – that was a big morale boost.

I also remember Alberto Contador arriving there at the camp. Levi Leipheimer was a big name in the team, and he had been flying, half-wheeling everybody and showing them all how good he was because he and Tom Danielson were building for the Tour of California in February. But even so, and despite Contador coming out late because he'd been delayed or something, as soon as he jumped off the plane he was on the bike and as soon as he got on the bike he dropped Leipheimer immediately. Then when Alberto was having the usual pre-season sit-down conversation with the team managers to tell them what his goals would be, as his surname begins with C as well, he was just ahead of me in the queue. Somebody left the door open, and I can remember standing outside and hearing the long silence of stunned disbelief at his sheer ambition when he told them he was going to try to win Paris–Nice, the biggest stage race of the spring. And then the same year he won the Tour too.

It wasn't just Contador who took to dropping Levi Leipheimer. Getting rid of Levi, if he and Tommy D stopped for a piss or something during a training ride, turned into a game for all of us. It was all just for fun, but seeing Grand Tour winners and other big names killing themselves to keep a couple of the other top guys out the back and freaking out because they couldn't catch up when they thought they were in good form, was a whole new experience for a rider like me. It showed me again how much I was operating in a different kind of league.

I pretty quickly got flung in at the deep end of that league too. Although they had a really strong one-day line-up, the team was very much Grand Tour-orientated overall, and so when one of their main Classics men, Hincapie, broke his collarbone, there wasn't a long queue of domestiques to plug the gap. I was in Mallorca, training like a madman, and the team called me two days before Sanremo, asked me to do that, and I was straight on the plane for Italy. I made a good impression there, because I was still in the thick of the action at the Poggio trying to help Allan Davis, who got second, and that was enough justification for them to put me straight into all the Classics for the first time in my career.

I had already learned fairly quickly that the cobbled Classics were never going to be my strong point. I had thought I would like them, but in Landbouwkrediet, where we did masses of one-day races in Belgium and the Netherlands, all it took was a few for me to realize the opposite. So much of it was based on positioning in the peloton and I didn't like that, because as I saw it, I could have great form, but a bad position wouldn't just lessen your chances, it could mean that you weren't going to get any kind of result in the race. Apart from technical short-comings, ultimately I think my engine was not made for

Belgian Classics as I was too much of a diesel – not explosive enough. It had been doubly hard when you were wearing a Landbouwkrediet jersey too, as nobody would let small fry from a small team like that into the lines that formed in the front of the peloton. But it proved very different if I was wearing a Discovery jersey and, at the time, my team-mates Tomas Vaitkus and Vladimir Gusev were doing really well in races like Flanders, so my job in the northern Monuments was primarily to help them.

I was still, at that time, trying to find out where I belonged in the cycling peloton, and how I could carve out a niche to try to be of value to a team and have a good career. Of course, I had had thoughts about how I wanted to get into a break and win something. But at Discovery, when you're with guys like Contador, you discover that at the top level it's a very different kettle of fish.

Someone like Contador operates at a completely different level to what I could be, and because you're thinking it's not attainable, you try to keep your spot in a team that has so many world-class domestiques. Guys like José Luis Rubiera, Pavel Padrnos or George Hincapie, who would be leaders or top 'Plan B' options in any other team. All in all, and given the degree of competition even to be a team worker, such a role didn't look so bad. I had a long way to go and I was still very raw. But then just a few weeks before the Giro d'Italia and as my unexpectedly intense Classics season was drawing to a close, I hit on a key problem: what do you when you have serious doubts about the ethics of the team leader?

*

The thing was that one of the biggest names in the sport, Ivan Basso, left Discovery Channel that spring because of his links to Operación Puerto, a massive anti-doping operation in Spain. Basso was defending champion in the Giro d'Italia and the top favourite for the race, as well as one of the guys I'd got to like when I saw the way he rode himself into the ground just to drop Leipheimer at the training camp. I'd known he was a top racer, but didn't know until then that he didn't take himself too seriously all the time and had a good sense of humour.

But then suddenly because of Puerto, he was facing a possible doping ban. That was when I started to question, seriously, the ethics of me devoting myself to a leader if the leader was not behaving in an ethical way. Why should I do that? The harder I looked at it, the more I started to question the whole sport, what the team bosses were up to… it didn't seem right and suddenly I felt uncomfortably close to how I felt about the team pursuit and going through the motions, rather than really loving what I was doing.

This wasn't the last time I felt in such a dilemma, and right then I tried to put it all out of my head, and think, 'He's all right, he's not "doing" anything, he's a decent guy…' However, deep down I had serious doubts. On the one side it was – what could I do about it? OK, everybody in cycling or in any sport probably has to face a decision at some point whether they are going to cheat or not and I absolutely didn't, ever, want to cheat. At the same time, even if you had to do your job on what you considered were the right ethical grounds, you couldn't beat the system and simply refuse to work for somebody because he was dodgy, or potentially dodgy. However, I'd think I absolutely didn't want to use medicine to get an advantage and I didn't like the idea of devoting myself, particularly if I was clean, to somebody who wasn't... ultimately at the end of the day, after much mental agonizing and trying to think it through, I found myself back at square one.

Looking at that situation now, it makes me realize that there is a key learning here, about the injustice of the world, how it is impossible to change, but all you can do is choose how you live with it. You may not win if you live within the rules, but if you manage to push yourself to the absolute maximum, you can hold your head up high when you walk away.

At the time, the upshot of all this doubting was that when Basso resigned from Discovery and left the team, it had really made me question everything, which wasn't very enjoyable. But I had to recognize that there was another side to it all, which was that as he was – obviously – no longer our Giro leader, I was brought in as his replacement. That meant, all of a sudden, I had my own opportunities, rather than these quandaries about team leaders. So I began telling myself that this was more about what I could do, rather than worrying about what other guys like Basso were doing. Plus I was growing in self-confidence too: having done the Classics, I wasn't supposed to do the Giro, but I finally did both. That was important because it meant that regardless of what else was going on, the team believed in me. Either that or they had no one else they could send...

Regardless of what their reasoning was, I loved the team. Whether or not it would have lasted I don't know, but there was a great vibe about Discovery, a lot of good humour and we didn't want for anything, either. There were good bikes, good kit, and we had things like the free laptop and headphones, all that kind of stuff. It was all above and beyond what the norm was at the time. I have to recognize too that I was naive about Discovery, because I would ask riders from the Tour group if they were clean and they would insist they were. It was only later when the scandals broke that I found out what the reality was.

As for me in the Giro, in some ways the pressure was off: I had been told I was standing in for Basso with minimal advance notice, just ten days beforehand, and it was unknown territory, so my only personal objective was to try to do the best I could and finish the race overall. I couldn't overthink it.

I also loved the fact that I was starting my Grand Tours doing the Giro d'Italia. I loved Italy, the level of passion the fans felt for the sport and for their home race, the food and the culture. Just from the way the world stops for a day in each town when the Giro comes through you can see how much it is wrapped up in the history of each place. I had to learn things fast about Grand Tour racing that I hadn't expected, like the mind-boggling length of time you have to end up on a team bus going between one stage and the next. When you're watching this at home, all you do is see it on TV. Actually being there, you understand, accept and deal with all the effort that goes on to make it all happen in one very different place after another. To experience a Grand Tour for the first time felt like I could see the pinnacle of the sport. But even so, I recognized how much I needed to improve too.

Having said that, it was just as well I was focusing on my development because from a team morale point of view, things went pretty badly from the outset. First of all my team-mates had lost Basso, our hypothetical leader from the race and the guy who was probably going to win it. Secondly, our back-up plan, Yaroslav Popovych, slowly slid out of contention and quit after a bad crash after about ten days of racing.

Then, weirdly enough, the Giro became fun.

This was even more unusual, looking back on it, because there were a lot of unhappy people on the team. Popovych wasn't going well, guys like Jurgen Van Goolen and Pavel Padrnos were pretty downbeat at the best of times, and all in all the atmosphere on the team bus each morning was shit. So, myself and Matt White, an Australian rider, formed a team within a team. Whitey would say, 'Come on, mate, let's go down the back of the bus and put the beats [music] on,' and for the best part of two weeks we spent all our time out of the hotel and off our bikes down in the back of the bus, with the beats on.

It wasn't just on the bus that we became close. Whitey swapped around the team hotel room list, got rid of the 'Czech nudist', as he called Padrnos – apparently he was always walking around the hotel room stark naked, all six foot five of him – and I shared with Matt instead. It all became a bit of adventure, and I was always laughing. Whitey had a big engine and I needed way more sleep, so often he would not be in the room by the time I nodded off and he'd be gone by the time I woke up. He was full of life.

He'd look after me in the race too. I learned a lot about the race route as he'd be poring over the race route book.

We'd talk about scenarios for hours on end, not just for the leaders but also for the *gruppetto*. On dangerous days for rookies, like a transition stage with an early climb, I'd find Whitey riding alongside me and warning me that 'Fucking hell, mate, this is a hard start; you got to be in a good position.' And then when Whitey wasn't helping me, he'd be helping other Australian guys, who weren't doing so well, like Nick Gates over on Lotto. So we'd be 'waiting for Gatesy', then he'd be helping me, and somehow we all muddled through to Milan, me in 110th, Whitey in 105th and Gatesy in 127th. But even if the racing had been hard, Whitey kept my morale up all the time and I was never in danger of not finishing, taking one day at a time, listening to the beats on the bus. Really, I could not have been with a better person for a first Grand Tour.

*

I'd just finished the Giro and my confidence was on a real high when a few weeks later I got the call-up to do the team time trial race in Eindhoven, with what was pretty much the Tour de France line-up for Discovery, plus me. I'd been asked to ride because with my team pursuit background I was pretty much the strongest on that kind of terrain, but then disaster struck. The guys in the team car had kept telling my team-mate Vaitkus to get out of the line because he was swinging all over the place, but he didn't want to do that – I suspect because I hadn't been dropped and he didn't want to lose face. Anyway, being so close to the limit, he skidded off at one point, right in front of me, and I went into him, highsided over him and slammed into the kerb: result, one broken elbow and two broken ribs.

This drastic reversal of fortune gave me a bit of an insight into how expendable you can be in a team too. Despite my injuries, it seemed like the team wasn't actually that bothered about me; they were more worried about Vaitkus given Thomas was supposed to be going to the Tour. I was really fucked, for all I played it down, but the team kept on in any case, saying, 'We think you're going to be fine.' As it was, the next day I got home and my arm was the size of a balloon. Having been told by the team I didn't need to go to hospital, it turned out it was broken. So I had a spell off the bike and by the time I got back into racing in the Tour de Pologne, the team had won the Tour with Contador so the pressure was off and the mood was rather laid-back, and to be honest my season was pretty much done. I raced through to Il Lombardia, meaning I'd made my race debut in four of the five Monuments in a single season, and done my first Grand Tour as well.

Sean was a great mentor too, but really he was mentoring me to be a really good team worker, which itself opened up another dilemma. All that year, I never really once thought about racing for myself. It was partly because I was operating in unknown terrain like the Giro, partly because when you're in a team like that that's constantly winning – Paris–Nice, California in the spring, the Tour de France in the summer, all the way to nearly forty victories – it also made it so much easier to be a team worker. You knew that more often than not, your leader was going to come away with the top place overall, so there was always a part of me that thought if just being a lead-out man or a domestique was the best I could be, I was happy with that.

I reached this realization just I was waiting for Discovery to renew my contract, as a part of me wanted to get re-signed and fit in and I'd only had a one-year contract so I had kept on doing exactly what they asked of me. I thought that given I'd done everything they'd asked of me, I'd proved my worth. Obviously, money was always going to be something of a concern, although I didn't really think about it that much in my career until my last contract came up for renewal.

But then the Basso situation arose before the Giro, which made me question that domestique's role. On top of which I was always scared of not getting the best out of myself and I realized that in order to get the best out of myself, I needed to keep that dream of winning alive. Otherwise I'd start going through the motions and that was fucking complacency, and I didn't want to be in that zone. I wanted freedom to do what I could as a racer, even if that meant I'd have to get used to a much more unpredictable world, where I was dependent on my own results for my future in the sport.

But with these two schools of thought in my head, outside circumstances made the decision for me. Instead of being renewed quickly, I was one of the last ones on the squad, if not the last, to get asked about 2008 and whether I wanted to sign for Astana, the new squad essentially recreated from the ground up by Bruyneel and Demol, partly from the soon-to-be-defunct Discovery Channel.

But by then it was too late and I just signed for the first team I could for 2008 – again, with Max, the former pro who had started working with British Cycling and who became a great friend, playing a key role in getting me the contacts. That said, the negotiations between me and Claudio Corti, boss of the middle-ranking Italian squad Barloworld, were the umpteenth reminder of what I'd been finding out since 2005: just how arbitrary the European professional cycling world could be.

Corti: 'How much a year are they paying you in Discovery?'

Me: '65,000.'

Corti: We'll pay you 70,000.'

I had genuinely forgotten to mention to Corti I was talking about my annual wages in dollars and Corti didn't tell me he was talking about my annual wages in euros. As a result, rather than increasing by a couple of thousand euros, my annual wages went from £40,000 to £70,000 overnight.

By the time I realized the misunderstanding, it was too late to change. So I figured I'd roll with it.

The doubling of my salary for the most random of reasons was exactly the kind of off-the-wall ending you might have expected to three insanely roller-coaster years. I'd now seen both extremes of the sport, in terms of what teams had to offer too, from the near chaos and limited resources that was Landbouwkrediet to the faultless organization and massive budget of Discovery Channel.

Either way, I'd realized that maybe I needed to get a bit wiser, and to get some results of my own because that's what actually gives added value to a ride for a lot of these managers. Rather than being steamrolled into a role that I found limiting, as a domestique, or not having any real support like at Landbouwkrediet, it was time to explore the middle-ranking, mid-budget teams and see what my chances were there. Whether they were paying me in euros or dollars to do that, I really didn't care.

Chapter 4

2008–09: Road or Track?

I f you wanted an example of how I think outside the box as a racer, I've always had a tendency to ride at the back of the bunch. Even when I was a junior, I'd be selective about when I'd fight for position, by sensing when the race was on. What really matters, if you're a stage hunter, is that you're at the front at the right moment.

Either way, for my entire career, nearly every director bar one would tell me the opposite was true. You had to be there at the front, all the time, no matter what.

Sometimes it wasn't about strategy, it was a question of team image. At Discovery, Sean Yates would tell me, 'Stevie, it's not the 1980s any more. I used to sit at the back for 300 kilometres. But you can't do it any more; there are too many cameras.' But other directors in other teams would also try different techniques for stopping me from riding at the back, simply because they thought it was right, without actually having a real reason. Dave B was probably the only one who understood my attitude: he'd ask, 'What was your job?' and I'd say, 'Well, they didn't really give me one,' and he'd try to be more specific going forward with the roles that the team would give me. But otherwise, and in general, I wouldn't be there. What was the point?

I'd reason things out differently. My alternative strategy could be summed up as: 'If I fight for position, I expend a lot of energy, so why don't I just stay here and then, when it's a key moment and I need to go to the front, I can move past everyone cos I'm stronger anyway.' In a hilly race like Liège–Bastogne–Liège, the first really steep Ardennes climbs on the course, called the Stockeu and Wanne, are always where there's an initial selection and every time in the race, riders charge to the foot of the climbs as if it's a bunch sprint. But rather than get mixed up in that, I'd just stay at the back and then ride past forty or fifty riders on the climb.

That'd be me sorted in that particular race, by playing to my strengths. But this racing at the front/back of the peloton issue also showed a big underlying problem throughout my career and that harmed it considerably. It was true I had some ideas of how best to exploit what I could do, but having ideas of my own meant I found myself constantly having to fight against other people's concepts of cycling and more specifically the way men's road racing is such a conservative-minded, insular sport that in many ways refuses to be open to different opinions, let alone change.

Which is frustrating for me, because when you do detach yourself from cycling and read and study and learn about larger-scale issues – as I was increasingly doing in my last years as a rider and even more now I've retired – it's like a light-bulb moment. You realize, 'Fucking hell; surely this could be done so much better.' You start asking really good questions and re-evaluating people's contributions to each team.

In an ideal world or team, you need to work with somebody with the same kind of mentality. But back in 2008, rather than working with a particular person, I realized if I wanted to make the most of my career, it was high time I started working inside the framework of the cycling culture of an entire country: Italy.

*

My decision to sign for Barloworld, South African sponsored but, crucially, with an all-Italian team structure and headquarters, was partly circumstantial, partly because I could see it suited me and partly to do with Dave Brailsford. Back in 2006 or 2007, Dave brought me into the office in Manchester and asked me all these questions about Discovery, like how much managers' salaries were and so on. Even back then, I suspect, he was planning on forming a road team – as would happen in 2010 with Sky – and in order to make a big splash when that happened, firstly he needed to be able to count on riders racing at the highest levels possible. So he did his utmost to try to place us in all these different teams. He used Sciandri as a manager to process the different negotiations and Max knew Corti of course, so that was how they got Geraint into Barloworld in 2007 – I remember hearing about Corti sitting there, pinching G's legs to see how much fat he had on him. And Bradley was in Cofidis, I got into Discovery, and another

British racer, Ian Stannard, was in ISD, an Italian squad. So when I met up with Corti to discuss my contract for 2008, for all it was last-minute, it was part of a bigger process too.

In a sense, signing for Barloworld felt like I was going down a step, as in this was a medium-sized, middling budget squad that wasn't part of cycling's top league, the ProTour, like Discovery Channel had been. Yet it had some advantages as a result: rather than automatically being classified as a domestique as I was at Discovery, Barloworld had some good riders like Baden Cooke and Robbie Hunter, both of whom were fast finishers, and Félix Cárdenas and Mauricio Soler, both of whom were great climbers, but they weren't leaders in the Contador or Basso league, and they weren't a million miles better than me. That's the point when you start to try to close the gap to become a leader yourself, or at the very least get your own opportunities to shine.

So rather than looking at Barloworld as being a setback, I started taking away the positives. All I needed at that stage in the game was a good bike, a reasonable race programme that suited me and some chances. It didn't always automatically follow that the best teams have the best equipment; it was more about finding the right balance. As for whether it was morally right or not to work for a leader who you didn't know whether he was clean or not – I decided to bury my doubts about that and get on with doing what I could.

Barloworld also had another major attraction: they were Italian-run and based in Italy as well. Ever since I'd started racing there and learning about the nation, I didn't just like what I saw, I also realized it could teach me a lot about life on and off the bike. Part of the contract with Barloworld specified that we had to live in Italy. But after a few months there, I never wanted to leave anyway.

As a young rider, Italy had a huge appeal to it because you'd see all these pictures of their top names, the Mario Cipollinis or Marco Pantanis of this world, out training in beautiful countryside and in the warm sunshine. Then when I got there, I started to recognize that there was so much more to appreciate about it, to the point where I grew to consider Italian bike riders to be masters of the sport. They always looked healthy and nearly always lean, and as I wanted to do the basics better, it was clear that these were the riders I needed to use as examples to progress, from the key building blocks upwards.

Italian food is a good, obvious example of that learning process: you could go there and just eat what they ate – pasta, chicken and a steak on the day off – and as a consequence you would become leaner and a better bike rider. What appealed even more was that in Tuscany, where I lived for all my professional career, there are all these beautiful play-grounds for riding a bike, networks of high mountains and little hills for your training. Finally, and perhaps best of all, so many Italian people have a long-lasting love of cycling as a sport and a way of life.

Max, who knew that area of Tuscany very well, was crucial for both giving me insights into that deep cycling culture, and what I could learn from that. His knowledge and experience ranged from how and where to live as a rider, tactics I could use when racing, and training strategies. Road racing has a very different kind of training cycle to track racing too, which is very intense for a certain part of the time, but then tapers off completely after big events like the Olympics. In road racing there are fewer 'off' periods, so you have to learn about how to lower the intensity a little bit and raise it when it matters, and Max showed me how to do that. It wasn't that I could go off and drink fifteen beers in a single sitting because I needed to relax, simply that you needed periods when – to use swimming as an example – you're going to stay afloat in the pool rather than try to get another length or three in, because you can't live like a monk for ever. So thanks to Max, I learned all about moving between different levels of 'monk-ness', being a good professional all year round. He also helped me see how, if I wasn't careful, and didn't remember to enjoy what I was doing too, my desire to do well could damage what I wanted to achieve. But getting that balance right took me a long time to achieve.

Max was also turning into a great friend. He seemed to know, without actually being told, what time I would be finishing training. So often when I was living alone in Tuscany, the phone would ring and he'd say, 'Hey, why don't you come over and eat something with us?'

He paid attention to all those little things, looked after me a lot and I'm still very grateful to him and his family. Sometimes he'd sit there in his office, multitasking with conference calls, drinking coffee and telling me stories, all at the same time. It wasn't just about Brits in Italy. He'd never stop trying to bring Italian cycling culture and lifestyle into the GB team too. No matter how small a part that was, it had its importance and deserved real consideration. I remember in Madrid during the 2005 Worlds I was sitting there with Dave B and Brad having a coffee and Max came over: 'Hey, Dave, dinner's nice here but why don't we get some Parmesan for the dinner table too?' (After that, whenever Bradley used to do his Max imitation – he was an expert mimic – it'd invariably start with 'Hey, Dave, the hotel's nice but there's a nice piano in the lobby; why don't we put it in the bus?!')

What this idea of Max's in Madrid really showed though, was Max's never-ending enthusiasm and interest in trying to get everything right that could be made right, down to the tiniest last detail. Even the Parmesan had to be there where it should be, on the table, or he wasn't happy.

*

I also liked the way Italy worked on a social level, a strange but very effective combination of being a bit more liberal in some ways, a bit crazy in others, and above all just getting on with life and living it. Put it all together and it made for a kind of common-sense attitude to things that allowed you to live in a much more pleasant way. One simple example: whereas in Britain if there are 'no parking' yellow lines on a street and everybody respects that come what may, in Italy you can park in the middle of the road if you're reasonable about it and don't block the traffic. The traffic warden might ask you where you're going, but as soon as you explain you're just grabbing a coffee and you'll be back in ten minutes, they accept that and move on.

Another Mediterranean country that could have appealed was Spain, particularly as Mallorca is well-trodden ground for British cycling. When I first went there my first thoughts were, 'Jesus, this is paradise.' But after I'd been to Italy and then gone back to Mallorca like I did with Qhubeka in 2015, I'd start realizing the island's limitations, like having to do the same climb time and again because that was all there was. I'd end up thinking, 'What the fuck are we doing on this climb where I have to slow down because the corners are so tight?' On top of that, I didn't want to go to these places and be disturbed by all these cycling tourists like you can be in Mallorca. I don't want to sound ungrateful for having the opportunity for being there, but in a sense, in terms of cycling, Italy's a bit more off the grid and was ideal for me to get the best out of myself.

There were also reasons for leaving the UK. Living in Italy, as I discovered, meant that there were long periods when I could do everything for my life on the bike, and at that time, in the UK, that wasn't possible. There were too many distractions and temptations that I didn't want or need to be exposed to. It's as simple as it being a Friday night on the Wirral and all your mates are going out, whereas in Tuscany, if you look out of your front door, you're surrounded by mountains, and it's like they're telling you to go out and ride them. On top of that, after a few weeks, you'd find there are certain climbs that you have to do again and again, and you can't help but look at the times you're doing for them, and how you're performing. Just like the mountains, the times are there, unavoidable and in your face, so the next thing you find yourself thinking as a matter of course is that if you weighed one kilo less, that's a thirty-second gain on a particular climb. So because of the place, and the culture, and the lack of distractions, you're always thinking about your bike, and how to be faster.

Sometime early in 2008 I drove all the way from the Wirral to Tuscany in my VW Golf that I'd bought when I was seventeen. God knows how it got there – it wasn't very roadworthy, had no insurance (I had very little money at the time), and I remember being stuck on the ferry when the train was about to go because the car wouldn't start. But I did get there, and for a long time I'd drive it around Tuscany despite (full disclosure here) the lack of insurance issue.

At first I lived in Quarrata with Cavendish and Geraint. I didn't want to be in Lago d'Iseo where the team was based because I liked my own space and I knew what Corti was like and that he'd be coming round and checking to see if there was any Fanta in the fridge. Claudio was really passionate, very traditional, a bit nervous, and he'd smoke like a chimney, and sometimes when he lost the plot and started shouting he really lost the plot. But you could see him two hours later and he'd be back to normal again, and he really cared about the riders, and for that I was grateful to him.

Even so, I wanted my own space and to be away from the team, and that's something I learned to do with all of them, to be close enough to the team headquarters to nip by if you needed something, but far enough to say, 'Nope, sorry, I can't make it.'

I had the same strategy of keeping my distance while sharing the flat in Quarrata. The lads at British Cycling all wanted to train together, which was good for them but not so good for me. I was a few years older, and although I wasn't desperate, I couldn't afford to fuck around too much and I was still on my way up, trying to perform at the highest level. So I did a lot of my training alone. Then at the end of

59

that year, Nicky and I first bought a flat and later settled on getting a house out of town.

Italy wasn't all great training rides and sipping cappuccinos on the terraces of Quarrata's bars in a sunlit central piazza. The house we finally bought was quite damp and at first we were using camp beds; being so close to the ground and what with the wet conditions I woke up one morning with a frog sitting on my face. Nicky killed herself laughing, saying I'd been kissed by a frog. But I wasn't to be discouraged about Italy whatever: too much good stuff was happening to me on the road, at last, for that to happen – and even if 2008 also turned out to be a year where I was still too entangled in the British Cycling track scene for my own good.

*

After missing out on it in 2007 while I was with Discovery, I felt an obligation to go back to the GB track team in 2008. As I saw it, it was partly completing the four-year Olympic cycle and partly because I felt I owed it to British Cycling after all they had done for me. I wanted to see their project through to Beijing.

This situation, and the way it dragged on through 2008, meant that even though I was performing at a lot better level than I had done up until then on the road, I still wasn't at my natural level in that area.

On the plus side, as those better road-racing results started to come through, the pressure lifted and I was more relaxed and not trying to force things. So I started to race even more effectively, and could reflect more deeply on what I had done well or badly, using those race reflection documents again for a lot of the events. At the same time, I was settling down more and more in Italy, and we had that network of English language speakers with Cav, G and Rod Ellingworth too. Even if I didn't go training with them so much, it was a good time to be there. I was having a breakthrough year.

But then there was the track, which was doing my road-racing performance no good at all. And that was killing my morale, despite 2008 turning out, with hindsight, to probably be the second best season I ever had all round. I knew that to get the best out of myself, I needed to jump out of bed in the morning and be able to say to myself, 'Right, I know what I'm doing and this is why I'm doing it.' But I wasn't, I was crawling out of bed, thinking to myself, 'For fuck's sake, this isn't working, but I've got to do it, and this is not a nice place to be in.' I needed empowerment, the feeling of taking ownership of your own journey, objectives and goals. To put it bluntly, the feeling of owning your own shit.

*

The better I got on the road, the more the track situation needed resolving. As early as spring 2008 I finally got my first professional road win, and given how unsure of my condition I was at the time, raising my arms in triumph one cold day in February in the Giro di Reggio Calabria stage race in southern Italy was a colossal surprise.

There were a lot of fans and it was a good atmosphere that day, even if it was the usual chaos of the south with dogs running around the race, and really dodgy road surfaces. But

I loved it all, and the more time I spent in Italy and with Max, the more I enjoyed being in those kinds of places. Our team was really happy too, even if the local Italian teams were not too chuffed at being beaten by a foreigner in races that were very much their bread and butter.

I wasn't anywhere near my race weight where I needed to be as I found it a real challenge to manage my own weight when I was track training, but for some reason when the race split apart on the second stage, I was able to hang on at the front. I was feeling better and better as the front group shrank to thirty and then on another climb when it went down to five. The first split was basically due to my having the legs to stay in contention, and then as we'd been through the finishing circuit once or twice on finishing loops, the second time I went for it was down to having the legs and working out exactly what was best for me to make my move: 300 metres from the finish on a slight uphill, through a chicane.

Getting the win was a big boost to my morale, particularly as I wasn't at all in a great place in terms of my condition. And that brought me back, yet again, to what to do in my situation regarding the track.

Up until that point, thanks to their farming us out to teams like Landbouwkrediet, essentially I did the team pursuit because it helped me pay the bills and it helped me get where I wanted to go. But in 2008 or so there had been some big changes in the GB team pursuit training programme and, as a result, we'd begun doing loads of weight training – leg-press work, squats and so on – and I kept on popping my knee out with all the efforts. I was bigger than I should have been as a result of all this building up of our muscle mass, and it wasn't just me; if you have a look at photos of team pursuiters from that year we all looked like balloons. But the track management didn't seem to care about that. They wanted us to be ultra-fast starters and this was their system of ensuring that happened.

The short version of the explanation of why I no longer fitted into the team pursuit's overall training philosophy and why it was actually damaging my road performances was that, deep down, I wasn't really a team pursuit rider and I didn't want to do it. The slightly longer version would be that I simply didn't have the kind of ultra-fast acceleration the team were now demanding to ensure the four of us were reaching our maximum speed in the minimum time possible. For the fullest version of why the track team's training strategy had changed radically over that winter of 2007 though, it all begins with Ed Clancy taking over as the GB team pursuit's Man 1 – the first to start in the chain of four pursuiters, with me as Man 4 – while, at the same time, Matt Parker had replaced Simon Jones as our trainer.

Up until that point in time the standard distance for Man 1, like Ed, to do at the head of the string of racers when the starting pistol was fired was three quarters of a lap. But then Matt decided that it would be better if Ed did a lap and a quarter – which is a heck of a lot longer, and went against the conventional view of the time that it wasn't possible to do that.

At the time we all raised our eyebrows, and with hindsight I can see that it was brave and a stroke of genius to have that idea. It also highlights what I have written previously about thinking outside the box and trying new things. As it turned out, Ed managed it: he got to a lap and a quarter and that kind of breakthrough instantly acted as a game changer for the rest of his team-mates, including me.

If you want to know what all this meant expressed in terms of power output, Ed's maximum was about 1500 watts, maybe more. Now I can do 1100 or 1200 watts so even to follow him before all of this meant I had been on my limit and instead I'd focus on holding the team together in the last part of the race – a classic endurance effort. But as a result of this change of strategy, whereas before Man 1 had protected Man 4 early on to the point where he could almost recover, now, with Ed riding on the front for that extra half lap, that no longer happened.

It was also true that the hardest part of the team pursuit for me had always been the start, as I'm not the kind of explosive rider with the acceleration that all Man 1s have in a team pursuit. But what made it much worse for me was that with Ed's new strategy locked into place, the team pursuit training programme became much more heavily focused on doing a lot more work around our starts: half-lap starts, quarter-lap starts... I could have trained for that kind of start for the whole of the rest of my career and I still wouldn't have improved, because I never had the kind of explosive acceleration they were trying to sharpen up. What I needed, as a 'diesel engine', was a lot of threshold training work and the best I went on the track was after big blocks of road training. But for all that was my strength, the track team weren't interested in doing that any more, and that was when the criticism began from Simon Jones (he may have been the messenger – I was never sure if he was actually the origin of all that) that I wasn't riding as a team player. I was fully committed, but because I lacked the communication skills I needed to put my case to the team, I couldn't get through what it was I needed either.

The end of it all though came at a holding camp for the Olympics in Newport and being told there and then I wasn't going to be one of the six team pursuit riders selected for Beijing. Ironically enough, given the margins between a very good and an excellent performance are so small, I probably could have still raced well enough to get into the team pursuit. And for all some of the staff had felt that 'Steve's not buying in' – which was bullshit – they hadn't realized that I just had a different attitude to it all, which was if they were going to change their strategy so much and I wasn't going to fit into the team any more, that was fine; I could have handled that.

*

A few weeks later, I was in a shopping centre in the UK and I walked past a TV shop just at the moment when the GB squad were doing the Olympic team pursuit final. I stood there, watching them win, through the window. I was pleased that they won, because on a personal level things between me and my team-mates were good. But I felt both sad about how it had all ended and also quite angry because the only reason they had kept me in the squad so long was because they needed to intensify the competition for places. I understood it, I accepted it, that elite sport has to be ruthless, but I didn't like it. They'd known already in 2007 that it wasn't going to work for me, so they probably should have said to me then, 'If you don't like it, then just concentrate on the road.'

On top of that, I had gone back in 2008 to try to finish off the Olympic cycle, and I had missed out on the 2008 Tour with Barloworld because of that. Instead I had had to do the Giro because of this bloody track programme, so that was an opportunity missed. Perhaps I should have been brave and left the track after 2006. But as I stood there in that shopping centre watching them get their first team pursuit Olympic gold after ten years of racing with them, no matter what had happened and what the reasons were, it was over. So if I'm honest, another feeling I had, apart from happiness, sadness and anger, was a sense of relief that I was no longer part of it all.

After being told I wasn't doing the Olympic team pursuit, the GB team management said that they were prepared to offer me a ride in the road race and time trial instead. So to make the most of what condition I had, I agreed. I went back to Italy from Newport and the data I got from my training rides in Tuscany that July – for the specialists reading this, I was doing four ten-minute blocks of 450 watts – were good, solid times and numbers.

However, when I finally got to the Olympics I did a terrible road race because I wasn't prepared for the humidity and the heat. To make up for that, I think I could have run top ten in the time trial – I was running fifth on the split times after the first lap – but disaster then struck when my chain fell off three times in a row, and I had to stop three times to get it back on.

This was a balls-up but it all kind of happened without anyone from the GB team saying anything afterwards. I know that British Cycling prioritize their resources and where the medals are going to come from, which is good business sense, but judging from their attitude, and perhaps rightly so, I obviously wasn't considered much of a resource. To make matters worse, I used a British Cycling road version of the UK track bike for the time trial which caused me no end of problems with Barloworld because they had wanted me to use their in-house Bianchi and perhaps naively I was concerned with which bike was the fastest and didn't care too much about anything else.

It didn't help that Barloworld were already having a very tough time of it, because of their Spanish rider Moisés Dueñas testing positive for EPO in the Tour de France. I had been really surprised by his performances in the Tour – he got a couple of top ten places while we were training for the track – and I remember talking to Geraint about it, saying, 'This guy's going all right, him with his fat little sausage legs.' Then when he tested positive, my thoughts changed to, 'Now we know why.' But it was also a surprise, because suddenly that whole issue, something you'd only read about in the doping scandals with Festina and never seen directly, felt as if it was coming very close. I didn't speak to Dueñas very much, although I did a few races with him, but there was a language barrier. I do remember him being a very nice guy, who then, it turned out, did something really, really selfish and stupid that affected so many people.

The team was definitely affected by it – and particularly the management. I was relatively young, and I was in the track team so I didn't really worry about stuff like that, although I probably would have later when I had a mortgage to pay and more responsibilities. But there was a concern that Barloworld would pull out and it did affect me, finally, as the team didn't do the Tour in 2009 and, from a selfish point of view, that was an opportunity lost.

Anyway, as seemed to be a recurring theme for me in the 2008 Olympics, I had mixed feelings about the road performances. I was disappointed about the repeat chain-drops, but was also pleased to be at the Games and turning in what could have been a good performance without the mechanical issues. But while Beijing was a massive triumph for British Cycling elsewhere as the 'gold rush' of medals kicked in, the biggest thing about the Games for me personally turned out to be seeing Lionel Messi in the Olympic village, although I did kick myself afterwards for not getting my picture taken with him.

I also used my time in and flying to and from Beijing to reflect on how it was time to kick on, to feel pleased that the never-ending six-week blocks of track training were over for good, and that I need never stress out about time splits on a track lap and all of that stuff again. Most importantly, finally – finally – I had the real opportunity to go and do my road racing without any interruptions. I could really get into it like I had wanted to for so long. However, what I didn't allow for as my optimism grew were the potential bust-ups with other figures in authority and fighting against a stick-in-the-mud director or two...

*

Post-Beijing I flew over to Milan, ready physically to do the Tre Valli Varesine one-day races in August, a series of very hilly events that take place over a week or so across northern Italy. Mentally, though, I was really tired from the flights from Beijing and then to Italy and my Barloworld director for the races, Alberto Volpi, showed no empathy or understanding whatsoever of my jetlagged state of exhaustion.

At the first race, the Tre Valli, the peloton had thinned out over the first couple of climbs but I was still up there, riding in my usual spot towards the back of the pack. But when Volpi brought the team car up to the back of the peloton to see what was going on, he started shouting, 'Go to the front, go to the front,' pushing his weight about. I didn't reply, just eyeballed him and put my finger to my lips and mouthed, 'Sssh, sssh.' This didn't improve what was already a fairly tense situation given my tiredness and the next day when we had another race that was beyond my physical capabilities, the Coppa Agostini, things got even more difficult.

Agostini that year was like Liège–Bastogne–Liège but with way steeper climbs. I was down to ride this event with Geraint, who had got back by this point from the Olympics too. Given what had happened in Beijing and his gold medal success, let's just say when G's head has gone off from racing mode, his body might be there in an event, but his head is doing the rounds of paradise. So when I said, 'G, this is too hard for me but tomorrow could be really good for both of us, let's do two hours and then stop at the feed,' he quickly agreed. But given the Volpi situation, I knew we had to be a bit subtle about it.

I remember Mario Pafundi, the soigneur whom we later took with us to Sky, was killing himself laughing because we hid behind the team car with our bikes so that Volpi wouldn't see us when he drove past. Then we were just putting our bikes on the roof rack and laughing because he hadn't seen us when the race radio announced that we had quit. So that was our cover completely blown and, of course, it made for an even more furious Volpi.

When we got to the Coppa Bernocchi race the following day, Volpi announced before the start that we would be working for a bunch sprint for our fast man, Robbie Hunter. This rather went against my strategy of getting in the early break and when Volpi came storming up to ask me what I was doing there when I duly got in it, I answered that I was acting as a policeman, making sure the team was represented and acting as a brake on the guys ahead. But the brutal reality was I couldn't be arsed with him any more, and to judge by the way he refused to bring the car up behind the break so I had to get drinks from any other team, he wasn't exactly that pleased with me either.

Anyway, the break shrank down to just three or so and I won, outpowering the other two guys close to the finish. But as I crossed the finish line my victory salute consisted of me putting my fingers to my lips. It really wasn't premeditated, but given how I'd used the same gesture with Volpi a few days before, it caused a lot of shit to go down with the squad. Things were already difficult because of the Olympics time trial bike, and then Robbie piled in on the general row, bawling me out on the bus because I had been supposed to race for him. So my second victory of the year didn't exactly pour oil on troubled waters – just the opposite.

But I fucking won the race, and winning Bernocchi felt, to me, like a huge breakthrough. The Olympic non-selection had been such a big rejection it felt like I'd been injured, and on top of that, it had been very tough getting back on the road from the track, because I had lost endurance and put on a fair bit of weight. So I'd had to be mentally strong for a number of weeks following Newport and accept that my results on the road for that period were not going to be great, and that was tough. Then there was controlling my diet, because having to lose weight and balance that with a race calendar is never easy.

But I'd just cracked on and handled it. I still had a long way to go, but I was starting to accept things and move on quicker and quicker. I didn't like the situation I'd found myself in at the Olympics and part of me was really pissed off. But ultimately I was as resilient as I could be and used it all as fuel, and thanks to that I got a good win and a good start to the next part of my career.

So while one chapter, that of track racing, was closing, another was simultaneously opening up. In some ways I felt sad about leaving that part of my life behind, but quite apart from how it was affecting my road career I had always hated the being famous side of it, that people would recognize you more in the supermarket after an Olympics and I'd probably have had a hard time handling all the fuss winning a gold medal brings.

To an extent, locally and among the cycling crowd, I'd already been through it all after getting a silver in the 2004 Olympics, when it hadn't been that long since I left school and in that period I was out socializing a great deal, so I knew a lot of people who probably thought, 'Hey, that's the guy from the pub. How did he do that?' Also, I've got two brothers, a big family network and we live on the Wirral which is almost like an island really so people probably recognized me for that reason too.

There was weird stuff too, like getting upgraded on flights because you were in the BOA or being invited to see the Queen. I know Brian and the rest of the 2004 Olympics team went, but I never felt an affinity for the Royal Family. I would rather go to Anfield. So I stayed at home. But the basic point was that if some people like that kind of fame and recognition, I'm the complete opposite. I just wanted to do my best.

With that in mind, I felt that seeing what I could do in the WorldTour, cycling's top league of road racing, was a fairer, more balanced environment than the Olympic track world, and my results would count for more as a result. I didn't complain about it, but in that era I felt and thought a lot about how Great Britain had an unfair financial advantage, and at times that made me feel uncomfortable. And neither did I buy into Britain having these superstar athletes as a matter of course.

*

Was the Olympic track scene truly a level playing field? I do wonder whether some of these British cycling athletes at that time would have been so successful if, to put it bluntly, they had not been born with a silver spoon in their mouths. Only a few of them had that experience of going to different teams and appreciating the difference in financial muscle power between, say, Landbouwkrediet and British Cycling – which is like the difference between Britain and the other cycling nations when it comes to the Olympics. So I don't think they realized what an amazing platform they were operating on, and then if you look at the other countries and ask yourself, do they have that same platform? Do they get millions of pounds spent on R & D? I'm not so sure. Especially back in the 2000s, GB's special equipment got rolled out, went back in a box and then came back in the next Olympics. But if the difference between Britain and the other top cycling nations was already extreme, it was only when you get to the poorest parts of Africa – as I did with Qhubeka, my team from 2015 – that you suddenly realize, 'Fuck me, we were all born with a silver spoon in our mouths just to be able to go to school.'

That's why I think of one of the current Ineos Grenadiers top riders, Richard Carapaz, and how hard it's been for him, as an Ecuadorean cyclist, to get to where he is without that federation and back-up grant and being able to train for three years for one event. I take my hats off to the people, because if Carapaz made it, then there are probably lots more Ecuadorians who didn't and that's because although they are just as good athletes, they don't have that financial platform. In the British team you didn't really appreciate that element because you were living in a bubble.

Lastly, the disparity of platforms and opportunities that exist explains why a team like Qhubeka, which works hard trying to develop cycling in Africa, has an amazing opportunity to leave a legacy. It's hard to measure that legacy, but which teams and riders have even tried to do something like that for their sport?

For me the Tour truly is the pinnacle of the sport, and if you can't win it outright, then trying to do the next best thing by winning a stage has to be your goal. I'm very proud of what I achieved on the track, but in terms of my medals, at the same time I don't care about them. I recognize they are part of me, but there was a time when I had to move on and, given that context, it means more to me to have tried to succeed in a different way.

Chapter 5

Man on a Mission

The first time I met Bradley Wiggins we were both racing, and we were both doing our best to ignore each other. It was at the Junior National points track race in the late 1990s where he was so far ahead of me that he had about double my points total, and I knew from far earlier than I liked in the race that he was faster and stronger and I couldn't possibly beat him. So I focused on staying ahead of the others, racing for second, just let Bradley – was that the guy's name? – do his own thing.

Yet as hard as I tried not to, I found myself sneaking the odd look at Bradley. I could see this guy was exceptionally graceful on the bike, with his legs going like two perfectly gauged pistons and his faultless position in the saddle. He was looking so good riding around the track it was as if he had some kind of aura about him, and everybody would stop what they were doing and watch.

Not only that, in the last kilometre of the individual pursuit, Bradley would suddenly shift his pace up a gear and almost sprint round. This is perhaps not the ideal pacing strategy to get from A to B as fast as possible. But it didn't matter as he was still faster than anybody I knew. In four words: out of my league.

At one of the brief points when I stopped blanking him at that first Junior Track Championships and went over to say hello, he came across as a nice kid, if pretty introverted. It wasn't only me interested in Bradley as everybody wanted to talk to him since he had just won at the World Track Championships earlier that year. But he didn't say much back, just stayed close to his mum and stepdad, who'd gone there to support him.

However, just because he was shy, I grew to appreciate that didn't mean he was a pushover. A year later, from about 1999 onwards, we were both on the GB National track squad and riding the team pursuit, and there were times when our little group of riders would be dragged into some kind of team management political showdown. It wasn't nice because we risked being pulled in one direction or another for no reason or benefit to us. But whereas I'd end up nodding politely to whoever was asking us to take sides and then go off and do my own thing – because I worked out that as long as you performed and didn't clash, verbally, that was preferable – Bradley would nod politely too and then simply say to their faces: 'Fuck off, I'm not doing that.' He'd literally use those words, partly because he would do it in a way that was funny and which would defuse any tension (as well as getting his message across), and partly because he was Bradley Wiggins and you can do what you want when you're that good. But it was also partly because that was one of his ways of dealing with challenging situations. Me, I had no choice but to lie low and try to be more diplomatic.

But for all he could be so direct, his shyness was so extreme that there were other times when he'd withdraw into himself completely. I think one of the best descriptions I heard of Bradley was made by Steve Peters – whose work had been so important to me and who was fond of making animal comparisons – who said that Bradley was a lion. By this Steve said he meant 'You have to leave him alone in the jungle and he'll eventually come back out. Either that, or he'll have been killed by another lion in the meantime.'

But Bradley would always turn up alive, eventually, even if there were times when he took the disappearing lion act to extremes, like once when he was with Sky and he went off-grid for two weeks with his phone switched off. In a way it was quite funny: there's our Bradley, a price tag of two million quid a year and for a fortnight nobody knew where the heck he was.

In other ways, though, I'm convinced that that ability of Bradley to tune himself out of situations and disconnect at will was one of his greatest gifts as a racer, because it could manifest itself as a skill: one of being very, very selfish, but in a good way. When it was time to be full on for an event, Bradley would blank out any white noise. He'd be in that tunnel and he wouldn't hear anything he didn't need to hear, or see anything he didn't need to see. He'd be a man on a mission.

Even more amazingly, and again, that shows how much of a champion he was, he could vary that level of mental commitment at will. From a really early age, Bradley would be sometimes 100 per cent concentrated on events, but he could simmer down to exactly 90 per cent or 80 per cent of that focus, just as he chose.

The question of how to stay really focused and blank out the rest of the distractions is something that maybe has a historical angle too. Guys like Bradley, myself and Geraint are all part of a particular generation of British pro racers who were sometimes pushed out to race abroad for months in foreign teams, on our own. Personally, I'd found that in some ways British Cycling was so far ahead in the sports-science angle and the foreign pro teams' approach seemed so backward in comparison that I would tune out at times. On top of that, objectives and goals that were so clear with GB became all fuzzy and blurry in a foreign team – or it felt that way at first. But at least that cycling 'education' abroad taught us how to think for ourselves, establish our own priorities and make our own choices when they mattered. That is not something that would be so necessary, say, in a British Academy house abroad where there's a group mentality and a group to support you. Those kinds of places had other downsides as well – which is why I turned down the option of staying in a shared house with other young British Cycling-backed riders in France in 2001.

On top of that, when you've no one to talk to because you're living abroad alone, and handling a different environment, language and culture to the one you grew up with every hour of every single day, you naturally become more introverted and get tunnel vision. That's because you know whatever white noise there is out there beyond the cycling world when you're abroad is guaranteed not to be very helpful. You just say 'fuck it' and do what you've got to do to be sure to switch off all the other rubbish. You can't, and you won't let it affect you. And Bradley benefited massively from that – as I did, to the point where what seemed at the time to be a huge challenge is now something you laugh at and wonder why you even considered it to be so daunting.

But for all Bradley's capacities for individual commitment, independent thinking and prioritizing were enormously useful, it didn't always make him friends. In the 2010 Giro d'Italia, for example, after a fortnight he was lying seventh overall and had done really well on one of the toughest stages in years, when the race ripped itself apart en route to L'Aquila a few days before. So he was clearly on form, then all of a sudden he just decided that he didn't want to fight for the GC (General Classification) because he was going too deep before the Tour. So he eased back, dropped out of the GC battle and it turned out we'd done two weeks' full-on riding for our GC leader for nothing.

In one sense, that was typical Bradley and I understand if it pissed some people off, particularly those who hadn't been on the track racing with him and who didn't know his background. But it also showed Bradley had eyes on one thing. He wasn't doing it because he was a cock, he was doing it because he felt it was the right thing to do for the Tour de France, and given that kind of single-minded focus, it didn't matter what the team thought.

That ability to home in on what mattered and stick to it no matter what couldn't make up for some gaps in his talent set. For example, when I think about stage racing stars in my era, the Italian Tour de France winner in 2014, Vincenzo

Nibali, could float around at the front on a bunch in a race, feeling and looking totally relaxed. But in the same circumstances, you could always feel the stress fields surrounding Bradley. That's not to say that when Brad put his mind to it, he wouldn't find a way to get to where he wanted to be. But he wasn't as much of a natural in that sort of situation.

It was the same in one-day races. I remember watching Bradley in Paris–Roubaix one time, once there had been the usual initial split, and he'd drift to the back then ride up to the front again. Classics stars like Tom Boonen, Fabian Cancellara – and among the sprinters, Cav of course – were, or are, the ones that could be floating around in the bubble on the front without making an effort. Those guys are always there, whether they're going well or badly. But if Bradley was in a bad way, he'd be right at the back of the bunch with me, having a laugh.

*

From about the winter of 2000 onwards, as National track team-mates, we started rooming together, and that was when I got to know him a lot better. It wasn't just the track, either: in 2001 we did a ton of races in France and Spain with the parts of the Under-23 National road squad, events like the Circuit des Mines and the Cinturón a Mallorca. Bradley won Mallorca and I was on full team worker duty for him there, but if we rode so well together it was partly because the mood in the team was so good. We were always laughing about something for one thing, and as I'd learned he had a wicked sense of humour.

Bradley's speciality for getting a laugh was mimicry, starting with the management in the GB squad like – off the top of my head and recalling that particular era – Pete the soigneur, who was a builder and used to work for Bradley off season, Gary Beckett, another soigneur and friend of his, Doug Dailey the logistics guy and a total legend, Dave Brailsford of course, and John Herety, the road team director up until 2005. No matter who, he would often be taking the piss out of the staff and riders in a way that couldn't help but make you laugh.

Probably the best example of this would be the spoof 'Godfather Trilogy', a video we made during the Circuit des Mines one year. Morale wasn't great because we'd done a big block of track and put on weight. Now we were back on the road at a race where we were getting exactly the battering you go to those races for, to help you lose those extra kilograms. So over the race Bradley had a new computer with a camera, which was a novelty back then; I'd never seen one on a computer before. As the video-making trilogy proceeded, one of us pretended to be John Herety as Don Corleone (complete with skull cap for John, given his lack of hair); the other would ask the questions and then they panned back to John/ Corleone and we kept adding another pillow under the bed to simulate John/Don Corleone getting larger and larger.

But he wouldn't just take the mickey out of the guys on the team. When he got to be famous – and was mixing with other famous people – that didn't put him off either. I remember when he was on the BBC Sports Personality of the Year – before the cameras started rolling he really took the mick out of Lee Dixon, the former Arsenal defender and a well-known footballer. Bradley went up to Lee and said, without batting an eyelid, 'Oh, you used to play up front for Stoke, didn't you?' However much Lee insisted on the opposite – and he tried – Bradley would deadpan him back, 'No, it was Stoke, I'm sure.' 'It was Stoke, I remember.'…

When Bradley was young, it didn't seem to matter what it was – everything was funny. I remember staying up late, even on a race as hard as Circuit des Mines, just laughing and laughing.

For sure, it wasn't always easy if you were the butt of his humour, particularly because Bradley used it to bring people down a peg or six at times. If somebody mouthed off too much about having a fit new girlfriend or a nice designer shirt, say, they'd find themselves getting a full blast of Bradley's piss-taking.

But at other times he used it to capture and take the mickey out of our own particular cycling world. I remember at Chris Newton's thirtieth birthday party, there was a brass band on a stage, and Wiggo suddenly went up there and started singing a kind of bluesy rap containing something about everybody we knew… 'Tony Gibb – slip-on loafers; Simon Jones – Cornish pasty; Paul Manning – loves his glasses; Steve Cummings – lives in Heswall.' it just went on and on, all off the cuff, and the band picked up the melody and backed him up as he singlehandedly ripped the piss out of the team pursuit squad and everything we were doing, Ali G style. It's moments like that when you think – this guy is a genius and not just when he's on a bike.

But either way we'd race and train hard and I was selfless for him. Despite the laughs, there was always a serious edge to him too, and for all the humour, if things weren't going well, he might yet stop laughing and close up. But I recognized that reaction for what it was and it never really bothered me at all. In the end, I'd laugh at him and my mickey-taking would take him through to the other side of getting the hump about something. Before you knew it, he'd be turning the tables and taking the piss out of me, saying, 'Oh, Steve's got the hump now,' and that way, we'd move out of the minefields and on to the next thing.

It helped, of course, that when we switched off in the track team, we'd really switch off. One example that probably sounds like nothing special, until you remember that in the GB squad anything that wasn't deemed ideal for performance was frowned upon and at times it felt suffocating, was in the middle of a training camp when we sneaked on to the hotel roof somewhere in Spain to go sunbathing. Or to give a rather more extreme example (although Bradley wasn't there) there were the infamous events of Christmas 2002 in Mallorca when Heiko, our German trainer, had just come on board the GB track team. While Simon Jones took him off to a restaurant for a meal and a chat, the track team went for a coffee, decided to have a beer, ended up drinking ten beers, finally all got blind drunk in a pub and finished off by jumping in the sea. As our trousers got completely soaked and really heavy and kept falling down, it seemed like a good idea at the time to take them off and wrap them round our heads as we headed for the hotel. So that was Heiko's first sight of the illustrious GB team pursuit squad as he sat eating his meal at a table next to the restaurant windows: a bunch of lads walking down the street clad only in our underpants and with sopping wet trousers round our heads and over our shoulders. (I have to add that Heiko dealt with it really well: the next morning he lined us four up and with a completely straight face said, 'OK you're Man 1' – the rider who starts a team pursuit rolling – 'you're Man 2, you're Man 3 and you, you're with the swimming team.' After which, 'Guys, do we want to be cyclists or make the swimming team?' became a running joke within the squad.)

But those laid-back times only happened occasionally, and there were always going to be times as the big events drew close that the pressure would rise and rise. Leading into those kinds of races, I knew the process with Bradley would invariably be based initially on 'if he talks and you want to have a laugh, then great.' But I knew that a minute or two after that, as the focus levels went up and the humour levels went down, he wouldn't be sitting there or talking to you at all. He was a man on a mission and you had to respect his space, and accept that at times it was best to leave him alone.

That was the thing: for all his piss-taking of people, he still had a very serious edge to all his racing. Occasionally, the two sides of him would combine, like in 2003 or so when we were doing the pursuit together and I was given the role of team captain. (Basically, I'd realized that we needed to push for an extra level of professionalism and we couldn't be swimmers and get hammered after every World Cup if we ended up finishing second, third, fourth or fifth.) If some of the lads weren't in great form, say, or were (as young lads all are) scatty and forgetful and needed a talking-to, initially Bradley would just be in Bradley world and he'd maybe say something to me about it at most. But then he'd also take the piss out of the guys as a way of dealing with it too, and in the process show that actually what they were doing mattered to him more than he let on: 'Oh, fucking hell I see you've brought your shoes today, lads, well done. Nice of you to turn up.'

We kept each other going during our own tougher times too. I remember doing the Tour de l'Avenir stage race in France in 2005 when he was in Crédit Agricole and I was in Landbouwkrediet, and we were in a similar position: he was stuck in Nantes, France, living alone and hating it, and I was stuck in Belgium and hating a lot of it too. At the Tour de l'Avenir, Bradley did a terrible prologue by his standards, which was his one target in the race, so afterwards I tried to get his spirits back up, telling him that if he'd done the hard yards beforehand, he shouldn't throw the toys out of the pram and that maybe it'd work out in the next few days. At the same time, I found I was trying to convince myself along the same lines, because I had similar doubts about my own performance.

So because of those mutual doubts, we kept on pushing each other to the edge of quitting, but then holding each other back, saying, 'OK, we're abandoning here after this stage, because there's an airport close by, and we can get back to the UK and rent a car to get us home.' And we planned our abandons, and then planned another, and another. But as things turned out, by taking it one day at a time and looking out for each other, we stuck it out one day after another and somehow we finished the whole thing. In the middle of all this, Bradley ended up winning a stage from a break, and I got third the same day, so it worked out really well – and he really appreciated what I'd done for him too. He even made sure the Crédit Agricole soigneur got me into their team car for a lift back to the airport after the race, even if it was so full of equipment and kit there wasn't enough space in the car, so I had to sit in it and then they packed bags on top of me.

As a training partner, we were equally close, and in terms of what I wanted to achieve form-wise, he always set the standard. When Simon Jones came on board at the GB track team and they made the whole structure of training programmes more professional, I enjoyed how it made me improve and the sense I had that Simon really cared. It had other consequences I hadn't expected: I also found that provided it wasn't a time trial, I was closer to Bradley on any kind of road training ride between two and five hours. With repeated efforts, at long camps, I would get better because one strong point was I could absorb a lot of work. But being that good a training relationship, sometimes we combined forces and ended up being unintentionally merciless to the other guys, like when we went to Mallorca one early spring in the early noughties, and the very first session was a three-up training ride with another GB track team-mate, and world champion, Rob Hayles.

We were supposed to do an intermittent zone three training ride for two hours – that's a tough pace where your heart rate is at around 90 per cent of its maximum capacity – but instead it morphed into intermittent zone five, where your heart rate is going at nearly 100 per cent. That's a scientific way of saying we were ripping it up on that training ride, because Bradley and I had been psyching each other up about winning the Olympics and how important every session was.

We didn't bother to inform poor Rob though, who was a bit heavy and had just had a great Christmas with the family. So in the training we just went on killing him and then killing him a bit more.

By going so hard in that first session and putting himself under such pressure, Rob really put himself in a box for the first half of the camp. As a result Brad and I would go on doing training rides for three hours in the morning and another couple in the afternoon with some efforts. But we'd look in as we went down the hotel corridor and poor Rob would be sitting there in his room for hours, doing twenty minutes in the afternoon on the rollers, as he called it, 'colouring in'.

After I stopped doing the track in 2008, Brad and I would keep in touch loosely, and he'd send me a funny video of him mimicking somebody from time to time. But then we both signed for Sky in 2010, and they wanted us to race together almost all the time so it was back to how things were in the track days.

Having been apart for a couple of years, I found he was as focused on his performance on the road as he had been on the track, which was fine, and I got to enjoy a lot more of his particular sense of humour, which was great. We'd have a right laugh, probably too much but just as before it was our way of filtering down the pressure.

However, it's also true that not everybody would get it. I remember Froome took a lot of shit – he used to call Froome the Froominator and laugh at his habit of wearing an African sarong thing because he used to get sore balls – and he'd be sitting at the back of the bus, putting chamois cream on his balls with his tackle in view. A lot of it was banter but I think

Froome maybe found Brad a bit too much, like some other people who'd take offence. I think it was Chris who said that Bradley was like a bollard or a traffic island in the road – somebody you had to go round rather than through. Sometimes that was quite a good analogy, even if when he was younger when I started racing with him he was less like that.

But it wasn't just Froome he'd target with his humour at Sky: if the management were doing something that wasn't fair, he'd impersonate them, taking that unfairness to extremes. It didn't matter that the rest of the team would be saying, 'Fucking hell, you can't say that, Brad,' – he'd do it anyway, be it Dave Brailsford or team performance director Rod Ellingworth talking about 'doing a little bit of threshold', which Bradley didn't like, or the videos he made imitating the team's first manager, Scott Sunderland, which we'd then put on the bus screen projector, much to the delight of the other guys. I ended up getting the shit for that particular private showing actually, but I didn't mind taking the flak because that was how things were at Sky: our friendship meant I felt massive empathy for Bradley and his predicament in the team.

In races, and unlike some GC riders, he didn't want a Sherpa rider with him all the time to keep him out of trouble. Sometimes he'd have a big guy like Christian Knees to open up a way through the bunch, but Brad had the advantage of being tall, and he knew how to steamroll his own way to the front of the race when the situation demanded. I think initially that he didn't want a whole team around him, perhaps because he was used to doing things his way and predominantly alone. Maybe he didn't want the pressure of having the whole team centred round him. But perhaps it took time for him to develop and accept that he needed that level of support and he had to learn to deal with it.

Initially, the team was convinced it would be better for us to room together at races to help keep the pressure down. But after a while he opted to head off by himself and stick with Mario the soigneur. The staff were very fond of him – they'd make sure he had his own pillow and kettle – and he just got by like that, without any excessive demands.

Focusing on what he could control was another strong point of Bradley's as a racer. If something wasn't good with his equipment, he'd certainly vent – what the fuck are these overshoes? – but beyond that he handled that area very cleverly. Rather than get too stressed long term, he delegated it all to the British Cycling R & D team. At that time there was a massive crossover between British Cycling and Sky, so whatever British Cycling found was what Sky, finally, got. The downside of that was that at the time, if you, as a rider, left Sky, in a way it felt like you'd left British Cycling as well.

Yet for all his happiness to delegate, he still had a real nerdy side to him about the sport and equipment in particular. Right back to when he was a junior, you could call him a cycling pervert: he'd remember not only who won what race, large or small, but also what shoes, glasses, helmet they were wearing when they won as well. It wasn't just the big names. He used to tell me that I hadn't been wearing a certain pair of Sidi shoes when I won some obscure race somewhere – 'No, they were the yellow ones.' He'd be right, of course. There are very few riders I know who are like that; it's another thing that makes him special.

Even more than when he was doing the track, in 2010 and 2011, the two years I spent at Sky, Bradley was under enormous pressure. That was partly because he was a professional down to his fingertips. But at the same time, given the scale of expectations when Dave Brailsford said that Sky was going to win the Tour, before Chris Froome started turning in his GC victories, there was only one guy at Sky who looked like he was actually going to do that, and that was Bradley.

That's a huge responsibility and effectively he was carrying the whole team. I watched that process develop, all the way through the Giro and the other races where I was supposed to be his right-hand man – and I did that quite well – up to the Tour, where we both weren't in such great shape. Whereas before we'd either been working flat out and I'd be admiring his ability to commit or he'd be Bradley the demon piss-taker and we'd be having a laugh, at the Tour I found myself feeling something new. I just felt sorry for the guy, because having all that pressure and not being able to deliver despite absolute commitment was such a lonely place for him to be in.

You could argue, maybe, people like Steve Peters were floating around and if Bradley had wanted to, he could have got some help. I'm not sure if he did or he didn't, to be honest. But he didn't appear to have done that because his personality is what it is – a lion in the jungle...

Team meetings exposed him in particular. In 2010, the year before he started winning races all over, he wasn't very vocal on the bus when the meetings were happening. He was more like a man with the weight of the world on his shoulders, because he wasn't really performing and neither was the team. It all seemed like a puzzle that everybody, not just him, was struggling to put together, and, finally, I was really happy to get away from that situation because I felt like I'd got too close to it all. It was intense and I was intense and the combination wasn't helping me. I wasn't coping.

Oddly enough, it didn't feel like the pressure got much easier for him to handle when he had won the Tour. We'd kept in touch even though I'd long since left Sky by then, and I was over the moon for him winning. I'd not talked to him much during the race itself, which I didn't mind because it made total sense in terms of where we were respectively that July: I'd had a terrible year, kept on crashing and getting injured. So while I was at the back suffering and trying to survive, he was at the front of the bunch in flying form, trying to be the first Briton ever to win the race.

We spoke at length on the last stage, though, which was great, and I'd gone on the Sky team bus before the start in Paris, which was awkward – although I was glad I did it, the atmosphere was too close to feeling like 'the enemy is on the bus.' But after the race and the Olympics, when he was probably the most famous man in the UK for a week or so, he organized a 'yellow ball' – vodka bottles at each table, all a bit Mod. Even though I'd largely finished with the partying and drinking phase of my life, I felt I should go to the ball to support him and I was worried about how he would handle the fame and attention, which can't have been easy on him or his family.

You could see that last question in the way that after the Tour he went through a spell where he was a bit of a tool. But that's my point: maybe anybody risks being a tool in those circumstances where winning the Tour thrusts you head first into the limelight. Not only that, suddenly you've got guys like Liam Gallagher on your guest list for your yellow party or whatever (and he never showed up, either). I remember Geraint saying it was mad after winning the Tour because you're doing things like going backstage with Elton John, and in situations like that Geraint seemed to be able to remain grounded whereas for Brad it seemed to be more of a challenge.

So handling that is a big ask. It's even more marked because of the contrast between being on a race, whether it's the Tour de France or a tiny race in Belgium, and when you suddenly get out of it and it's over, where you have to deal with what people in the bigger world have made of it. When he won the Tour, finally, it was almost normal inside the race itself because he'd been in the yellow jersey for ten or fifteen days, so we all – media, riders, Bradley himself – had time to get used to it. But afterwards, while I'd gone back to Italy and mostly avoided seeing what it was like for Bradley, I knew that he was up to his neck in the Olympics and then he'd been plunged into the whole business of suddenly being the most famous man in the UK.

He's taken some very different attitudes towards his own success, and again part of that is, I think, due to his need to withdraw from it all. At first he went through this phase of being a celebrity, knocking around with the likes of – as I've pointed out – Liam Gallagher. But then he went into a mode of 'fuck that, that's not me, keep it real' and headed to the opposite extreme. One day he came up to me and told me, 'I've sold all my watches and thrown out my trophies because I don't need that stuff – they don't define me.'

This takes me back to Steve Peters' idea of Bradley being a lion. The flip side of being so self-contained, and the way he can focus on things, is partly that I don't think there are that many people out there who actually understand him, and I don't feel he's good about opening up about things – at all, which is not so cool. He's very different to Cav in that aspect, because Cav will talk a lot, about anything and everything. But with Bradley, it happens so rarely that you always remember it. Other times, you won't hear from him for a while, and if you know there's something that could be wrong, it's worrying, as it would be with anybody.

He can have an aura of not giving a fuck about anything too, which I find oddly relaxing, but then sometimes it's not a pose and he really doesn't seem to give a fuck about anything. But either way the thing was you couldn't tell Bradley anything about how to do something. He's always had to go and find it out for himself, and sometimes that's a weakness, sometimes that's a huge strength. He never stops having ideas about what he should be up to either, and the ideas vary wildly. There's nothing that he could do that would surprise me and part of our being friends is accepting that. I remember when I invited him to my wedding I had no idea if he would actually turn up, given he's on his own road to wherever. (He did turn up, by the way.) And sometimes that part of him can be truly nerve-wracking. I remember once travelling up from Italy to go and meet him in Salzburg so we could see a football match and sending him a text from the railway station, saying, 'Look, I'm getting an overnight train – so make an effort will you?'

But at the end of the day, that's just Bradley: he's always wanted to take his own path in and out of the cycling jungle, and any other jungle he's found since retiring. He's my brother from another mother but now, then and always, he's his own man too. And I respect that.

Chapter 6

The Wrong Kind of Limits: Team Sky 2010–11

When I signed for Team Sky as one of their riders in their first ever line-up, I had this idea that I was really going to explore how good I could be. On paper the circumstances seemed perfect because I was on board there with Dave B and Shane Sutton and I knew how ambitious they were. Although they had publicly given themselves five years to win the Tour, it was a goal from the first day the team started.

When it came to winning the Tour, Dave was always asking rhetorically, 'Why can't you do it?' and certainly racing history was on their side. If you had wound back the clock ten years and looked at what Brailsford and British Cycling had achieved on the track for Great Britain in that time, Dave's question back then had been, 'Why can't you win an Olympic gold?' But he'd answered that himself, because he'd masterminded British Cycling's track performances as they went from netting bronze medals and the occasional gold in the Olympics and Worlds to a scenario where if you made the team and you couldn't get at least one gold, you were the odd one out.

So I was totally on board in Sky. I had faith in Brailsford. I thought they'd revolutionize cycling and I was keen to be a part of it. I looked at how far Wiggo had gone on the road and thought, given my past and his past on the track, that it'd be hard, but as I was in the right place and environment to explore my limits it didn't seem out of the question that I could do something similar.

The process of getting into Sky had begun, oddly enough, when I signed with another team, Barloworld, in 2008 and had shown what I could do on the road whilst still on the GB track programme. Then it continued, equally oddly, when I was approached by another team, Astana, at the end of 2008 with an offer of a contract for two years. I flagged this interest of Astana up to Dave B, and that was when he confirmed that Sky was going to start in 2010; they'd seen how I raced and they wanted me as part of the squad. He also told me how much he was going to pay me and said that instead of Astana I should stay with Barloworld for another year.

In one way it was hard not to sign with Astana, because I really liked the people I knew in the team. But the squad's Kazakh management side, which was obviously a very significant element, was a mystery to me.

So my idea was that I could and would get into a whole new world at Sky. I had a lot to learn.

*

It's a typical race day at Team Sky somewhere in the middle of the 2010 Tour de France, my first and the team's first and we're sitting on the team bus in the middle of the daily pre-stage meeting. Just as now, each rider has his own seat and table locker in the two rows of six, I'm sitting there in the middle near Geraint, Brad's at the back... but the star of the show is the overhead projector, which they use for the whole of the meeting, at every meeting. Your picture comes up on the projector and it says 'your role' under-neath. It's always this military stuff: Brad as commander, Juan Antonio Flecha, our Classics specialist, is the tank driver, I'm down as 'wingman' – all this sort of shit. You'd have a list of things to do below your picture and my list is always enormous. First hour: only six guys in the break. Or only four. No riders from this team in the break. Or that team. Or that team. Once that's done, keep Bradley out of the wind in this section. Get Bradley here in that section. Get bottles here. Get bottles there. Then there's the final. On and on. It's overwhelming. How am I supposed to memorize all that? I couldn't. But then it comes to Brad and the projector flashes up 'zero watts'. And you think 'Like – really? How the fuck are you going to race the Tour with zero watts?'

The meetings are novel in their presentation format, which is at first refreshing but then it gets tiring, particularly as they're really long too, and the upshot is I'm tired even before the stages have begun.

I was way too nervous to feel the buzz around the Tour. I know it's there; for one thing it's a sign of how big it is that I have to talk to journalists every day. But I found those interviews really hard because I didn't have anything good to say. Basically, I wanted something to swallow me up because I know I'm not on top form and the Tour is the worst race in the world to be in poor shape. You want to be there at the Tour – who doesn't? But not in these circumstances when I'm struggling and in a world of hurt.

On top of that there's Sky's race strategy to deal with, which for most of the Tour is the same as it's been since January. We have one main mission, and that's GC for stage races with Brad. But just because they've got one overriding goal and they've come out with these sweeping statements about winning the Tour in five years, you can't get away from the really negative atmosphere that undercuts it all. Or maybe that's only to be expected as even when Wiggo was lying seventeenth or worse in the Tour, they were still trying to race as if a multiple Grand Tour winner like Lance Armstrong was in the team. It might have been the necessary step they needed to get where they wanted to go, but at the time, if you added in the intensity coming at us from above, it was a challenge to tolerate.

It doesn't actually help that, after two weeks in the Tour and six months of this strategy, the management deviate, totally, from their previous approach of the whole season. Suddenly, instead of GC with Brad, they realize they're getting nowhere and they switch to a policy of 'All right, now we're going to try to win a stage.' But it's too late: there are almost only mountain stages left to race, meaning we've barely got any real opportunities even to get a consolation win.

We have had our chances before though. There was a first-week stage that went over some of the cobbled sectors of farm roads they use in the Paris–Roubaix Classic and I'd got up front after another team-mate, Simon Gerrans, gave me a hand. Geraint was already in on the move, and with two of us in the break, for sure there could have been a good outcome for Sky. But no. Instead, the team told me in no uncertain terms to drop back from the break and wait for Brad. So rather than me and Geraint riding off each other and one of us maybe getting away and increasing the team's chances of winning a prestigious stage of the Tour, we came away empty-handed.

But that was the Sky mentality: rigid and robotic, or that was my perception. It was those kinds of moments, like on the Roubaix stage, when I realized, 'I don't want to race like this.' It was taking all the fun out of racing and my attitude was: enjoy what you do or it can kill you! If I was having fun all the necessary sacrifices seemed effortless, but this was doing me in – physically and mentally.

What made it far worse was this strategy of 'all for Brad' had already fallen apart at the Giro, where at least initially we had done much better than in the Tour. He had won the opening prologue and then we had performed well by getting Bradley and some other guys from the team on a famous race-changing big break on the 260-kilometre stage to L'Aquila, the one that changed the race by nearly destroying the chances of favourites like Vinokourov and Cadel Evans. We'd not just worked perfectly as a team that day; we all knew the stage itself was something special – I remember the stage winner, Evgeni Petrov, saying as we rode along, 'Today we change cycling.' And we were really part of it, something of which the team could feel proud.

But then, as I already wrote in a previous chapter, Brad changed his mind about the Giro GC, and all that effort had been for nothing. By the Tour we were back to 'all for Bradley on GC, come what may'. It was like the Giro hadn't happened.

It wasn't just about the team getting crap results in the Tour or shooting itself in the foot at the Giro, even in the smaller races I'd suffered from rigid robotic style in Sky's strategies. At one stage race somewhere that first year, I'd been lying eleventh, which might not sound great, but I was in flying form and I knew there were some opportunities coming up for me to improve on that.

Instead, I was asked to ride for our sprinter and in the process ensure that on what were good stages for me to have a chance to get away, we stayed together as a bunch all the way to the line. I was so angry one day that all I wanted to do was drop everyone. Eventually, I rode on the front, all by myself, for 25 kilometres, and I went so hard it split the group. We didn't win the sprint, either.

So it was a different version of the same old story: at a big team like Sky the management's view was I wasn't good enough to lead, and that meant I was always falling into this domestique's role. Because I was good on the flat and OK on the climbs, everybody would say, 'That's great, Steve can pull. Steve can pull.' End of story. But why did it have to be like that? My view was that I wasn't good enough to be a consistent leader or GC rider. But I was hungry to win and I wanted to have fun trying, because that's what made me happy and without happiness I would never have got the best out of myself. I hated the feeling of not doing that – it was my biggest fear.

*

To try to treat this issue objectively, Dave B likes to be in control, which is fair enough when you have the favourite and you are on a predictable course with few contenders like the Tour de France.

But that same strategy was even applied in a race like the Tour of Britain, which is all but impossible to control. Britain consists of one very hilly stage after another. The time trial, when they have one, is very short so you don't get a clear pecking order from it, and on top of that there are only six riders in a team. I would have preferred to take risks, because I wanted to think and I wanted to improve and I wanted deep down to get the best out of myself. But they would focus on controlling the race a lot and end up fifth.

This serious mismatching of strategies filtered down to me, my morale and my performance. It wasn't so bad in the cobbled Classics group, led by guys like Geraint and Ian Stannard, but in the Ardennes Classics/Grand Tours group with riders like me, there was a real sense of negativity. Then to make matters worse they packed me into far too many races: in the first half of 2010 I did the GP Marseilles, the Étoile de Bessèges, the Tour of Andalucía, GP Almeria, Paris–Nice, the Tour of Catalonia, the Tour of the Basque Country, the Ardennes, the Giro, ten days of Tour reconnaissance with six-hour rides most days, and then the Tour de France itself.

The attitude was 'Steve's going well, let's put him in the Giro, let's put him in the Tour, let's put him here there and everywhere.' Then the comments started that 'Steve wasn't on it at the Tour.' But that was both harsh and skewed given the number of races I'd done.

It wasn't just the race programme that went against me or the race strategy. On top of that I felt like I was being used as a guinea pig in a lot of things. To give one example, which I suspect was to act as a test run for Wiggins before they tried it on him, I trialled a super-restricted diet of 1000 calories a day. It was centred on what they called 'fruit days': in other words, two pieces of fruit five times a day and half a pint of skimmed milk for your protein, and that'd be it. Our nutritionist would measure your body fat levels and say, 'OK, you're 10 per cent, pop in a couple of fruit days and that'll bring you back down.'

These were combined with a catabolic diet of no breakfast, ride your bike for up to five hours, then have 200–300 grams of meat or fish and salad for lunch and dinner. Five days on like that, then five days off.

The year Sky started I did that for three months at fortnightly intervals, and it certainly was effective in one way as I dropped to my lowest ever weight of 69.9 kilos. (Just to give you an idea of how extreme that is, at the Tour de France in 2015 and 2016, my two most successful years, my in-form weight was 75 kilos.) And on top of that I was really strong on short, steep climbs and going uphill.

Initially, I was happy to do this as I was keen to be as light as possible – what cyclist isn't? But the benefits didn't work more than short term because apart from not being super-healthy the problem with crash diets is there's always a rebound and they aren't sustainable. Your body ends up grabbing everything it can at a race, and then it becomes bloated. It just underlines that what you do at home needs to resemble what you do in a race, and when it comes to diet, I preferred sustainable practice – which 1000 calories a day, particularly when you're racing really hard for seven months, definitely isn't.

Overall, Sky's ideas and plans were due to them being on a huge learning curve. What cracked me up about that was that I was thirty and I didn't have time for ideas that I'd already tried in the track days and knew didn't work or hesitated to try them again. Don't get me wrong, I was all up for testing riders' strength and trying to use a scientific approach, and I understood the importance of weight loss, so I tried all this off-the-wall stuff. But another part of me quickly had had enough of it and just wanted to do normal, sustainable things.

I used to look at certain riders and think, 'Fucking hell, they're always tanned and lean, and they're in good shape from February to October. End of story.' The foundations for my strategies were about trying to do the basics better than anyone else. Sky, on the other hand, had the right goals, maybe, but they were hell-bent on having a go at making round wheels square and seeing if that worked out this time for once.

I still had it in my head that if someone was going to win the Tour with Dave B, you'd follow him because he'd been so successful, and in my own way I was following. But if that attitude of mine was positive, there was another side of me that was kind of icy, that didn't like being told what to do and if a sports director came up with some stupid strategy, I found it very difficult not to voice an opinion. Perhaps my opinion was legitimate, but at the time I didn't have enough communication skills so I struggled to articulate myself and often my frustration spilt over. I questioned the rigour, I questioned the science, I questioned the people, I felt like I was running out of time and needed to go away and find a simple, tried and trusted methodology.

After the Tour went wrong for me and the team, in the autumn and over that winter, rather than try to boost my morale for the following season, Sky unintentionally crushed it. For the 2011 race programmes, they had each rider on a big chart on a wall at team HQ, with a pink label for guys provisionally down to do the Giro, yellow guys who will be doing the Tour, and the red guys will be doing the Vuelta. And the colour of my label? That was black. Because you've been blacklisted, Steve.

There will be a lot of people reading this, I'm sure, who are wondering that if I thought Sky wasn't an efficient or effective team back then, why on earth am I working for the same line-up now? The answer to that one is easier than you might think: I'm talking about what the team was like over a decade ago, when Sky had just started and were still finding their feet, and when I was in a very different position in my career. Where we are now is, thankfully, a whole different story, and a wholly different time.

It helped that I never had a problem with Dave Brailsford. We didn't always agree, but I understood and always respected that he wanted what was best for the team – not necessarily what was best for me. But that was when I realized I wasn't there to win, I was there to be a robot, something that I couldn't adapt to and I knew it would be best to leave. The feeling was no doubt mutual.

Ultimately, the biggest problem for me, though, at Sky in 2010, was that as a person and as a rider I was a square peg that couldn't fit into any of the round holes. On top of which, up until the Tour I'd pop out these good results all the time, which actually threw them even more. I couldn't win the Tour, I probably wasn't going to be a super mountain domestique and I certainly didn't like all the fighting on the front of the bunch all day, which was the other option on the table – to become a domestique working on the flatter stages. Where did I fit into that?

*

It was always in my nature to be looking for something that gave me an advantage or represented an advance in my performance. But there was – and is – one clear condition to all of that. It has always had to be a legal advantage or advance – 100 per cent.

Medicine for me was a no-go area, something I didn't want to approach or experiment with at all, partly because there's a thin line between what's allowed and what isn't, and partly because I hated the idea of the Festina affair and all that shit, needles and so on. To be honest, it just scared the crap out of me and I didn't want anything to do with it. I considered medicine as something you'd only have if you were sick and that was it.

At Sky, the guy I really trusted on that question was Roger Palfreeman, one of the team doctors. I'd always be double-checking with him. Probably I was stupid about being so cautious but that's the way it was and has always been. I just didn't want to have anything to do with anything that could be a threat to that stance.

It is true I had missed a number of out-of-competition anti-doping tests when I was living on the Wirral and doing the track. But this was due to lax organizational skills, struggles with the 'whereabouts system', as the programme for riders indicating where they could be tested was called, or simple last-minute changes of plan. You always have to say where you are for at least one hour of every day on the whereabouts forms for out-of-competition testing and I'd always say I'd be at home between eight and nine in the morning. But then one morning I'd left to go to the velodrome at six and after they came to the house and failed to find me there, they refused to go over to Manchester to test me. So that was one strike against me. When I'd missed two, I decided it was high time Nicky took over sorting out the forms in full, because I recognize it's something I couldn't handle well. After that and for years in the second part of my career, there was never a problem.

Within the context of anti-doping I understood completely why this out-of-competition testing had to be done, even if as a process I found it very wearing and hateful. There'd be times when you'd have dinner, come home at ten at night and the inspectors would be outside your home, waiting for you to do the anti-doping test. Or they'd turn up at six in the morning, which is fine according to the rules, but it's not fun either. What was worse was that a lot of the inspectors weren't trained properly and there were times when they wouldn't put the needle in correctly so it'd take three or more times to extract the blood sample.

Apart from those missed tests early on, the other issue I had with anti-doping legislation was due to struggling with allergies throughout my career, allergies caused for reasons that we were never able to pinpoint precisely, and one of the consequences of them was asthma. I had a Therapeutic Use Exemption certificate in 2008 for a salbutamol inhaler, but a little later on you didn't need that certificate for salbutamol if you stayed within the permitted dosage. I'd occasionally need to use it.

In any case, I definitely needed something, because when I have an allergic reaction, even now, often it creates more mucus, so your nose gets blocked, you get a sore throat, a chest infection or worse still a sinus infection. This was the pattern of many springs until we found another kind of inhaler, ipratropium, which helped manage it. But it did mean I had to avoid certain races, like the Tour de Romandie in Switzerland, where there's a high pollen count, throughout my career. I got a last unwelcome reminder of why I couldn't handle Romandie when my last team, Dimension Data, sent me there in 2018 despite my requests to the contrary and I ended up lying on the side of the road barely able to breathe.

That was my personal situation. But initially I wasn't convinced, given the history of the sport, that it was possible to win the Tour de France clean and, rightly or wrongly, this cast doubts in my mind whether winning the Tour was achievable for Team Sky given their strong anti-doping stance and policies. When Brad won the Tour and that was followed up by Froome and G's victories, that had a significant effect for me because it proved, more than once, that it was possible to win at the very highest level without doping.

This period also saw a shift in my mindset to 'Yes, dream of winning, but put that to the back of your mind and focus on doing your best – refine the process and the outcome/results will take care of themselves.' I'd also reached a stage where I realized perhaps I could not win big races and be more consistent, even at Sky. But I wanted to make sure before I left the sport I had got the best out of myself.

That, though, was in the future. All I knew was there were a number of reasons why I wanted to leave Sky and do things differently. I wanted to take on the discipline and the structure of the Italian professional racing scene, to be the kind of guy that didn't have to think that much about what the cycling lifestyle actually is because they know that if you just eat well, sleep well and live well, you'll progress. Sky were tactically too one-dimensional, and given the number of life lessons I was getting in Italy at the time, you might even say they were too British for me. They were too unwilling to recognize some things have to be left to chance. A lot of the management had been used to working in a track environment where the racing is very controllable barring the mass start events. On the road, while strategically you can plan in advance, tactically you can't because you have to accept the scenario changes at the drop of a hat. But Sky tried to plan everything down to the last detail, without allowing for all the elements of uncertainty that always come into road racing – the weather, the terrain, the number of teams...

I didn't just struggle with that attitude. On top of that I also needed a sniff of victory. I didn't want to be a robot – no way – and I certainly didn't want to be in the team just because people thought it was a cool squad and they had one of the biggest budgets in cycling.

As things worked out, I started 2011, my second year with Sky, very strongly. I won a stage in the Volta ao Algarve in 2011, ahead of my old Discovery team-mate Alberto Contador, a double Tour de France winner, and briefly led the race. Even then, another squad, BMC, were already talking to me about 2012. Then if I needed more convincing it was time to move on, I had another reminder of my descending position in the Team Sky priority list when I caught pneumonia after Liège.

The illness was horrendous. Forty-eight hours after I'd come back from Liège to Tuscany, I found I was lying on the couch with a fever and shaking and coughing up a lot of blood. It got so bad that I couldn't move, and Max drove me to the doctor in his car, who sent me immediately on to hospital. Max rushed me there, and I remember he even parked in the helicopter bay, abandoned the car with the doors wide open and carried me straight into A & E where I was in a daze for forty-eight hours. When I awoke though, it was anything but pleasant. I had severe pneumonia and I was in a ward with all these old people that kept dying and getting wheeled out. But my mum, dad and Nicky were with me and that was very comforting.

We were a bit worried about my chest as it seemed like I had a shadow on my lung, and I lost a lot of my form and strength. Finally, when I went out for a ride with Sean Yates and Max, they took me up the San Baronto climb in Tuscany. But Max could see I was in terrible shape and I could barely follow them, so we packed that in in favour of a black sepia pasta his wife Valentina made for lunch. The latter act of kindness was the kind of gesture they often made towards me and which helped me feel even more like one of their family.

All through this illness, I hadn't yet signed a contract with BMC, but their boss, Jim Ochowicz, had kept in touch, as had their team doctor Max Testa. So I felt it was the right decision to leave.

The situation unravelled so quickly at Sky that it wasn't that I didn't like it. I actually hated it. I couldn't wait to get out. I'd been put on the blacklist, literally, for 'not buying in', which I thought was very unfair because I'd done my best to do everything they'd asked, even if I wasn't perfect and made lots of mistakes. So after one year, in my mind I was already saying to myself, 'Fuck this, I'm going.' And that was that. Time to move on.

Chapter 7

No Stress Man

Y ou could sum up this chapter in a dozen or so words: nothing seems to stress Geraint Thomas out, and that's one of his greatest strengths as a person and an athlete.

I remember back in our track days, Simon Jones organized a camp for us in Australia, staying out at some golf club holiday resort in the middle of nowhere, an hour away from the velodrome, so we could get out fast on the bike for training on quieter roads. The idea was that it was good to be away from distractions. But because we were so far away from anything or anyone it was like living in the *Big Brother* house. I was rooming with G, and there was nothing to do. People were just cracking mentally at the tedium and intensity of it all and while I wasn't sleeping well as a result, G was snoring. I was ready to kill him.

In fact, though, you can't ever be angry with G. Other people, yes, but not G. He's so nice, so harmless and so incredibly calm. I've seen Froomey win the Tour, Brad win gold track medals and the Tour, Cav have huge success, and they've all started from scratch and gone to being superstars. You can see how it affects people, and you can understand why it would. But after winning the Tour in 2018 G had barely changed. He came to my home in Quarrata for a dinner after Strade Bianche in 2019 and I told him to let me know if he needed anything special to eat, thinking that as a Tour winner he was bound to be on some kind of special diet. Instead his answer was: 'Do you want to have a roast?' So you could see he was not fazed by it all, which was quite refreshing.

He was even laid-back during the time at Team Sky when he always found himself in Froome's shadow. He's a really loyal team-mate and person. Maybe I'm biased but I'm not sure if Froome would be so loyal if the shoe was on the other foot. I think G has super-clear thought processes, but Froomey – and this could be the kind of leader he is – is more ruthless. Even when Chris has poor form and he's been in the same situation for a week, he is the kind of leader who would still be thinking, 'This is just a bad day; tomorrow I'll be stronger,' and try to convince everyone else they are doing well, along with themselves. Other types of leader would say, 'I'm no good, I'm no good,' even if they are, and that's because they just don't like pressure and the possibility they could let people down.

G, meanwhile, has his own style of leadership, one that means he is harder to read in some ways, particularly as he's not a great talker for its own sake; he just gets on with it. At Sky we'd have all these meetings and everybody would have something to say, but G would just listen, take it all on board. G hates confrontation – and will do everything to avoid it – so if he disagrees he is likely to withdraw and go quiet and just crack on. But no matter what actually happened afterwards and no matter how testing the situation was, G could handle it, because one of the things that's made him such a great athlete is his ability to deal with almost anything that gets thrown at him.

Just to revisit that extremely challenging training camp in Australia, for example, quite apart from how tough it was off the bike, on the bike we'd have to ride a particularly testing training programme called 'Intermittent Zone Three'. In my case that meant G and I riding in turns at the front for two hours non-stop and normally at an average of 40 km/h on dead-straight roads, with these big trucks roaring past us all the time. It was horrendous. Then we'd get changed, ride 30 kilometres each way to the track and do a series of ten 6-kilometre low-gear efforts. Add it all up and we were doing something like 200 kilometres or maybe six hours on the bike, which is – if you keep on doing that – a heck of a lot.

Even Sean Yates, my road *directeur sportif* at the time and a legendary training animal, would say he thought it was too much and we should be careful. But if I was freaking out, and that's something I had to work on to improve, to G, that situation in Australia was all about just buckling down and getting on with it. And that is his default response to everything. It's a colossal talent to have.

I didn't suspect any of this when I first met G in the very 'glamorous' location of an Asda branch just outside the Manchester track, when he and Matt Brammeier were buying themselves lunch. As a first-year senior in 2004 or so, he'd made that transition from being a junior, and everybody was saying he was going to be really good. But to be honest, I'd heard that before about juniors who'd just moved up and they rarely turned out to be so great.

When I saw them on the bike and when I met them, though, I could appreciate that both G and Ed Clancy, who came on to the track programme at the same time, were seriously talented. Apart from liking them, I knew pretty much straight away they were better team pursuiters than me. That didn't make us rivals though; at the time, I was trying to get away with doing as little track and as much road as I could and they were going in the opposite direction. I think what was perhaps unique with G is he seemed to constantly improve – and was pretty steady with it. He would have the odd bad day like anyone else but when you looked at his trajectory it was always going up and his grounded personality surely helped him in that. He never seemed to be too high or too low, just stayed on the level all the time.

We got to know each other even more from 2008, when we were team-mates together on the road at Barloworld. Initially, I'd felt like I had to look after him as he was a bit scatty like every twenty-year-old can be. On top of that he was so laid-back, and you'd always have to be check he was going to be ready for the training ride at ten or whenever it was. For his part he was very sociable, and he'd bring me into the group of different riders for get-togethers and so on because I was naturally a bit of a loner. If G hadn't been involved, I'm sure I wouldn't have bothered. But it was good for me.

Our living together was something that happened by chance. Max had said that G had a spare room in his flat, and so in 2008 we shared for six months, together with Cav who'd borrow my room when I wasn't around. G used to drive me crazy with being spacy, particularly when he'd do things like go off for a race and for three days I'd be trying to work out what a smell was, and it'd turn out he'd left a bowl of cereal under the sofa or forgotten to switch on the dishwasher. He was the complete opposite to Ben Swift, an occasional visitor, who was such a fusspot he was always making sure his sunglasses were in a straight line and who couldn't leave the house without it being spotless. But it was never because G didn't care, just that he's naturally relaxed.

That time was very much a lads together atmosphere, because we were all young and starting out – or close to – on our careers. There were plenty of fun memories to share, like the barbecues we'd set up on the back balcony, which led to G dropping a sausage onto the baker's yard at the back and which somehow never decomposed, so we were joking about that for months. Then there were the long journeys in G's Polo, partly because my Golf, having got me over from the Wirral, began playing up, partly because his car had air con, unlike mine which you had to drive with the windows down and towels on the seats. But even then, we'd always have to do a three-hour drive to Bergamo and the team HQ before most races, and for some reason stuff would always happen on the way. I remember once when we were coming over the hills round Bologna that smoke started pouring out of his car and we were losing power to the point where we were doing 20 kilometres an hour. At first we said if we get to the top of the climb we'll be OK, we could freewheel down the other side. But the car kept on getting slower and slower and G was asking, 'What shall we do? Who'll know what to do?'

Finally, G had an idea: 'OK, let's call "glasses",' aka Paul Manning. If I was like a big brother to G, Paul – who's a sensible, very straight sort of bloke – was big brother to all of us. So we called up Paul, over in the UK all the way from the top of a hill near Bologna, to ask him how to fix the car. He instantly fired back, 'Have you got oil in it?' And we sort of looked at each other and answered, 'Erm, yes, that might be it.'

It wasn't just oil in the car, Geraint was so absent-minded he'd forget his key when he went out training, borrow mine and then lock both in the house. I was kind of used to this, but it didn't go down so well when Shane Sutton, one of the key figures in British Cycling at the time and with a notoriously short fuse, came out to stay with us. We came back from training and G was asking me if I had the key and I fired back, 'What do you mean, have I got the key?' and of course he had left it in the house. Shane was absolutely furious, yelling, 'You muppets, you stupid muppets,' and then he said, 'Right, hold this bike,' walked down the road and grabbed the first roadworks barrier that he could see and carried it back to outside the flat. Fortunately, it was June and warm and we'd left the windows open. So Shane put the barrier on its side and used it as a ladder to shin up to the balcony, jump over the railing and get inside through the windows – all the time shouting, 'Fucking hell,' 'You fucking idiots,' 'You muppets,' at the top of his voice as he did so. He didn't stop shouting until he opened the front door.

So we'd have our little dramas like that, but overall it was fun, probably the most we ever had. We were all pretty humble, so there weren't too many egos getting in the way, and we were living the dream and making money doing what we loved. Cav would be bouncing in and out, as he was on a different programme, then we'd go off and do our races, come back and talk them all through. There were no huge responsibilities, no major pressure to perform other than the pressure we put on ourselves, and in my case I was that bit older and keen to perform. But either way, it was a special time.

It helped keep us going that there was a bit of a clique of us English speakers in Barloworld too – me, Daryl Impey, John-Lee Augustyn, G, Froome and Robbie Hunter. Enrico Gasparotto, who won Amstel Gold twice a few years later, was in on the gang because he spoke such good English, while Robbie was the best Italian speaker so he kind of glued it all together. But it was me, Geraint and Cav in the flat, with me constantly looking out for G a bit – 'Have you done this, have you done that, have you bought the milk, G?' But that was fine. I knew he wasn't behaving like that because he was selfish or took things for granted, simply that he wouldn't remember the basic bits sometimes.

In the races it was a similar story, all of us looking out for each other, even when we were on different teams and no matter the terrain. When he was at Sky and I was at Qhubeka I remember trying to help Geraint out in the 2015 Tour on the Alpe d'Huez because he was having a bad day and I was on a good one, plus I'd been in the break so I was ahead and in the right position to do that.

That mutual support stretched all the way back to 2008 and the complete opposite extreme when fighting for Grand Tours could not have been further from Geraint's list of potential targets. We both did the Giro together for

Barloworld and Cav and Bradley were there too in Highroad.
The four of us messed around quite a lot in the race and G
likes a beer, so on his birthday we all went to a hotel bar
and got a few rounds in while we watched Cav trying to flirt
with a woman cycling photographer. But before fingers start
wagging about drinking on a race, please understand that he
was still only twenty-two or twenty-three, and on that Giro
we didn't really have a plan at all other than get through it
– you need to think, 'Ah, fuck it, chill out; enjoy life a little.'
Anyway I remember G ended up having a few beers, but the
next stage was in the Alps again and it started on an uphill
and poor G was saying, 'I feel rough.' It was comical. Anyway,
I don't know if he had a bad stomach, but we were joking
around saying it was a dodgy pint and Geraint was simply
praying nobody would start attacking. But sure enough, Felix
Cárdenas, our team-mate, attacked right at the start, and G
was almost dropped. All day I was telling G to 'stay with
me, stay with me', looking after him as best I could. And
we fought really hard for a good position in anticipation of
getting into trouble again, and then when it split on a downhill, somehow we were in the front group and we ended up
nearly finishing in the top fifty, which, at the time, was a
really good result for both of us on a big mountain stage.
What made it even funnier was the way Dave Millar, who
was super-focused and serious, kept on asking what on earth
we were doing so well placed on a fairly tough mountain
stage? He couldn't understand it, but thanks to Geraint's
'dodgy pint', we'd actually done better than expected!

I think that a lot of the time, given he is so laid-back
and quiet, he's easy to underestimate, whereas in fact, if

you could design a perfect cyclist, Geraint would be the ideal team member. Rather than hammering his fist on the table at the team meetings to get what he wants when he's the protected rider in a race, the impression I get is that he leads by example. He is naturally inclusive of all the team members, defuses tricky situations with humour, and even if he's not that vocal, that makes him one of the best I've ever seen. But probably his biggest talent is how he's so good at making situations work for him. Take early 2019, for example, when he'd won the Tour the year before, but everybody was fussing over Chris Froome with no mention of defending Geraint's Tour title. He was talking about leaving Team Sky at that point but he didn't and I think that was the right call – at the time I told him that Team Sky was the best place to get the best out of himself, because regarding the Froome situation, he was second-in-command there, and that's almost the perfect place to be in because you don't have to handle all of the pressure that comes with being top rider. Geraint realized that, and he used that situation brilliantly. He's a very canny guy.

He's got a reputation for being unlucky because he has had more than his fair share of accidents, and for being tough because he's had a lot of injuries from those crashes but has battled through. Both those things are true, but I think they're not quite as exceptional as the media make out: bike riders crash a lot and often, like in the Giro in 2020 when he ran over that bottle and crashed so badly, Geraint's just been in the wrong place at the wrong time. And it is more common among bike riders to be resistant to pain, because that's part of the job.

I think it's a sign of his wisdom that he knows when to ignore the coaches too. To go back to that 2008 Giro d'Italia, for all there were some good results – I ran eighth in the last time trial and was in a big mountain break in the last week – essentially it had been like a three-week training camp for the track and the upcoming Olympics. So when we'd finished, the GB coach said we should do some of those zone three capacity efforts that had been such a nice feature of our horrendous training camp in Australia all those years before. G's very wise response was instantly, 'Fuck that,' because he knew he'd just come out of the Giro and didn't need to get that extra-hard training.

I wasn't so clever and did everything the coach had suggested, as a result of which, two weeks later when we went to the track, I was as strong as an ox but lacked explosivity. I hadn't recovered properly after the Giro and had carried the fatigue instead of resting up. Whereas I had put my faith in the coach, and was proved totally wrong to have done so – as I later realized, after a big block of road training for the track, you need to stop completely, then restart at a very slow pace, otherwise you overtighten the screw and it'll snap – G knew what he needed to do. He claimed he felt shit and wasn't up to the post-Giro training so he wouldn't have to do it, and ultimately came through in much better shape. Conclusion? I should have done like G and taken ownership, rather than keep pushing and being killed by desire.

That confidence, decision-making (which I found particularly hard) and discipline when it comes to training is something I have to respect about him, and from a track perspective he had it nailed pretty quickly. But he's always absorbing new ideas and advice from different people. One day a few years back he said, 'I think I'm turning into you; I just want to go training alone and I don't want to go to training camps!'

On the track, as time went by and even though I wasn't around to see it, I heard he'd started questioning everything a bit more, not just his training regime. That is only normal because as you get more experienced, you develop your own opinion of what's going to make you faster and what works for you in training. But his greatest strength as a rider is that despite any setbacks, he'll keep fighting and he never had to learn that from anybody: on the contrary, it's G that is setting the example for others to follow.

Chapter 8

Roller Coaster

My friend Giacomo the chef takes one look at me as I walk into the restaurant – my favourite, then and now, in Quarrata – and immediately says, 'Right, that's it. Basta. Basta. We're going to get you sorted. I'm taking you to see a pal of mine who does a bit of...' and he makes a few signs of the cross gestures and says, '...tac-tac-tac-tac.'

I don't have a clue what he was talking about. But the next day, when he comes out of the restaurant kitchen after his lunchtime shift, we get into his Fiat and drive down the main road for a while, then up a side street – him still wearing his whites and apron and red trousers with pictures of chillies on – and I find out.

After three crashes in three races that spring, each of which have ended up with Giacomo watching me walk into his restaurant either on crutches or with an arm in a plaster cast, Giacomo is taking me to see a genuine Italian witch doctor. As he sees it, he, or rather the doctor, is going to lift this curse on me and my 2012 season once and for all. Basta.

(This seems like as good a point as any to point out that not all crashes are automatically a problem for a bike rider. I remember during the RideLondon Classic in August 2016 – a race I loathed because stress and fighting for climbs were the last thing I needed after the Tour – there was a pile-up and I went down, fortunately not badly. I lay on the ground for as long as it took so I wouldn't have to continue, thinking, 'Thank fuck, I can go off and do a training ride now.' However, injuries caused by crashes are obviously another story and that spring I had had more than my fair share of both. Hence the witch doctor visit.)

I'm not exactly experienced in this kind of doctor or treatment. I'd heard vaguely about it, of course, but I had no idea it still existed. It's symptomatic of my confusion that when we stop at a house I make the mistake of thinking the first person we come across, a woman with crazy orangy-pinky hair who is doing the washing and looking at me oddly, is the witch doctor. But no. To judge from the way she goes in, perhaps checks my appointment in a diary, comes back out and beckons me across the threshold, it turns out not to be the case. (In fact, apart from being his receptionist, I think she was his wife.)

Anyway, in I go. I walk down the corridor, which is dark and has walls covered in bronze crosses, pictures of Padre Pio and at the back in the kitchen there's a very smartly dressed Italian man – from Reggio Calabria in the south, as I find out later – sitting there with a walking stick and Ray Charles-like wraparound dark glasses and a fancy waistcoat. There's some more religious bits and pieces around, more pictures of Padre Pio and the guy looks at me, but talks to Giacomo – it's as if he doesn't want to talk to me – and starts muttering, 'si, si, si, si,' and the chef says, 'He thinks you've got malocchio,' (the evil eye). So the witch doctor then flicks his hand to the chef and starts muttering – 'fu, fu, fu, fu' – that Giacomo should leave us in peace.

Giacomo hurries out and then the witch doctor opens up his wallet, which has a gold ring inside it, unties a ribbon round the ring, and starts making crosses with it around the areas where I'd crashed – my pelvis and wrists. He might have said a few words or a short prayer too, I don't rightly recollect. Then he puts his ring very carefully away and starts making little 'shooing' gestures, as if he wants to wave the evil malocchio spirit out of the room, just like Giacomo had been sent out before, but hopefully a whole lot further.

I don't know if all these magical remedies worked or not, at the end of the day. Maybe. It was trying something I'd never tried before, and at all points, as long as it was legal, I'd try everything that I thought could help with my career. Also, I love Italian culture, so I'd like to think it worked and in fact we tried to go back another time, but the poor guy had died in the meantime and we never found another witch doctor. I guess there aren't that many in Italy.

I do know that I went to the Tour de Suisse afterwards and wasn't very good, which probably made sense after so many crashes and injuries. Then I did the Tour de France and had another really painful crash, right at the end. But in a sense what was truly heartening and morale-boosting was seeing how Giacomo had tried so hard to help me out. He wasn't the only one: some of my friends who'd heard about my witch doctor cure started buying me bracelets with good luck

Italian peperoncinos and Irish shamrocks. I really appreciated that, at a time when I needed it badly.

Short term some people like Max Sciandri, who was now my director at BMC, took a very practical approach to what the future might hold. As Max put it: 'Fuck, what else can happen now? Nothing else can happen. With all those bracelets, you don't need to brake no more, the gods are going to keep you safe. You can close your eyes and just go.'

*

The irony of so much bad luck in such a short space of time in that first half of 2012 was that my first few weeks with BMC earlier that season had started very well. I didn't just feel good. At one of the team's first training camps we had had a time trial day to test our form – it was slightly uphill, a twenty-minute effort – and I turned out 460 watts of power all the way up, which was faster than our leaders.

As it was my first time with the team, I was nervous though: after that I said to my sports director Rik Verbrugghe, 'What do I need to do, what do I need to do?' And he answered, 'Trust me, after what I've seen in the last ten days, you don't need to do anything!' That TT ride, then, was confirmation I was flying and racing couldn't come soon enough.

So I was anticipating a good ride in the Volta ao Algarve, my first race, and in one of the first stages the break had gone and I felt like I hadn't touched the pedals, so things were fine. But I was on the outside of the bunch, somewhere towards the front, when someone swerved into me on the inside of a corner and they took me out.

With Andy, my elder brother, 'fixing' our bikes. My dad's racing bike is in the background.

A National Junior Points race podium with Bradley in the late '90s. I never enjoyed podium visits until much later on.

The countdown to the Olympic team pursuit final 2004, thinking 'Shit, how did I end up here. Oh well, I'd better go full gas now.'

Landbouwkrediet, 2006, on my way to taking second in the Trofeo Laigueglia. This result made me realise I really could win some pro races.

Tuscany, 2008. Considering how raw we all were here, it's amazing (and quite amusing) to think how well Froomie and G have done since!

Fishing with G in Florida. We bumped into him and his family when we were on holiday there in November 2015.

With my mum and dad after getting silver in the 2004 Olympics.

'Stevie, get some tats and harden up.' Sean Yates, my director here in Discovery Channel in 2007, was like a big brother. He taught me a lot, and we laughed a lot.

My first victory as a pro, 2008 in Reggio Calabria. I couldn't believe my luck, my shape wasn't great.

'Look, that girl has got your Bermuda shorts on from the 1998 National Track Champs podium.'

Worlds, Copenhagen 2011, en route to Cav's victory. An immense sense of personal satisfaction and feeling of joy for everyone involved.

Vuelta, 2013. An emotional victory, that led to increased confidence, and a strong belief I could fight for a stage win.

Max Sciandri: a great friend and mentor. We talked and talked about all things bike and bike racing.

Suffering in the Dolomites in the Giro d'Italia, 2013.

Brad and 'Keith Lemon' recording a podcast in Soho shortly after I'd retired.

Suspended from the shed ceiling to reduce the weight through a fractured sternum, clavicle, and scapula. My legs felt good!

Mandela Day, Tour de France, Stage 15, 2015. Waving to the French president who happened to be at the finish line.

Alone, reaching the top of the Col d'Aspin, Tour de France, 2016. This was an extremely cool feeling.

A moment of reflection during the Vuelta a España, 2018. My body was at the race, my head was somewhere else.

Tour de France, 2016. Unlike 2015, I had time to think about my family and friends, the work, the sacrifice, and how this victory was for them.

Winning the 2017 Road Nationals. The biggest victory was being able to make the start line.

2016: Cav won four Tour de France stages and I won one. Five out of seven stages in the Tour is something to smile about.

Apprehensive before my first TTT as an Ineos Grenadiers DS, with Brett Lancaster.

Perla helping me clean the bike in Italy, part of our daily winter routine.

I went back and got the spare bike from the team car, but it took me about 20 kilometres to get back on to the main peloton. But as soon as I had, I knew it was pointless. I dropped back down to Rik in the team car and said, 'I'm fucked, I need to stop; something's not right.'

Rik asked if I was sure. I said I was. So he called up the doctor, a bit baffled because I didn't have any road rash or outward signs that anything was wrong. But I quit and we went to the hospital where the diagnosis was clear: a broken pelvis.

Pelvis breaks are never simple and the effects of one can vary a lot. Geraint Thomas once bust his pelvis in the first week of a Tour de France and he managed to finish the race, but others take a week to ten days to get back on to their bikes again. My break was bad, though, and it was awkward for a cyclist because it was right on the point where you sit on the saddle. It was going to take a lot of rehab.

I went back to Tuscany on my own and as I couldn't ride the bike I went into Pisa every day, all day, for magnetic and water-based therapy. I focused on cardio fitness, moving my arms a lot with all kinds of different machines and using a swimming pool training circuit to walk round with my legs under the water, first of all very, very slowly and then eventually pedalling. Finally, after six weeks, I was ready to get back into riding my bike and, at the Vuelta al País Vasco, racing again.

We got to stage four and I was just starting to feel OK again, because with all that time stopped I'd gained a bit of weight and lost a lot of form. But it was wet and there was a crash on the right, and when a bike came flying across, there was nowhere to go. I hit the bike and keeled over. I tried to finish the stage but ended up in the broom wagon – that's the vehicle that picks up riders who've crashed out – and going to hospital again. This time, I'd ended up with a broken wrist.

Overall, despite the injury, I felt reasonably OK and I could still ride the bike, and at that point, with the training camp performance in my favour too and constant training data numbers, the team still had really high hopes for me. So they decided I'd go to the Tour of California – an important race for BMC as they were American-registered – a few weeks later. The only problem being on stage three when I was snugly placed with the team in the front of the peloton, someone fell in front of me, I went down and that was it again. Another broken wrist. And after three bad crashes in as many races, my mind was a bit shot as well.

I don't think that's uncommon for pro bike riders to have runs of crashes like this: one rocks you so much that you get nervous and it's almost like a vicious circle. But despite the crashes and that pretty rubbish Tour de Suisse as my come-back event, the team still decided to put me in the Tour. Although I was getting better I was still some way off my best because of the lack of real depth due to three or four months of broken and inconsistent preparation. The vibe in the team wasn't very good either: our leader, the previous year's winner, Cadel Evans, was acting up and was fighting a lot of the time with a youngish American racer, Tejay van Garderen, because Tejay was doing better overall. Cadel was super-stressed and nervous, but I can understand now that he was perhaps struggling to live up to his own expectations and didn't want to let anybody down after winning the previous year. As often happens too, off the bike Cadel is a lovely guy while on the bike he could be quite different. But Tejay eventually finished fifth in any case, two places better than Cadel, and by that point though I had fresh worries of my own.

By this stage in my career, I had largely learned to ignore what was going on in other parts of the team and just be accountable for me, my form and my behaviour. But on this Tour, given I was struggling physically after all the crashes early on, it was a huge challenge and that played on my mind. To cap it all with three or four days to go, I had another bad crash, on the Port de Balès climb in the Pyrenees, the second last one of the day. I really took a battering. It all began when my rear wheel was damaged shortly before the start of the Balès because somebody had crashed into me. I didn't realize at the time that my wheel was in a bad way so I did the climb, and then on the descent, my bike wasn't responding as it should have done. Hindsight is a wonderful thing and I know now that if in doubt, change your wheel, particularly if the race situation permits and you're in the *gruppetto* – as I was that day. As a result of not having that hindsight though, I slid off the road and into a drainage ditch shortly after the summit.

It was awful. I lost a heck of a lot of skin and I was bleeding pretty badly. The look on the face of my sports director, Fabio Baldato, couldn't have been more expressive – put simply, you could tell he was thinking, 'Man, you're fucked' – and he wanted me to stop. I was in real pain down the whole of my left side and I could barely pedal, and my power output had dropped to 300 watts at most. It was going to be a challenge to finish the stage, particularly within the time limit. Tyler Farrar and Sebastian Langeveld, friends of mine in the peloton on the Garmin and Orica teams, caught up with me and were kind enough to help me off the descent. (They'd both been having a different version of a bad day, though perhaps not as bad as mine had ended up!) Then we started the final climb, the Peyresourde, and I went to the race ambulance to get my injuries checked as I was bleeding a lot. I finished, over half an hour down and towards the back of the *gruppetto*, but the next morning I was far from convinced I could start the next stage. I had hurt my coccyx and it remained one of or the most painful crashes I ever had.

But I did start, and eventually I finished the Tour too, the second of my career, even if the Champs-Élysées was shit and I could feel every cobblestone. Paris wasn't a celebration, I just wanted to go home. I felt in pain and frustrated and the team even brought me dinner up to my room as it was too uncomfortable to get to the dinner table. Then after the Tour, I slept downstairs at home on one side, with my knees bent and a pillow between my legs to ease the pain. The road rash was really bad, to the point where I only felt comfortable moving around. Put it this way: when I got back to Italy, I didn't have to go back to the witch doctor, but people were buying me a heck of a lot of those good luck bracelets.

*

Whenever I got a win there were four people I'd always ring. My default people, as you could call them, were Nicky, my mum, my dad and my first proper trainer, Keith Boardman. Even after a race like the Tour, I'd call Keith, no matter how much chaos there was with all the press stuff and being in demand. It was that calming voice on the end of a line I'd always had since I was a young guy. Whether I'd been in Birkenhead Park or the Club 10, or if I'd just won the Worlds, I'd still have the same conversation, and I really loved that. I also like to think he'd enjoy having that call, maybe even felt a bit surprised that I'd remember him.

But if you'd told me that five weeks after that Tour I'd be ringing Keith to celebrate the biggest breakthrough win of my road career, I wouldn't have believed you.

*

There was less than a month between the Tour and the Vuelta. Physically and mentally I was done. I'd barely done anything for a week after Paris; I was too sore from the crash. But I got the call-up for the Vuelta from the team anyway.

I went out for one training ride and felt terrible. I went out for another and felt even worse. I rang Max and he told me that the best thing to do was go to Spain, ride the Clásica San Sebastián and then the team would make the call.

Somehow, it worked out. Part of the reason was that BMC had a physio and osteopath called Anthony Pauwels, the brother of Serge, a team-mate in a couple of my squads and now with Deceuninck–Quick-Step. Anthony began turning things round with really intense treatment and he continued working with me during the Vuelta. The most important thing was he worked hard on my back. I'd hurt it badly and that had a very negative effect on my overall power output.

I think it's definitely worth mentioning at this point that a team carer and/or physio and/or osteopath can be worth their weight in gold, both physically and mentally. That one hour you get to spend with them can often be the best part of the day. As for the summer of 2012, while not feeling cured by a long way but a lot better, I tried to go to the Vuelta with the attitude that I was just going to enjoy it and recalibrate. That meant nailing the basics like fuelling, sleeping and resting well and trying to do the right things in the race. All this, of course, while inwardly knowing it was never going to be that enjoyable when you're suffering and getting your head kicked in every day on a Grand Tour for three weeks as a consequence.

On the plus side, I had a good group of team-mates in BMC at the Vuelta that year: former or soon-to-be-crowned world champions like Alessandro Ballan and Philippe Gilbert as leaders, and some class team workers like Amaël Moinard and Brent Bookwalter. Like me, Brent didn't want to be at the Vuelta either, he just wanted to go home to the USA, but Philippe was great at keeping our morale together. He was determined to have a good race, but to enjoy himself and have fun too. Philippe ended up being one of my favourite leaders I ever worked with. He remained professional and he never seemed under pressure because he defused it with humour. It was a privilege to have raced in the same team as him.

I certainly needed his upbeat attitude. I was still going terribly. I even got dropped from the main group as soon as stage three when in theory that early in the race everybody's still feeling fresh. Then on the first big climbing stage, I can remember getting dropped again.

I really thought that was the end of my Vuelta. But I was making my way through the convoy team cars following behind on a downhill and somehow, without even pedalling, I ended up back in the bunch. I remember thinking, 'Oh, for fuck's sake,' because I really didn't want to be back there and had thought I might get lucky and get to go home early.

But after ten days of the Vuelta, things changed. Max came up to me and said, 'Look, what happened, happened. I just want you to go full gas, for one hour, every day. Just one hour.' In other words, I had to try to get in the breakaways.

So that's what I did and I instantly felt better for trying to do something each day. It's always a challenge when you're faced with a situation like that. But your attitude has to be, 'I'm not good – OK – accept it – deal with it – and do everything you can to be as good as you can be. Then let's see.'

I was getting better at dealing with these situations, which helped at the Vuelta. But on top of that I started to feel better physically as well. It was like after three weeks of intense treatment from Anthony, I was finally opening up. Then when we got to a transition stage like stage thirteen, I hadn't felt as good since the Volta ao Algarve, nearly seven months earlier.

By that point we were up in Galicia, racing along the coast from Santiago de Compostela to Ferrol on what were big, wide roads. This being Galicia, it was still up and down all day long. But I always felt like I had an extra gear. It didn't matter who was going up the road, I could go with them. Finally, I went off with a very strong group of half a dozen guys: two from the Orica squad – Cam Meyer and Simon Clarke – another big breakaway specialist like Thomas De

133

Gendt, and two Tour de France stage winners, Juan Antonio Flecha and Linus Gerdemann.

It was just as well we were strong in that break, because we were going full gas all day. The bunch behind was chasing hard and the gap never came down from three or four minutes, so it was always in the balance that it would stay away. It's quite unusual that a break does manage to stay out there like that when the peloton wants to bring you back. But we did.

With about 20 kilometres left to go, people started attacking all over the place. But I was able to tell myself to stay calm. I had that feeling you get when you're strong that you've got time to think, and I could identify the most powerful riders in the group no matter how much they played off each other or tried to hide that. Above all, I could sense that Flecha was desperate to win, perhaps too desperate. That in my opinion was a weakness in that kind of situation because that's exactly when you have to be prepared to lose. He was a big-name Spanish rider, with not too many opportunities to go for it given his team, and when he attacked on a climb, I went with him. That sank a few of the rivals, and then he launched himself away with 5 kilometres to go. But it didn't bother me. I wanted him to stay out there and cook himself, so I could use him as a launch pad. I knew that if I wanted to I could close on him really fast, and in any case I gambled on the Oricas, as a duo, being more likely to work to bring him back. Which is what happened.

Then immediately after that, I attacked. It was a good moment, a slight uphill, when everybody was a bit on the edge and I could use their slowing down as a slingshot to move forward. There were 4 kilometres to go, and I looked back from the top of this little rise. I could see Cam Meyer was once again pulling for Simon, who's faster and who could have brought me back because it was a little bit downhill. But they didn't.

I had a few factors in my favour, apart from my own strength. There were a few roundabouts and they were fast, and you had to get them right technically which was tricky. But we'd gone up one side of a big road, done a loop and then were coming back down the other, so I had a rough idea of what was coming. Then in the back of my head I'd go back to my visualization in the team pursuit. Given the run of crashes I'd had I was fighting not to be overly cautious. Whenever a voice said, 'Fucking hell, you're going to crash on the corners,' I'd tell myself, 'No you're not, think about the good corners, think about the good corners.' Plus I had Max spurring me on and yelling, 'Don't look back! Don't look back!' in my ear.

This raises an interesting point. People talk about radios and whether what we hear from the director through the radio, other than factual information, can actually make a difference. And in this case, I have to say 'Yes', because Max was 100 per cent right. I remember what he said, even now, because it was so useful and so simple, removing any doubt and keeping me focused on doing one thing and one thing alone. That was going full gas and 100 per cent. On top of that I was feeling the best I had in months. It all helped me get through to the end, alone, although after the season I'd had, I refused to think I had definitely won before I crossed the line!

I was buzzing with a sense of relief that I'd got it, and it switched a light on for me in terms of confidence and satisfaction. I didn't know if that was the only way I could win a Grand Tour stage. But even as a junior that was always how I wanted to imagine it: alone from a break, delivering on my own expectations. It was a true reflection of my best, in a big race and that was the most satisfying thing – finally getting it out on the road in a top event for people to see. By this time I really felt I was becoming quite polished on the bike in terms of position, weight, training, the whole regime of racing, and while it may not have been perfect, I felt fast and strong. And you instantly have the feeling, OK, you can win at the Vuelta, so why can't you take it up a level and win at the Tour?

From the outside, after all the crashes I'd had, it looked as if I was reaching the end of the season so much better than I went in. That was particularly true as a bit later in the year I took another stage win, in the Tour of Beijing. But in fact, when I'd kicked off the year I'd been in phenomenal shape and then everything had gone wrong.

So I had felt a bit angry and hard done by, but here at the Vuelta I felt like I wanted to show people what I could do, which brought me satisfaction, but it was also a relief in a bigger sense than just the injuries: I had felt frustrations but now I'd managed to bottle those feelings and by sticking to the process, having a laugh along the way too, I was physically able to release those frustrations in the right way – on the road. There'd been glimpses before but nothing on the bigger stage. A hard-core cycling fan might be impressed at winning a smaller race like the Tour of the Med, say, like I did in 2014. But here, at the Vuelta, this was for everybody to see.

It was also satisfying that the team were so pleased with me, guys like Philippe Gilbert and Jim Ochowicz, but also the team manager, John Lelangue. John even used me as an example afterwards in motivational speeches on the team bus, saying, 'One stage win can change your life. Look at Stevo: one stage, your life.'

One change I certainly noticed was my contract and pay rate, both of which improved. After I'd won in Beijing I went to see 'Och' in his hotel room and he got out his black book where he kept all the riders' details and he said in that gruff US accent of his, 'Heh, you are a little underpaid, heh?' So I said I was OK with that and I got the extension through to the end of 2014 and a rise.

The other thing was that the combined effect of the crashes and the Vuelta meant I really started riding a lot more at the back. I'd been doing it a fair bit before, but this was when I really realized that even if you could do a good job for the team, you could easily struggle to get a good contract. Negotiations would invariably run along the lines of, 'OK, what have you done?' and your reply would be, 'I've worked for the team.' Then they would say, 'Yes, but what have you done?' And your only answer could be, 'I haven't done anything, I've worked for the team.' So after 2012, I began thinking, 'Fuck it, do what you want.'

But it didn't work out. In fact, the goalposts changed and having gone from one extreme to the other in 2012, rather than building on the Vuelta win to go on to greater success, I went to a point where I was ready to quit bike racing altogether. The issue this time wasn't anything to do with injuries; in fact for the rest of my time in BMC I only had one other bad crash, breaking my wrist or elbow (I can't remember which) at the Tour of Belgium in 2014, which knocked me out for six weeks. Rather, where things fell apart were, it felt to me, at a managerial level.

When I started at the team, I'd got on fine with John Lelangue and I felt I could have cracked on in the squad if he'd stayed in charge. Ultimately, I knew that with John, if you performed, then he was going to back you whether he liked you or not.

At the same time I'd found myself with a group of world-class team leaders and directors including three former world champions – Gilbert, Thor Hushovd and Ballan – as well as Baldato, Max and Rik Verbrugghe. It had felt very different to Sky because collectively BMC had been much more on the artistic side of racing rather than the robotic attitude I'd experienced before. I didn't just really like it, I also felt there was a real opportunity for me to do well and that I had to raise my level to do that.

Things were not straightforward all the time, because it's always hard when a team invests in bigger riders and they don't perform. Often the pressure bypasses the leaders as the management don't want to upset the key men so the heat lands on the guys further down in the pecking order. However, when Allan Peiper came in at the end of the 2012 season as manager, straight away things got a lot worse.

Put simply, I felt Allan didn't rate me at all. Everything suddenly became a lot more difficult, because when it seems like a manager doesn't want you in the team, you're always up against it and your race programme becomes very unpredictable, which is challenging if you're never sure what you're preparing for. No one likes uncertainty and unfortunately bike riders sometimes have to live in that space for long periods. Allan had some good points and he did raise the level of the team professionally, using things like wind tunnel testing. (That wasn't actually new to me, in fact if a team didn't do it I usually did it at my own expense, in the belief that investing in yourself is rarely wasted.) But although he got everybody dialled, he was authoritarian, telling me how the team needed me to do this and the team needed me to do that. I was never the kind of guy who liked being told what to do, particularly if it wasn't logical. You explain it clearly, then I might not like it, but I would accept it and crack on. But at the time I didn't have the skills I needed to deal with that effectively, even if eventually I realized how much I needed to learn about how to deal with different people in different ways. Either way, suddenly I was in an atmosphere where I couldn't thrive any more and where I felt whatever I did wasn't good enough.

*

And so 2013 began. We'd started off well by winning the team time trial in Qatar, although I would say if you'd taken me or Taylor Phinney out of the equation, they probably wouldn't have won it. Then the team opted to put me in the Giro d'Italia, which wasn't a great idea because I'd discovered in previous years that if I went to race in Italy at that time of year, I'd end up suffering a lot with allergic reactions.

They seemed to get worse as my career went on. We'd done tests twice and never found either a cause or a solution, and I explained to the team perhaps it wasn't wise to go. However, even when I got there and found I couldn't breathe properly, they started asking why I wasn't performing so well.

So I wasn't firing on all cylinders and I couldn't do what the team expected. On top of that I was having run-ins with Cadel, who – perhaps understandably given I'd not been the help he wanted on other stages – didn't like it when I finished quite close to him in the time trial. But I wasn't the only one who had problems with him of that nature.

As I had observed even when the Tejay–Cadel stand-off happened in the Tour, Cadel is a really lovely bloke off the bike. But as a leader he was both strange and sometimes difficult. Everything had to be Cadel's way – to call him picky would be an understatement – and he didn't like anybody putting him even remotely or unintentionally in the shade. For example, his big mate in the team was Ivan Santaromita, but in that Giro for a couple of days, Santaromita was ahead of Cadel on GC. So Cadel was at a finish sitting in a team car on the back seat to get back to the hotel and when Santaromita got to the same car and got in the front, Cadel told him to get out of there.

But it wasn't just what he said, it was how he said it too. Whereas Philippe Gilbert would be funny about it if you weren't performing at a top level saying, 'Hey, where were you, man, come on!' and he'd try to encourage you, Cadel was the opposite. Not only that, he was fussy: he'd ask you to go and get some gloves during a race and you'd come back with them and he'd get furious and say, 'Not those gloves, the blue gloves!' All this when the peloton was in one line, people going out the back, you're struggling and he'd expect you to be riding like a motorbike, when getting frustrated with them is never going to help.

In 2013, I didn't enjoy being around him, particularly in the Giro d'Italia, and me, Adam and Taylor would try to avoid him. Steve Morabito, who's a soft-spoken, wonderful guy, tried to act as his counsellor and intermediary and everywhere Cadel went, Steve would follow him, telling him in his quiet little voice, 'Don't worry, Cadel, everything will be OK, Cadel...' He tried to defuse the situation between us, saying maybe we could go to dinner with Cadel and we'd answer back, 'Fuck, no, you go and have dinner with him.'

Things got to a kind of extreme when we did the stage into Firenze and the next day was a rest day with a transfer. We finished so far down on the stage that everybody had gone when we got there, and we passed by Quarrata, so the three of us thought we might as well drop in and have a bite to eat. We had a good laugh and hung out a little with some friends. I saw Nicky and we would have had to have had some supper anyway, but the next day Cadel went absolutely mental. Max was so upset that he had upset Cadel he was almost crying.

Anyway, trying to enjoy myself a little while remaining professional was my strategy for getting through a situation where I wasn't the rider I needed to be performance-wise. On top of that, this situation was out of my control as I had been suffering with the allergies. But I can't see the point of being grumpy and sad because I don't see that that helps things.

However, while that attitude might have got me through the Giro d'Italia, it couldn't get me round Peiper. It turned out there was no way round that situation, not even when I won races on a BMC-made bike that I disliked, like the Impec. BMC had spent a fortune on this factory in Switzerland that made them but from my point of view – and others may disagree – while it was a beautiful model, it had one problem, it was heavy. I even won the Tour of the Med one spring on it though, and got third on a climb as tough as the Mont Faron. Those early races are super-tricky because it's often wet, and the Faron is very difficult. If you look at the *palmarès* of its winners, a lot of them (not all) are either prestigious names in the sport and/or have then done well in the Spring Classics. So at the time its history meant more than a new, possibly harder, race like Abu Dhabi. But it never felt like it was good enough for the team.

By this point in my career, I was really ready to stop. I'd had enough of being pushed around and it just felt too hard and no fun whatsoever. I hated this new authoritarian leadership style. It was almost identical to Sky, because their attitude was equally either you do what we want you to do, and you're buying in, but if you're not buying in, you're not with us. The net result was to make me feel like I was being used as a filler, and at the end of my time there I was completely and utterly fed up with the team politics. Beneath that sensation though, I still loved riding my bike and if you took away those politics and that bullshit and put me in an environment in which I had a good bike and a good programme where I could fight for big victories, I knew it would be a very different story.

But when you're in a dark moment, and I was in a dark moment for a long time, it was fucking horrible. You're going through the motions and you can't get out of it; it's like a trap. Knowing I could win in top races, like a stage at the Vuelta a España, had opened a door for me in the sense of how high I could reach. But what teams like BMC wanted were the biggest hits of all, bigger even than what I'd done. I was in the wrong team because I'd realized by this point that while I couldn't ever win Tirreno–Adriatico outright like BMC would have wanted, I could win stages there. At the same time, I was realizing more and more I needed to improve off the bike as much as on it, and I needed to learn how I could improve and effectively cope with unreasonable people and tough situations.

I did find a way out of this situation, by signing for another team, MTN-Qhubeka, in 2015. But that didn't take away the fact that in the case of BMC I had signed for one team and halfway through the management changed and the new management didn't want me there. It had been a roller coaster from start to finish, but finally the goalposts had shifted. Having won so many battles in 2012, suddenly it felt like I was losing the war.

Chapter 9

A Human Time Bomb

Whe hen Geraint (Thomas) and I first met Chris Froome, we couldn't figure him out. Nobody could.

It was in a Barloworld training camp early in 2008 after he'd moved from Bergamo to Quarrata where we were but he didn't go out much. It seemed like Chris, who'd grown up in Africa and had very few connections to the European cycling scene as a young lad, was still in his own little world. So when we got to the training camp – which was easy, traditional Italian-style training after the British Cycling camps, which were much more structured and intense – we spent our spare time, and we had lots of it, trying to suss him out.

We were asking ourselves, 'What kind of rider is this guy? He doesn't look like a sprinter or a rouleur and he can't be a climber cos he's too fat...' All these people who ask about how he's managed to improve don't understand cycling because back in 2008, before he got to be really good, Froome was 5 kilos too heavy, probably more.

Then there was that habit he's famous for of looking at his stem, particularly when he's climbing. Later Sky did something about it to stop Chris doing it so much. But back then in Barloworld he did it all the time, and sometimes he was staring so hard he'd just veer off the road.

While he was looking at his stem, me and G would be looking at each other, and saying, 'What are we going to do with this guy? Are you going to follow him round a corner and down a hill?' The answer to that being: 'Erm, no...'

Technically, he was bloody terrible. But we'd laugh about it, and after he got used to the British sense of humour, he'd laugh as well. In fact, when it came to taking the mick, he'd give as good as he was getting.

As for the mystery Geraint and I couldn't resolve over why he was in Barloworld, I think he'd done a couple of outstanding races in Italy with a small team called Konica and the Barloworld manager, Claudio Corti, had seen him. If it had happened that way, it wouldn't have been surprising. Sometimes on a race at Barloworld he'd do something amazing on one climb and he'd drop everybody, but then afterwards, all too often, he'd be dropped himself. It was just crazy. Froome would explain it by saying, 'Hmm, maybe I didn't eat enough.' So it was pretty clear Chris was raw, like an unpolished diamond that needed a lot of work, but his attitude and eagerness was remarkable.

You'd most notice how basic his understanding of cycling was when he talked about races. In his first year in Barloworld, he did Paris–Roubaix and some other really big northern Classics and rather than being pleased he came back from Belgium scarred. I remember he told me, 'I'm fed up with these shit races, you know?! I just want to do some nice races in Portugal' – where the racing scene is actually pretty low-key – with klaimes, as his accent made the word 'climbs' sound like. And we'd answer, 'Nice races in Portugal? What are you on about?' And he'd say, 'Yeah... with klaimes.' So he just didn't have a clue about the significance of Paris–Roubaix, but it was funny and it was refreshing.

The one point of comparison we had for Chris was John-Lee Augustyn. John-Lee was a South African rider with the most similar sporting background to Chris, and who was probably the most talented rider we had in Barloworld in terms of how he was racing at that time. On a good day John-Lee could get a top twenty in a race like Liège–Bastogne–Liège, something that at the time for Barloworld was a bit of a 'wow' moment. But John-Lee's potential was maybe affected by the fact he'd had a bad crash and had pins in his hip as a result and then he had visa problems in Sky. Chris, on the other hand, was an unpolished diamond whose flashes of talent suggested he had a heck of a lot more to him as a racer in the future. It was really a question of when those flashes appeared.

Meanwhile, there was no getting away from the fact that Chris was really different. We used to ask him loads of questions about where he was from in Africa and his upbringing, and he'd tell us all these stories about being chased by rhinos while training. He'd say utterly improbable things like, 'You've got to be really careful with rhinos; they're the really naughty ones,' or 'Naughty sand sharks. You go in the water and the sand sharks get you.' I even remember one anecdote which involved a hippo and Chris being stuck in a tree for twelve hours and, as he put it, 'I didn't have my phone or anything, just waiting and saying, "Go away, hippo, go away!"' And this is one of the most dangerous animals in Africa!

There were other mysteries as well. Sometimes he'd talk about his house and having 'people in the room'. And we'd say to each other, 'Does that mean he's got servants?' 'Have they got silver service?' The bottom line was that we didn't have a clue.

Then he'd tell us about riding through townships, like one time when he'd had a puncture and these guys stole his bike, he was trying to fend them off by flailing about with his pump. We'd laugh, but secretly we'd be thinking to ourselves, 'Wow, this is really scary.' But Froome, he'd ride through it all, saying, 'Those fuckers, they stole my bike.' It was brilliant to hear about, completely out of our usual worlds. And apart from him being great company, thinking about those stories now, some of them had signs of how resilient he was too.

*

Barloworld was a great little team, we had good riders and we got to do things like going to South Africa, to race the one-day race series called the Cape Argus. It was a pleasant trip, even if, coming from a European winter to 46 degrees, I was dead in the heat. But I won a race and Froomey won another when there were four of us in a fifteen-man group and Froomey attacked with about 55 kilometres to go. I wanted to win the race and do it with as little effort as possible, but that was Froomey all over; he'd just have these days when such long-distance attacks were possible. Then there were days when he'd be dead.

The Barloworld directors did not have a clue what to do with Froome. They would just say *'Madonna, queste Froome!'* ('Holy Mother of God, this blooming Froome!') When he first lived up in Bergamo with John-Lee, the director would come round and look to see what was in his fridge. If he had Fanta in there, the director would be saying, 'No good, no good.' They didn't speak that good English and (director Claudio) Corti used to call Max to complain. Max would put him on the speaker phone and we'd listen to Claudio yelling about Cazzo Froome (Friggin' Froome) and Cazzo Coomings and Cazzo Thomas for drinking too much Fanta too, because G, like the rest of us, was a little bit fat back in those days.

When we moved to Sky I don't remember seeing either Froome or John-Lee in 2010 at all, apart from in the Giro along with our half-Italian team-mate Dario Cioni. Half of Dario's family were from Reading in England and he spoke very precise Queen's English, almost like he was from India, and he would always come out with things like, 'One is a bit tired.' But he had this thing with Froomey too, saying in his perfect Queen's English pronunciation, 'What the fuck, Froomey? If I've told you once I've told you a hundred times, stay behind; you are a fucking human time bomb.'

Froome was really keen and he wanted to help in everything, even in the sprints. Froomey wasn't scared of anything. His eagerness to learn and improve, which you couldn't help admiring, was perhaps one of his biggest strengths. The problem was, nobody wanted to ride behind Froome – it was so unnerving because of that thing he had of looking at his stem all the time. I remember Mat Hayman saying Froomey had nearly ridden into a traffic island no matter how hard they had been shouting, 'Froomey! Left! Left!' And Dario's sitting there eating his pasta and listening to Mat and muttering between mouthfuls in his Queen's English, 'Time bomb.'

Then with a few days to go on a mountain stage in the Giro, Hendy (team-mate Greg Henderson) stopped for a lengthy natural break and he and Froome rode together back to the bunch afterwards. They made it to the top of one of the hardest climbs in Italy, the Mortirolo, together but Hendy dropped him on the descent and Froome missed the *gruppetto* and ended up riding alone up the valley to the finish. If you're in that situation on a tough day like that in the Giro, you're fucked and that's when he abandoned. Initially, we were all upset, but after a while we could laugh about it a little. And Dario sat there that evening at dinner saying in his posh English voice, 'It is so much better one no longer has to follow this human time bomb.'

*

Froome had had a long-time chronic disease called bilharzia, which even though it had been funny the way he'd talk about it – he'd say, 'I've got this naughty little parasite in my system, you know. It's fucking me right up.' – it was clearly a problem. Once Froome's bilharzia illness was sorted out, he got better and he just grew, and when he found Bobby Julich as a trainer that was a great match for him too. I remember we were sitting on the bus in the 2011 Tour de Pologne before the Vuelta when he told me, 'Yeah, I'm flying in training. I did two x twenty minutes at 460 watts, I'm 70 kilos, you know, but I just can't seem to get it out in the race.' And I said, 'You did what?' because these are ridiculously good numbers and I said to Chris, 'Look, if you can put out that sort of power in training, you can do it in the race as well.' He was OK in Poland and one day we had to pull on the front, and he was really strong. However, he didn't think Sky were going to keep him – he showed me an email from Bobby Julich saying, 'Sign this guy now.' But they didn't, at least not then.

Then things changed, firstly because Chris wasn't even sure he'd get a ride in the Vuelta, but something happened, somebody got sick or something so they took him.

I had said to him, 'What do you want to do in the Vuelta? And he'd answered, 'I want to help Brad and be strong on the klaimes.' We hadn't really seen any evidence of this for a while in Sky but he was confident and after he told me his numbers, I said, 'Yeah, with those numbers you can be good on the klaimes.' And that was it, he won the Vuelta! He had these red Sidi shoes and I kept texting him during the Vuelta saying, 'Froomey, can you get me a pair of these magic shoes?'

Compared to other British Tour winners like Bradley or Geraint, he's more ruthless, possibly. But perhaps that's the way it came across and there's an element of ruthlessness in them all – there has to be to be a winner. On the other hand, I can't remember if it was 2015 or 2016 but he was genuinely happy that I'd won my Tour stages, hugging me and that, which was nice. It took me back to 2008, 2009 at Barloworld when we were two kids living the dream. Cav says you never get used to the magnitude of the Tour and it wouldn't surprise me if Froomey still pinches himself at times at what he's done.

The best time, though, was at Barloworld. We were all at space cadet level, and someone would always fuck up. But we had a good laugh too. What is really refreshing is that despite all his success since then, Froome can still laugh at himself and you can have a good laugh with him. And you can still ask him if he's been chased by any hippos lately.

Chapter 10

Mandela Day

In Africa Steve Cummings is a hero after winning a stage at this year's Tour de France on Nelson Mandela Day. In France he is perhaps seen as a villain after beating local stars Thibaut Pinot (FDJ) and Romain Bardet (AG2R La Mondiale) on the summit of the ultra-steep final ascent to Mende airfield. For Cummings' MTN-Qhubeka squad it was an historic day, taking an African team's first ever Tour de France stage victory. For Cummings personally, it was a day of celebration and redemption after years of injuries, doubts and misunderstandings with his teams and himself.

Cyclingnews, 18 July 2015

Joining MTN-Qhubeka in 2015 was a huge relief, and it truly felt like the start of a new chapter of my career. It wasn't just that the team was heading in a good direction with signings like Matt Goss, Edvald Boasson Hagen, Tyler Farrar and Theo Bos – all solid, very powerful riders. It was also humbling when I started learning about Qhubeka, which is a charity aiming to provide bikes to South African communities with major economic and social difficulties and where students have to cycle huge distances to school, as well as what I found out chatting to some of the African guys who were on the team.

MTN-Qhubeka had started out as a South African squad, formed in 2007, and initially it was pretty low-key, racing only in smaller events. But four years later Qhubeka came fully on board and its unusual but inspiring aim helped raise its profile enormously.

I liked not just what they were doing but how we formed part of it. Every July, before the Tour, the boss Doug Ryder would do a presentation with a team photo from each year and it was pretty cool to see how the team had grown. It made you feel special. But it wasn't just about racing by a long shot. Every year the team would go to places like Khayelitsha, Cape Town's biggest and maybe most dangerous township, to understand more about the lives of the people Qhubeka were trying to help and to hand over bikes. That visit turned into something much bigger and felt much more commercial and too corporate an operation for my liking. During the past few years it's been held as a sort of ceremony in a big stadium on the outskirts of the township. But back in the winter of 2014–15, our visit was low-key, without any media and in a small minibus, and that approach made appreciating the difficult conditions people were facing much more real. We could walk around the township and were even taken inside some homes. At the time they had a few eye-catching side projects for the unemployed, such as planting trees locally as a way to getting a job.

Team-wise, things had already got bigger in 2013 when MTN-Qhubeka became Africa's first squad in the Pro Continental series, one division down from the top league, the World Tour. But as I found when I joined two years later, one of the knock-on effects of racing for a team with strong links to a charity was it did wonders for your motivation. I sometimes feel sorry for myself, as everybody does. Then I'd hear what the Africans on the team like Songezo Jim or Adrien Niyonshuti had had to go through just to get hold of a bike, let alone build a career in cycling, or hear about some of the communities that Qhubeka was trying to help, and my self-pity would stop right there.

Yet after racing for three years with BMC, when I got to MTN-Qhubeka I also said to myself, 'Fuck this, I'm setting up some boundaries.' From this point, I would have clear limits to what I would do for my team-mates, and my big goal was to go for personal success. I had tried to be a top team worker but I just wasn't that kind of rider. I'd learned the hard way that in cycling you can be loyal, but you don't always get rewarded for it. Plus this was maybe my last chance, so I wanted to do everything I could: not get frustrated, be strong, be calm, be cool, be ready to perform whenever the opportunity arose. And who knows, I might even get to ride the Tour again.

*

There had been points in the 2014 season when I'd hated it so much I thought I'd end my career there and then. It was partly because I had had those bad moments with BMC when I'd crashed a few times, broken my wrist and so on. But the worst part was that someone in management had told me BMC were going to sign me again for 2015, and then I got wind of the fact that, actually, they weren't.

I wasn't bothered that BMC weren't going to keep me but I was bothered that he had told me the opposite. So my attitude was like, 'That's a no-no, that's out of order.'

That summer was already pretty intense, with the Tour de Pologne and then the Eneco Tour, with a single day off between the two. I could have been wrong but the team's logistics guy seemed to be making my travel as difficult as possible, and I'd already wanted to walk out of the team. Then in October I got sent to the Tour of Beijing. This was the one event that BMC and I had agreed at the start of the season I wouldn't do because I'd raced it four years, every autumn, on the trot. On top of that, I'd had a silly crash in training and had hurt my knee a few weeks before the race, which turned into tendonitis. My season was done.

But BMC sent me anyway, claiming I only needed to start. The only reason I can see to send me when they knew I was injured is that they wouldn't have to pay a fine for having fewer riders. Perhaps they could have taken a rider that wasn't injured? Starting a race injured is, I think, against professional cycling regulations, but apart from this my thought process was: It's clear the team doesn't value you – OK, that's fine – but I value my knee and my career.

So I flew to China, we drove three hours to the start of stage one, I rode 2 kilometres of the stage, then I turned round in the road, and that was it. I was quitting. As I passed the BMC team car following the main bunch of riders, I slowed down and told the team's sports director, Yvon Ledanois, in no uncertain terms that I was going home. I paid for my flight back to the UK, as I couldn't be bothered dealing with the logistics guy again, but my falling-out with BMC didn't end there by a long shot. The team told me they were going to fine me €5000 for failing to show up at the Tour of Beijing team presentation before the race – I'd missed it because just when the team got their call to go on stage, I was in the toilet. I replied by saying I'd settle for a €500 fine at most. Then BMC stopped paying my wages altogether, a situation that continued for the last three months of the year. I don't remember ever being concerned about the money in itself, but I was just keen to be out of it all. Either way it was only when my agent, Andrew McQuaid, intervened that BMC paid up, and thankfully it was all over.

*

The two teams were radically different and it wasn't just in terms of stature. BMC were in cycling's top division, the World Tour, and had won thirty races including some top Classics in 2014, while MTN-Qhubeka were in the second division, lower budget and their biggest win in 2014 had been a stage of a small early-season race, the Tour of Andalucía. What mattered more was that, organizationally, things at MTN-Qhubeka were at times chaotic in comparison.

Even if the chaos cracked me up at times, I tried to make it work for me, look on it as an adventure. I remember that Doug used to say that in Africa 'we build a house from the roof down,' and that'd make me laugh, rather than complain. I focused on what we had as opposed to what we didn't have. So my attitude was that I'd got a great bike and great wheels, and all the other equipment such as the clothing was good, even if it wasn't perfect. When I found out that the power meters weren't working well, for example, I just went out and bought my own for training.

Then there were times at MTN-Qhubeka when things turned out well for me almost by accident. My Eritrean team-mates didn't have email accounts, for example, and in a top-tier team like Sky or where I'd been before BMC, if you're not on email I'm not sure how long you can survive. At that point in time I wasn't a great communicator and I wasn't the best in the world at answering emails either. But at MTN-Qhubeka I somehow became known as one of the star guys for replying to them.

I had the same determinedly positive attitude right from the start of the team's year in Mallorca, when we went to an early-season training camp. Usually, I'm not so happy at camps, because if you're riding in a group with ten or twelve guys you end up riding at an easier pace than if you were out training on your own. So I deliberately turned the Mallorca camp into an easy week for me, almost like an adaptation period, winding down from a period of more intensive training by myself at home. And I didn't have to do any washing or cooking, which is always a plus!

All in all, being so upbeat about my team was paying dividends, and I'm sure it helped me to be consistent throughout the season, right from the start. My weight was down, for one thing. Then in my first race of the season, also in Mallorca, I beat Spanish cycling star and future world champion Alejandro Valverde on a short climb on the road to Formentor, and I knew I was going well.

That day I thought Valverde would beat me in the uphill sprint, because he's one of the best in the world at those, so

I attacked on the climb halfway up before the finish, and that tactic helped net me the win. My team-mate Jacques van Rensburg had attacked early on, forcing Movistar to chase, and so when I went for it, they were exposed – thanks, Jacques. And that was typical of Qhubeka – everyone got a chance there to play their card as long as you were strong enough. But the best thing about this new season was that it felt as if whatever racing I did and no matter how hard I raced, it wasn't tougher than what I was doing at the time in training. To put that in a nutshell: train hard, race easy.

Another big new impulse to my career was Perla's birth. Towards the end of the 2014 season, Nicky had been pregnant for some time but I'd been so absorbed in my own world that all I was thinking about was 'bike', and that I didn't have a contract for 2015. I was hating life, actually, and it was only when I'd signed the contract with MTN-Qhubeka – Brian Smith had approached me during the Tour of Britain that autumn and we quickly reached terms – that she sat me down one evening and pushed a photograph of the baby across the table, and all I could think was, 'Bloody hell, I'm going to be a dad.'

It didn't all go right. The week that Perla was due, I went to the Tour of Andalucía. I shouldn't have gone, because my body was there in the race, but my mind wasn't. I couldn't sleep and one night I found myself sitting on a team food box – it wasn't even ours, it was another team's, FDJ's – in some random hotel corridor at getting on for three o'clock in the morning, saying to myself, 'What the fuck am I doing here?'

I ran into Dave Brailsford the next day at the start, and he said, 'Look, some things are more important than a race. Don't miss the birth of your daughter, go home.' MTN-Qhubeka convinced me to do the stage two time trial, but because I hadn't been sleeping well, I went down with really bad bronchitis and I had to come home mid-race anyway.

I spent forty-eight hours in bed, sweating, then I went on antibiotics and finally I came round a bit. I couldn't go more than half an hour away from home though, doing circular training routes round the flat, trying to maintain my form. But then, finally, Perla was born.

Her birth unleashed a whole chain of thoughts in me, such as, 'I've got to grow up,' and 'All I've got to do is do my best and stay strong, mentally.' I kept thinking about the ideal strategies for racing and training, what I call 'process', so much so that I'd wake up in the mornings and know I'd been dreaming about the 'process'. I desperately wanted to make life easier for Nicky and Perla, to be sure that when I was spending time away from them, I was maximizing that time, not wasting a single moment. If I finished twentieth in a race, I was twentieth, if I was tenth, I was tenth; that didn't matter. I just wanted to make sure I got the best out of myself. And if there were things that weren't fair I had to learn how to deal with them effectively. I wanted extreme ownership – I was only thinking about my behaviour and how I could influence situations. I no longer cared too much if I encountered someone I perceived as awkward. I'd shrug my shoulders and say, 'OK, the world is not perfect, can you do something about it?' If I could, I tried. If I could not, I didn't waste time thinking about it. I guess the bottom line was I wanted to be a good example for my daughter.

Brian Smith, the team manager, was really helpful at this time. Sometimes I've let things fester in the past, or I've approached management about something and it falls on deaf ears, or they simply told me I was too old. But Brian would call me every weekend without fail and listen to what I had to say.

Massively boosted by Perla's birth, I went to the Tirreno–Adriatico race, and things started to look up again. First, the organizers took out the team time trial they had planned, because of high winds which had caused trees to fall in the area, and replaced it with an individual prologue. This was way better for me personally and I ended up sixth overall. All year, it seemed, the good results were going to keep coming. Not great ones, maybe, but I was consistent.

After Tirreno–Adriatico I rode in support of my team-mate Louis Meintjes in the Coppi e Bartali race. Swifty, a rival at Sky but also a friend, had been leading but then when Louis won a stage and took over at the top of the overall ranking, he came up to me afterwards and said, 'You bastard, you made my legs hurt.' This was exactly what I needed to hear to confirm it wasn't just me who thought I was going well. Also, as a squad, we'd made some good decisions tactically and we'd then had the power to make them happen.

Being in MTN-Qhubeka that year was just like a big, fun adventure. The morale in the team was amazing and the African lads were great. In June in the Dauphiné race, Ambesa, as we called Daniel Teklehaimanot and which means Lion King in Eritrean, won the King of the Mountains classification for best climber, and in the last stage I got a good chance to win by getting in a breakaway move ahead of the bunch. What with my move – which didn't work out, but which had come close to succeeding – and Ambesa's King of the Mountains win, Doug Ryder, the passionately involved MTN-Qhubeka boss, was absolutely made up.

Earlier in the season MTN-Qhubeka had their first ever wildcard invitation to the Tour de France, which was massively important for a Continental level team such as ours and good for me too, because I hadn't been to the Tour since 2012. I'd always struggled to trust anyone but I really trusted Brian, with his knowledge and passion about the sport, to ensure that MTN-Qhubeka would get to the Tour, as previously he'd worked with teams such as NetApp-Endura that hadn't really got big-name riders or a big enough budget for the race, but had ended up being invited anyway. Obviously, I was pleased we were going, but in any case I'd signed a two-year contract with MTN-Qhubeka. At the time I thought, at my age, this could be for my two last seasons as a pro. I wanted to end my career with no regrets. So from the Tour of Mallorca to the Tour de France and beyond, when I found I'd got the right balance between opportunities, responsibility and support, with no sickness or injuries to worry about, it felt like the planets were aligning.

In the prologue of the Tour de France that July, I was the team's best performer, finishing tenth out of nearly two hundred racers. Everybody was pleased, as it was our first Tour de France (and the first for an African team in many decades) and we weren't a big team, so that night, even though we hadn't won, we drank champagne to celebrate our good start.

But what really mattered to me personally, in the Tour de France, was trying to do just that – win.

In 2015 it was the first year I'd ever raced the Tour without a designated leader in my team for the overall classification, so my strategy of getting in the breaks suited MTN-Qhubeka's aims for the Tour, of getting maximum visibility, down to the ground too. After not doing any Grand Tours in 2014, I wanted to show what I was capable of doing in cycling's biggest arena too. Even if I was in my mid-thirties, when lots of riders of my age were close to retirement and had long since forgotten about trying to win anything at all in the Tour, I wanted to build on that Vuelta victory. I felt I was technically better, smarter, fitter and leaner than before. I felt I could do it again.

I'd identified five days as 'my' stages for breaks, and marked them with an X in the Tour route book. Of course, if I could help out a team-mate in the meantime, then I would. But I didn't feel I could be much use to Edvald (Boasson Hagen) in a bunch sprint. In any case, as there were no real leaders in MTN-Qhubeka's Tour line-up, everybody was pretty much treated the same, meaning we were all allowed to push for our own chances.

I'd viewed the prologue as a test of my own strength, and taking tenth had been a confirmation of that. From then on, I just got through each stage where I couldn't do anything because it was a bunch sprint or major overall stage thinking, 'I'm going well, the form's there and I've worked really hard, so fuck everyone else. If they want to get stressed, they can get stressed and all I have to do is stay on my bike.' Really, that was all I was thinking: in all this first week chaos, stay on my bike. I was in my own little world. I was going to enjoy the Tour. I was going to use my strengths in the right moment. But above all I was going to nail my stages.

18 July 2015: Tour de France stage 14 – Rodez–Mende 178.5 km

I know this is a day for me. It's like a mental switch. Dave B has a way of putting it. He says, 'Intent. When you leave the team bus – intent.' And the switch is on. There's intent.

*

The Tour was deep into its second week by that point, and it was working to a set pattern. Chris Froome and Team Sky had got a real grip on the race. Froome was leading by more than three minutes – barring accidents he was going to win overall – and the other teams were mostly looking around for stage wins, either in sprints or breakaways.

That was always MTN-Qhubeka's plan anyway, but at this point in the Tour all the other teams apart from Sky, even the ones with overall contenders, had shifted over to the same idea. This made our Tour mission much, much harder, but we'd got to stick at it, and Rodez to Mende, the fourteenth leg of the race, was a hilly transition stage. In other words, one that was made for me. More or less...

Doug made a big speech before the stage on the team bus about how it was Nelson Mandela Day and how that was really important for a South African-sponsored team such as MTN-Qhubeka, and his speech was absolutely brilliant. But I've got to be honest, at times like these anything external was a distraction.

When I put my leg over the bike that day, I wasn't thinking about kids on bikes from Africa, or Mandela. I was thinking about getting out of the bus and on the bike with intent, starting on the right foot, following the right wheels. It was the process. My process.

*

There's an unwritten rule in cycling strategy about how the best way to get into a break is always to go with the first move. And while a lot of good riders say that and I don't have a crystal ball, I'll never do that because I don't go in a break just to wind up getting caught by the main pack with 3 kilometres to go to the finish.

I need to be sure that the break has riders in it that are strong enough not to get caught, to become what we call 'the break of the day' or 'the right break'. The one that has the best chance of winning. So I wait, and rather than sitting towards the back, as is my habit, I do what I have to do: stick close to the front at the points when it matters, and keep watching for the break of the day to form.

There are certain points when you think, 'The right break might go here.' It could be when the road narrows, or at the top of a climb, or on a tricky downhill technical section when the pace of the leader's team, normally at the front of the bunch, lessens slightly, and their control on the riders in the bunch eases a little. You try to identify those parts of the route beforehand: that way you don't constantly stay so far forward in the main pack when there's nothing to gain and your stress levels are lower. So you've got more mental energy for when things hot up and you have to fight for position.

There are 180 riders, give or take, in a Tour peloton. So which riders do you keep the closest eye on, because they're most likely to form a good, long-lasting break? You watch the guys who look on edge, or the guys with special equipment on their bikes, such as CeramicSpeed chains, which they wouldn't normally have. Or – back in the day when it wasn't as common or most people wouldn't bother – the guys wearing skinsuits for lower air resistance. Or they'll start the stage with one bottle, so they're carrying less weight, just to get in the break. The golden rule is never to think that you are going to follow one rider in particular. Apart from the top riders in the battle for the overall classification, who tend to take transition stages as an opportunity to ease back a little – although not always – it could be anybody.

Time-wise I give myself up to an hour and a half to get into that 'right break', with sixty to ninety minutes as the 'sweet spot' for doing it. If a break forms later on, there are fewer kilometres left to race, so it's got less and less chance of surviving, partly because there's less time to build a significant lead and the closer you get to the finish, the greater the chance the GC guys' teams will start working. Also, as there are fewer kilometres to go, there's a greater chance other teams will think, 'It's only an hour to go to the finish, so let's pull anyway.' To sum up, there's always a balance to adapting to this on the road, and when you have limited bullets, you have to stay aware of this stuff and maybe accept that another day is better. But whatever the stage throws up, I know I need to be smart and, above all, make damn sure I don't miss anything that matters.

*

That stage fourteen to Mende was 178 km long, so there was well over four hours of racing, and it was very hilly – we were in the middle of France, in the Massif Central. The main challenge that would decide the stage was a horribly steep 3.5 km final climb to Mende airfield, with the finish just a kilometre beyond it. But there were a few tough early ascents too, and it was a baking-hot day. We started so fast that soon the heavier sprinters were already going backwards on the uphills then getting back into the mix when they picked up speed on the descents.

We bombed down a hill, all strung out and carving through the turns, and at the bottom the road was narrow enough for Sky to try to block it. That way they could stop any breaks getting too big and simultaneously prevent any dangerous rivals to the race leader, Froome, from making a move. But I was feeling so confident I made my move anyway. I shot past the Sky team workers with Simon Yates, a racer from another rival squad, following me closely. I didn't bother to ask him to collaborate because I was going so fast on the flat – going uphill would have been different with a climber like Simon! – I knew he wouldn't have been able to do that even if he'd wanted.

During the stage I went to my physical limit three times just to try to get in the right break. But then, on the third try, Simon and I made it across to a group of riders who had already formed a move shortly beforehand, which definitely looked like being the break of the day. This was good, but when I got into this particular break, I immediately realized I was really going to be up against it to win.

For one thing, the break was big, even if that was kind of normal for that sort of stage. There were eighteen guys in it, rather than the usual six or so, and there were so many top names that people kept attacking and getting dropped. We were a good hour and a half into the stage – my personal deadline for getting into breaks, as I've said – before it settled down and definitively took shape.

Among those big names there was Yates, who came across to the break with me and who would win the Tour of Spain a few years later; Rigoberto Urán, a gifted Colombian climber, silver medallist in the Olympics in London; France's two top stage racers, Thibaut Pinot and Romain Bardet; and the rider ranked number one in the world, Peter Sagan, who was already holding the green jersey as the Tour's points leader, the most consistent rider in the sprints.

I spent a lot of time, as much as I could, evaluating the strengths and weaknesses of each rider. I knew I could shake off Sagan on that last hard climb in Mende, given his build, but as well as all these riders there were top Classics racers such as Greg Van Avermaet, who had captured the Tour stage into Rodez the day before, and Luxembourg's main man, Bob Jungels. All of them were potential winners; all of them had the form and the experience to go for the victory. And I had to beat all of them too.

On the plus side, these efforts I'm making in the first part of the stage are no different to what I've been doing in training, and that gives me confidence, because I know I can handle them. Another bonus is that none of the riders in the break represents a threat to Froome's lead or the other GC challengers. So Sky, the strongest team in the race, will probably let the break go clear and go to the finish, even if having so many top names is not going to make my job any easier.

The quality of the break is an obvious cause for concern – this is the Tour so it's really high calibre, basically – and there is one equipment issue at the back of my mind too. After the stage, when we're getting changed, Sagan asks me how much I weigh. I tell him 75 kg and he's impressed. He says, 'You must have put out a lot of power on that last climb.' But actually I had no idea what power I'd produced all day because, as I said, in all my races that year I had had to use that saggy power meter that didn't do proper readouts and wasn't reliable. It was like getting on your bathroom scales when you've had them for a while and they say you weigh 60 kg when you're 75 kg!

Anyway I'm in the break, saggy power meter or no saggy power meter, and the first obvious thing I notice, apart from all the big names, is that there are three riders from the French FDJ team in it too. They're a popular squad, but with uneven results so far that year. That's one of the first things I do in that situation – I immediately count which teams have how many riders. In this case, with just one of me and seventeen rivals, it's actually better that there are so many FDJs. I know that if any mini-breaks develop out of the main one, all I have to do is make sure that FDJ aren't in it, because then they'll chase that mini-break for all they're worth, and I can wait for my moment.

I don't recall talking to anyone, and that's my way. When I'm in a break I'm very aware of who's friends with whom, who might help each other even if they're not on the same team but who might be former team-mates or neighbours or buddies, and because of that, how things might evolve in terms of who attacks and when. There's also a nationality issue here: Italians, I think, would rather another Italian wins than someone else, and the Belgians are the same. Often two Italian team directors from rival squads will talk to each other to ensure that even if their riders don't collaborate, they don't race against each other either and there'll be some payback – not financial, but inside a race – at a later date. So there's not a negotiation between rider and rider but team to team, because they know that, working together, the small chance they have of winning increases a little.

But the French and Brits sometimes do the opposite, because it's like they don't want to be beaten by another Brit or Frenchman. In the smaller races that's particularly true, but also a little in the Tour de France. The French teams are often seemingly fighting each other as much as they're fighting their rivals. If they showed a bit more solidarity, they might benefit the country's sport as a whole.

And it's useful to know (or remember) who's directing each team car – are they friends and perhaps therefore more likely to tell their riders to work together, or sworn enemies? Some teams or riders may be very competitive, and are likely to mark each other out. There are grudges, old and new. All of this is often an unspoken discussion, just taken for granted. Sometimes you can sense with the older French teams that there are a lot of underlying back stories about who's helping whom (or not) you don't appreciate. But if you figure out which teams want a similar scenario, sometimes even when they don't want to and it's all a bit frosty, then you can start to understand the flow of how the race is likely to go.

*

The break's advantage stretches and stretches as the day goes on, all the way up to seven minutes. It's clear somebody from the break is going to win and Sky are happy for that to happen. With such a big advantage too, it's no surprise that some attacks in the break start quite a way from the finish.

The MTB-Qhubeka team car drives alongside, we discuss tactics for the finale, and somebody inside tells me, 'Go from long' – in an ideal world I would start attacking early as they suggest. But the game changer is that FDJ have three guys to chase me down. Even if I got a minute's margin or more, they'd probably reel me in without any problems before the climb, and I think I'd have needed at least a minute at the bottom of the ascent to have a chance of surviving. So I'm not moving. For now.

As I saw it, the biggest problem was that I was surrounded by rivals who would, on paper, go faster up the final climb in Mende – but only on paper. One thing in my favour was that a climb is very different when you've been riding in a break all day, as in our case, rather than when you've been tucked away behind team-mates in the main peloton. Second, I was a lot more aerodynamic than many of the other riders in the break, and the energy I'd saved during the hours we spent riding together before the Mende climb was going to be mine to use up on the final ascent. Finally, I knew I'd got a 450-watt threshold for my power output and the climbers had maybe a 400-watt threshold, and when we were on the flat, driving along before the final climb, I was using a lower percentage of my total power. Or to put it in a nutshell, this was a four-hour-long stage, not one single effort up one steep climb, and on top of that, the finish came a kilometre after the top so my higher power threshold could be useful there. All that gave me hope.

In any case, I've no choice but to wait. My only chance of winning is to hang on in the break with FDJ setting the pace at the front, and then go up the final climb as fast as possible. But for most of those four hours, I'm not thinking about actually winning, I'm thinking more about getting to the main, steepest climb with the stage still in my grasp. Then I'll time-trial up it, basically, going at my own pace while letting the others do what the hell they want.

It so happened that I'd been up the climb to Mende airfield before, in the 2010 Paris–Nice race, and five years later that was a good advantage. I'd also watched videos of previous races with the same climb. I knew that Mende was really hard when it started coming out of the town, then it got a little easier, then it was really steep again to the top. The key thing was not to go all out at the start, because if someone went bonkers and ramped up their power output to 700 watts and way into the red, they wouldn't be able to keep racing that hard for that long on a climb that steep and they'd lose the momentum they needed to stay in contention.

My time-trialling strategy for the climb was that for all bar the last couple of hundred metres I'd try to use the draft of the others where the speed would be higher as it wasn't so steep. But then I needed to be sure I was racing on the upper limit of my possible effort, but without actually forcing myself so hard that after twenty or thirty seconds I'd crack – a balancing act. That sort of threshold strategy, going steady for a long time at a high pace, was something I practised in training twice a week, three times in each session. You learn to feel your limit and you become good at finding the red line beyond which you'd crack, and staying right on that line. But then – and I also did this in training – the key part of this strategy was that when you saw the top of the climb, the end of your effort, you suddenly tried to do the exact opposite of what you'd been doing up to then.

In other words, when you see the top of the climb, with maybe 200 metres to go, rather than staying steady, you'd push yourself beyond threshold and you'd give it everything you had. The pain would build and build, although actually I'd kind of enjoy that, because it'd confirm my sense of leaving it all out there and I'd trained myself to go through this process and deliver that in the race.

This tactic consists of learning how to blow right at the top of a climb, exactly at the summit and not a metre before, which would be catastrophic. As I get to the top of a steep climb near home in Tuscany, I'll be telling myself, 'Come on, you've got three more [heart] beats, eight more beats…' That's because my maximum for any effort under fatigue is about 180 bpm; that's the magic number when I know I'm riding myself into the ground to the point of blowing, but not beyond it. I don't know whether it is the physical side or the mental side of making that all-out effort so often in training that matters so much in Mende. Numbers are a guide and sensations are more important, particularly in a race. But I do know that's why it was possible for me to win.

The net result of that delivery is you'd arrive at the top of the climb with your lactate levels at a maximum. You couldn't go any deeper. But you'd also gone as fast as you could for that last part of the ascent and that could make all the difference between winning and losing.

At the top of the climb, it would almost feel like you were going to crack completely, because you couldn't sustain that all-out effort of 700 watts for a long time. But if the course went on beyond the summit and you were on a descent, your power output would drop down to 300 watts, which you could handle easily because the road was heading downhill. So suddenly you'd have momentum for a whole new effort, and hopefully, by that point, you'd have shaken off your rivals with your late acceleration on the climb. And ideally, you'd be on the way to winning.

It all comes back, yet again, to understanding your strengths and your limits and the opposition's. I'm not thinking about winning or an outcome. I'm thinking about the process, formulating the best plan given the situation, despite it not being ideal, because if you wait for the ideal moment, you may be waiting a long time or it may never come at all. Then there's being flexible to make a new plan as the situation develops, and then executing that plan with complete conviction. Staying calm and calculated. Thinking about the outcome wasn't wise; I'd learned that in my team pursuit days. Rather, it's thinking about the process and breaking that up into manageable sections is what makes it straightforward.

So when we get to the final climb to Mende airfield, at the bottom I don't chase when the other guys shoot ahead of me up the road: Bardet, Urán, Yates, Pinot. Rather than cooking myself by going too hard, I keep my pace high, but steady, staying in the draft even if it looks like I'm the first to be dropped on TV, and as we get higher on the climb, I find my strategy works. I fall back at first in the order of the riders, but then I bottom out and come back up again. And by time-trialling it, I pick off my rivals on the climb and I go past the other breakaways who have attacked or gone too fast too soon in the first part of the ascent, one by one. I'm thinking to myself, 'Fourth on the stage,' 'Third on the stage,' as I go past them. I come over the top of that horrible steep climb just as I'd wanted to, timing it so I'm exactly at the point where I've ridden myself to shreds as I go over the summit, and then just as I'm picking up momentum on the downhill, they are right there. Bardet and Pinot, the last guys from the break who attacked ahead of me and I haven't yet caught, are there, within sight, and I think, 'This'll be good – I'll get third on the stage.'

But it gets better. With my momentum picking up after the summit, I charge past them on a downhill just before the last, flatter kilometre to the finish. Rather than play games, I go straight to the front and take the lead. One thing you learn from being in breaks is your rivals' characteristics, and I know Pinot is cautious when it comes to corners. We've got two corners left, in a downhill chicane before we get to the long, flat finishing straight along an airfield runway. Bardet is much better at cornering, but as I go past it's Pinot who is swinging in right behind me and that instantly gives me an advantage. I go through these downhill corners flat out, and as soon as I've got a little gap on Pinot, I put my head down and go even harder. After climbing Mende in 2010 – one last advantage from all that time before – I know once I come through the last corner that there are about 600 metres of straight, along the airfield runway to the finish. I also know that, with my power and my position on the bike, if those guys give me ten metres advantage, they're not going to get back on terms. My position on the bike is so aerodynamic compared to those two bollards, sitting up like that. With the momentum I've got on a flat course, I'm going to be well on my way. I'm getting this.

In the very last part of the stage, almost at the line, the two of them get out of the saddle, all but flapping their arms around; they're making such a hard last effort to try to catch me. But to be honest, as soon as I catch Bardet and Pinot I think, 'There's no way I'm not going to win this stage. I cannot lose, I cannot lose. And that is a nice feeling, because for my entire career, I've been waiting for that moment, for the biggest win of my life as a rider. In the Tour de France. And as I pedal towards the finish ahead of them, I know it's here. I've got it. It's the dream. It's mine.

I was so grateful to the team for giving me the opportunity and freedom. I still am. But at the same time I know I've earned that opportunity through good results and hard work and discipline – which gave me freedom, and being strong mentally, trying to make myself better in every aspect of my racing, because I wasn't ever good enough at any one thing in particular.

As I explain to somebody later that evening, all through the stage I'd been thinking about strategy, what I call 'process', nothing but process. It had all been rational, and with a plan that developed as the race evolved, but that's how I am when I'm in that zone. I'd been there all day.

Then when I cross the line, all of a sudden the emotional side of it kicks in and it's like, 'Holy fuck, what have I just done?' It's the dream scenario, the schoolboy dream of winning against those odds. It's been super-nice too, because with 100 metres to go I know I've won. It's a relief, a massive weight off my shoulders because of the challenges we overcame on the journey to get there in the days and months and years before. All of a sudden, it's all become worthwhile.

Chapter 11

Why I Couldn't Train with Mark Cavendish

Maybe it's because it's where I first met him but if there's one thing I can't ever forget about Mark Cavendish it's that he started out on the Isle of Man. I was about seventeen, he was about thirteen, and he was standing outside a nightclub in Douglas, wearing a tracksuit and clutching a bottle of something that looked suspiciously like 'shit-mix'. I was chasing skirt and trying to sneak inside, and there he was yelling at me, 'Hey, you're Steve Cummings. I've got your picture on my bedroom wall from when you won the Soens.'

He was a chubby kid, standing there with his little posse of friends, but at that age getting or not getting into a nightclub is a matter of life or death, so my first words ever to the future world champion, Olympic medallist and greatest sprinter of his generation were 'I don't know you, piss off.' He's always reminded me about that, and if my first words to him weren't exactly complimentary, I'll never stop saying this either: in terms of raw talent, Mark Cavendish is the best I've ever seen. There were periods of his career when you could give him a brioche to eat and a shopping bike to ride and he'd win.

It says a lot about Cav's innate ability as a sprinter that he got to the top of his sport and his speciality almost without any team support. He was fighting to do that long before Team Sky/Ineos Grenadiers existed, way before the 2008 Olympic 'gold rush' of medals for Britain's national cycling squads. He did it at a time when the British Cycling Federation was still fighting to get major funding and Continental-based European squads ruled the roost. There was no career path for British riders wanting to race at the highest level of the sport in mainland Europe, no home team to cover your back. As I'd found out, you got out there and did it yourself. Sink or swim – and if you sank, nobody noticed. British Cycling has its own talent-spotting system now, but back in the day it was more hit and miss. So it's scary to think how easily he might never have made it, and how much the sport might have lost as a consequence.

Later as teenagers, after that first meeting, our paths would cross again, and the fact they did showed how determined he was to get ahead in cycling, no matter what. It was at the Merseyside Divisional Championships on Liverpool's Wavertree Playground course, and I saw him winning a bunch sprint in his yellow-and-red Isle of Man jersey. The Manx team was included in Merseyside's championships and that meant a long ferry journey over each time you wanted to take part. But we didn't hit it off then, either: I have to say my ideal of a bike racer wasn't – and still isn't – a sprinter. I admire and appreciate a bunch sprint and the characters in it – Cipollini, Cav, Alessandro Petacchi are three names that leap to mind – as well as the really high levels of skill involved in bike handling. But I prefer riders who get results without taking so many risks and potentially putting others in danger, and some have colossal egos too.

We ran into each other again in 2003 or so when he was racing with the Cycling Academy in Manchester on the track and battling against the odds just as strongly as ever. For me Manchester was an easy trip from the Wirral, but for him it meant living away from his family and home for weeks or months at a time.

He hadn't changed in some ways from when we first met – he must have been eighteen by then and as he was working in a bank he had a bit more money than the average Academy lad. So because he had to get around, he'd spent it on a car, in his case, a Vauxhall Corsa. It was gold with a gold sticker on the windscreen which I'm pretty sure said 'Goldfinger'. He was a cocky so-and-so, but you liked him anyway because he had such good banter you couldn't help but laugh.

In Manchester I was in and out of the velodrome, racing with Chris Newton, Bradley Wiggins and Paul Manning in the senior GB team pursuit squad. Every so often, we'd hear stories about these Academy lads like Mark and what they'd been up to and it was just hilarious. When they'd fucked up, Rod Ellingworth, the former Academy manager, used to make them ride together in a line round the top of the velodrome banking. That's where it's steepest, and if you're using a fixed-wheel bike it's the worst place of all to ride round a track because the transition from banking to straight is so extreme that if you're too slow you risk sliding down.

Riding the banking so slowly like that was a good skill for them to master. But what made Rod's exercise so hard was it wasn't for a few minutes, he would make them ride round and round for maybe an hour. That wasn't the only punishment they got – once I saw Cav and the rest washing the team cars because they'd done something wrong.

Yet despite the tough regime, and the challenges of living away from home for months at a time as a teenager, with his raw talent and determination Cav was already progressing fast. It all went to show that no matter how difficult things were for him in those early days, you couldn't keep him down.

The first time I actually raced with Cav professionally, that hit home hard. It was at the Regio Tour in Germany in 2006, a good while after we'd first crossed paths. He was a *stagiaire* – an apprentice pro – with one of the most powerful squads of the era, T-Mobile, while I was there with Landbouwkrediet. I remember Cav spent much of the race working at the front of the bunch, which they eventually won overall with a star rider of the time, Andreas Klöden. In contrast, all we'd done in Landbouwkrediet was win one lousy hot-spot sprint prize – for the fastest rider midway through the stage – of a few kegs of beer.

It wasn't just Cav being in a major first division squad at such a young age that was impressive. The team were sponsored by Audi, and the riders had their own different model to drive after each race in Germany. So after the Regio Tour, Cav would be in his Audi zooming round wherever he pleased, while I and the rest of our team had to drive all the way back to Belgium, drinking our beer prize in a grubby campervan that smelled like an open sewer.

But maybe it wasn't just the right team or the nicer (much nicer) cars or even the talent that mattered most to Cav. To become the best sprinter of his generation he needed to have a brutally strong kind of self-belief. And he had lots of that. Even in T-Mobile, Cav was barely more than a chubby kid at that time, unlike some sprinters who are taller and more muscular, but he still always used to say to everybody: 'I am the fastest in the world.' And initially, like a lot of people, I didn't take him seriously. Then he beat two top names, Robbie McEwen and Tom Boonen, in the Scheldeprijs race in 2007. It's one of Belgium's biggest one-day races and is basically made for sprinters, and I found myself thinking, 'Wow, maybe he really is the fastest in the world!'

(After such a massive victory, Cav still managed somehow to slip over on the Scheldeprijs winner's podium. Years later, in the Tour de France, me and the rest of the lads used to put that bit of the race coverage on the team bus telly to remind him of his 'slip-up': 'What happened here then, Cav?' I'd ask with a grin and his answer to me would invariably be: 'Oh fuck off.')

Back in 2007 and 2008, though, while the rest of us road-racing Brits were stuck in no-man's land in terms of results, Cav was quickly becoming one of the biggest names in cycling. It didn't seem to matter that he had hardly any team support in the sprints, because at the time some of his older team-mates would have said that they wouldn't be prepared to help a young pro out. There used to be a thing where a young racer had to earn his stripes and carry bottles for five years before he could be taken seriously, although that obviously doesn't happen now. But back then Cav was too good and too fast so could win big races with or without their assistance and guidance, and after that they had to lead him out no matter what.

Back in the early days when he was getting successful, Cav was still that funny, wisecracking guy off the bike that he'd been as a teenager. But there had been one change. With his much bigger pro contracts, he'd also become a guy who liked to spend. Maybe anybody would if you were twenty-one or twenty-two and in his situation, but Cav had become like a kid in a sweet shop with unlimited pocket money.

Let's say we'd be going past a shoe shop and Cav would suddenly stop and say, 'Oh, lad, I love those shoes.' But the shoe would be available in three colours and he wouldn't be able to make up his mind which one he wanted. So Cav being Cav, he'd just buy all three pairs. Then you'd walk through his apartment in Quarrata, and there'd be clothes in bags and boxes that he'd bought and never opened. But he was enjoying himself, and good for him.

In other ways, Cav hadn't – and still hasn't – changed at all. I remember when my former Sky team-mate Ian Stannard got married, I was sitting there at the same table during the reception with Cav and his wife, but I was wearing a neck brace because I'd crashed. So I had to go and lie on my back in the hotel's reception area to take the weight off my neck and back. I was feeling terrible, looking up at the ceiling and who appeared in my field of vision, looking down at me? It was Cav, saying, 'Are you all right, mate? Fucking hell, that must be bad.' That's Cav all over. He's got his failings – everybody has – but he's got a heart of gold.

*

Later, during his time at the HTC-Colombia team in 2009 to 2011, it got to the point where Cav was so successful that I no longer came across him much in actual races. Like almost everybody else, I just saw him on TV, all the time, winning loads, winning everywhere, head nearly touching the bars as he tried to get as low down and aerodynamic as possible in his final acceleration, crossing the line with his big goofy grin and his hands in the air. But when our paths crossed, it was special, and that was why riding for Cav when he took gold in the 2011 World Championships will always remain one of the best moments of my career.

By then Cav wasn't just winning four or five stages a year in the Tour and nearly the same in the Giro d'Italia. He had become the single most successful British road racer of all time. British riders had done brilliantly in the Olympics in 2008, and Team Sky had been created in 2010, of course. But the Olympics only happen once every four years, and Sky had had two very average Tours de France (by their later standards) in succession, so essentially, Britain's best chance of road-racing success still hinged on Cav, and that autumn in Copenhagen, the World Championships course was unusually flat, so for a sprinter like Cav, it was a chance of a lifetime. Not only that, if Cav won, he could become Britain's first World Road Race Champion since Tommy Simpson in 1965, the only Brit yet to have that honour.

For Cav, getting selected for a flat course like in Denmark was a no-brainer. Britain's road coach, Rod Ellingworth, who'd moved on from the track, had been working on the project to win at the Worlds for at least an entire year. It wasn't easy for me to take part – some people in British Cycling didn't want to select me. I was leaving Sky and was perceived as difficult and I think in the end it was Cav's own word that meant I went. I don't know exactly why he chose me, although I'd guess it was because I was very fit and aerodynamic so could be relied on to pull for a long way, but either way I was able to pay him back in the race.

At the start of the race, me and Froomey were working for Great Britain to keep the race under control for as long as possible, by staying on the front, and keeping a high enough, constant pace to ensure there weren't any important attacks. A few other teams did come to help us, mostly some Germans, but it was basically us two doing the work, and finally Chris cracked before I did. Just before the Worlds, Chris had got second overall in the Tour of Spain, a result later raised to outright victory after the rider ahead of him, Juan José Cobo, was banned for doping. The fact that he'd raced so strongly in Spain but then left off riding in the Worlds, even before I had to do the same, makes me think that that day I put in one of the best performances of my life up to that point in my career.

In the Worlds at least our strategy was clear. When you've got the favourite – and Cav was the favourite as he was the fastest in the world at that time – all we had to do was deliver him to a position where he could sprint for the line without any problems. Simple in theory, though a lot can still go wrong. As a team we had the engines, more or less, to do it, and parts of it went very smoothly. Then Jez Hunt's experience proved invaluable, even if he was really noisy in his role as team captain. He kept shouting, 'Right! Left! Right! Right!' at the top of his voice to warn us if he saw there was a chance of us getting swamped by rival teams pulling ahead of us on one side or the other. Sometimes Jez couldn't take a turn on the front any more and he'd suddenly yell, 'In! In! In!' Jez went over his limit, we all did, but his – and David Millar's – experience helped give us an extra edge.

Then Brad took it up, and he went so fucking fast for a lap, for around 14 kilometres through the streets of Copenhagen. I only saw it much later on TV though I wasn't in the race by that point. I'd said to Froomey, who wanted to finish the race, 'Come on, we're going to drink some beer on the bus, you've got your new contract, I'm going to BMC; whatever happens, happens, we've done a good job.' So we quit. It might be odd in other sports to be part of the winning team without completing the event, but in a one-day race like the Worlds in cycling, it's standard practice. As the saying goes, cycling's a team sport where only one person wins.

Meanwhile, back in the action, Team GB had Dave Millar and Ian Stannard and G left, but the boys got swamped by the other teams and separated from Cav – G lost his position. At one point Cav's positioning was so bad that it looked as if he was out of the running for victory. So we messed up the last 5 kilometres of the race and Cav certainly didn't get a textbook lead-out from his team-mates. But even if this wasn't the same as when Cipollini – the last sprinter to win the Worlds – had got a lead-out from his Italians in 2002, Stannard still did a fantastic job bringing Cav back into position. And at the end of the day, we'd all done our bit; the team had worked very well that day, even if we weren't perfect. Froome and I had laid the foundations early on, everybody else had kept things running our way right up to the finale, and then Cav turned things around as he found his way through his rivals and he sprinted for the win. That's Cav for you.

We all wanted to celebrate and, after his victory, almost all the GB team sat in our hotel reception area, still wearing our race kit and drinking the hotel bar out of their stocks of beer. Cav was gone for ages, but like the party planner he always was for Team GB, Millar was glued to his phone, trying to sort out the 'drinks and nibbles' as he called them. But in fact it was a way bigger party than that.

Millar got us all into some kind of bar with our own area in the middle of Copenhagen. I'd made a music mix on my phone, something I enjoyed doing in my spare time – electronic, dance, heavy bass, that sort of stuff – and all evening we were bouncing around with the mix on repeat and Millar telling me how great it was. Wiggo and I stood by the door, inviting in anybody we recognized going past and emptying bottles of beer over their heads and cheering our heads off as they came into the bar. It was a big celebration, which was great because so often when you win a race, you're just straight on to the next thing on the schedule, but this time we all kicked back and enjoyed ourselves. To this day I suppose somebody must have paid our bar tab at the end of it all, but I have no idea who! (So to whoever actually did – thank you.)

The whole day of the World Championships will always remain one of the best memories of my career. It wasn't perfect, but everybody did their best. Cav, though, was the glue that stuck that team together, because when things were going well he was an amazing leader. He knew exactly what he wanted and our roles were made very clear. The feeling that win created inside the GB national team might be gone now, but it definitely helped boost collective morale for quite a few years afterwards.

But for me, racing with Cav wasn't just about the wins – I got some insights into aspects of the sport that I'd never seen carried out so effectively. Much later on in Cav's career, for example, when we were both riding with Team Dimension Data in the 2016 Tour, I was really grateful to have witnessed that sprinters' train of Mark Renshaw, Bernie Eisel and Cavendish himself and how they worked to bring Cav into the best position for the sprint.

You'd sometimes throw a few other riders and team-mates into the mix, of course, but those three in particular were the best sprint package I can remember since Cipollini's all-conquering 'Red Train', as they called Cipo and his band of support riders nearly two decades before.

Part of why Mark, Mark and Bernie worked so well was the ease and speed with which they communicated with each other, on and off the bike. It was so special and fast-moving that sometimes it would be comprehensible, but other times it would sound as if they were from another planet. What was astonishing to witness was the way they'd talk through a sprint. They'd go through dozens of technical questions, like which side of the road they needed to be on at each particular point and in which position: 'We need to be twentieth wheel here, and here no further back than tenth, but here we need to hit the corner in front, then it doesn't matter if we slide back.' It was like a giant clockwork system they were taking to bits and you could only see how bits of it worked, but either way the machine wouldn't stop there. When they finally got round to how and where exactly Cavendish would be sprinting for the line, they'd analyse that to death too. Some bits you'd get, like their starting point would always be planning back from Cav's last move. Cav would say, 'Look, lad, you need to bring me to 180 metres to go cos this is a slightly uphill sprint, and I need a 54 chainring cos 55 is too big.' That'd be followed with a little argument about the chainring – they were always arguing – and then Renshaw would suddenly say, 'I can go from this corner, which is 600 metres to go.' After which Bernie would have his say and it'd go back to Cav and Renshaw, yet again, and then briefly there might be other people dragged in, such as his team-mates Reinie (Reinardt Janse van Rensburg) and Eddie (Edvald Boasson Hagen). Reinie never said very much, but Eddie would be quiet for a while and then he would suddenly blurt out, 'Yeah, I can do that, I can pull from one and a half kilometres, no problem.' Which would be fed back into Mark, Mark and Bernie's collective way of thinking, and on and on they'd go.

The funny thing is that Cav would win, of course, and he'd come back on the bus and straight away they'd start the debriefing, with Cav shouting something like, 'Renshaw, you fookin' idiot. Why didn't you take me up on the right?'

Renshaw could be more restrained than Cav, but he'd still sometimes manage to fire something back like, 'Fuck, some dickhead was on the right.' But Bernie would chip in with, 'Yeah, but you let the wheel go.' And then Bernie would remember what the result was and say, 'Cav, you know you won.' But it didn't matter. The three would go back again to the start of the argument anyway. They'd probably had too much caffeine in the finale and perhaps it's not the best way for some to communicate, shouting and cursing at each other, but for a time for them and for Cav it worked incredibly well.

*

Generally speaking, during the summer of 2016 in the Tour, the atmosphere in the team was unbelievably good. We won four stages in the first week and the team held both the overall lead and the points classification lead. Every morning on the bus we'd yell, 'Bring out The Gimp! Bring out The Gimp!' because as points leader Cav was wearing a green skinsuit and he looked like he'd dressed up as the guy they call The Gimp in the film *Pulp Fiction*. But his success wasn't fictional, it was very real and there were some specific reasons, I think, why Cav was racing so brilliantly that summer: he'd been on the track too, preparing for the Olympics, an environment that always suited him well; there was a good camaraderie in the team (people to chat to, to train with and to laugh with as well); and he'd got a clear direction to follow and clear motivation to try to get there.

Fast-forward five years and when he then came back to the Tour de France in 2021 to replace Sam Bennett in the Deceuninck–Quick-Step team and won again for the first time since 2016, I was there too, with Ineos Grenadiers, but no longer a rider. But whenever I saw him out on the road, he would always be smiling, ear to ear, like I'd never seen him smiling before.

I did think he would win a stage in 2021 just because he's so bloody good, technically, particularly when the shit hits the fan as it does in those chaotic Tour bunch sprints. And apart from having that skill of being in the right place at the right time, he had the best lead-out train.

It was also striking what he said about how nervous he'd been in the first hour of the first stage of the 2021 race, asking himself what on earth he was doing there. I think that's because Mark's confidence levels tend to go from one extreme to the other: when it's good, he's unbeatable, but when it's bad, it swings to a real low and that's probably what gave him those feelings. But I think he also benefited from a big easing of the pressure by coming in so late to replace Bennett. They played it very smart and I suspect they might well have known longer than was publicly made clear that it was possible Bennett wouldn't end up racing. But either way, as the team manager Patrick Lefevere said, their only other option was Cav, and if he won they were all kings for a day. It's almost like reverse psychology: before he'd gone into the Tour feeling scared of not winning, and this year he went back to how it was when he first started out in the Tour, with an attitude of 'Bloody hell, I'm so grateful to be here.'

Another analogy could be Cav went to the edge of a cliff, almost jumped, but someone grabbed his hand and pulled him out. Sometimes you need to go through all of that to realize how much you love what you do. I've certainly been in situations where things aren't going well and you'd rather be doing something else, like at the end of 2014 when I just wanted to pick up my bag and leave, but that feeling, bizarrely enough, can become a strength. Because you've got nothing to lose, you then say, 'Right, I'm going to enjoy it and start doing the basics to the best of my ability again.'

You recalibrate and reset, because if you're always under pressure, it's much harder to do that. But in this case, because he hadn't won for so long in the Tour and because no one was expecting him to go to the Tour, plus a lot of people were expecting him to fail, anything really, barring abandoning straight away – and then at least we'd have known that was it – was going to be good. In his case, it certainly helped tip the balance.

Getting not one stage win but four and the green jersey was unbelievable, and I couldn't be more impressed and it reminded me how much of a privilege it was to race with him.

But to put it into context too, starting with his team, Mark did have the advantage of having a super-strong squad, partly because of the way they supported him, but also because the sprints would have been a lot messier without them there. More chaotic sprints wouldn't have played out in his favour, as he'd been away for three years from the Tour so it might have been difficult for him to handle them by himself.

On top of that some top sprinters like Caleb Ewan, Nacer Bouhanni and Arnaud Démare either crashed out or abandoned ill. It felt like a year where you said to yourself, 'Where's all the sprinters?' To counter that argument, Cavendish didn't go home because he's bloody good at staying on his bike and he was in the right headspace. I remember where Caleb Ewan crashed out injured after going down a small climb near the end and Cav wasn't in that finale alongside Caleb. But I'm pretty sure he wasn't in it because he didn't want to take a risk when he wanted to go for the sprint the next day. That decision shows wisdom and confidence and experience, and it also begs the question, would Caleb Ewan have won four stages if he'd done the same? I'm not sure about that.

Some people were surprised as well that Cav had managed to get through the three weeks and not come unstuck with all those tough climbing stages in the Pyrenees. These are just my opinions, but I think his fitness level was the best since 2016, and he was 100 per cent on it and had a good, solid base of physical condition that his illnesses hadn't let him have before. He was consistent, and as I found too consistency gave you that real depth, and when you're on a roll it allows you to absorb the little niggles and minor issues that can sink a person who's not feeling as stable, physically.

The other factor is that we've seen time and again that Mark does get better as a race goes on. It's true he didn't win in Paris this year, but there've been times when we've got to the Champs-Élysées and apart from holding the all-time record for wins there, he's won those final sprints by several bike lengths.

As for what came in between those wins in 2016 and how he performed in 2021, I once read in an interview that Cav said, 'As soon as I turned pro, I was winning straight away, so I don't know what it's like to not be under pressure.' It's true. I think he was under pressure for so many years that it perhaps got to a point where the demands started to overwhelm him. He'd become a victim of his own success.

When he was at the peak of his powers there were only a few times I saw the pressure get to him, and that was because it was even greater than usual. The worst instance was before the 2011 Worlds, where everybody expected Cav to win and he knew it was a once-in-a-lifetime opportunity, and he gave one poor mechanic a very public bawling out for messing up a bike that needed some late changes.

Thinking about it now, the underlying problem perhaps wasn't just the pressure Cav was under, it was (and remains) also that in this sport, as a young pro rider, nobody teaches you how to handle those sorts of situations better – by, say, getting a team director to explain to the mechanic, quietly and in private.

Shouting at mechanics apart, for years there have been countless positive aspects and consequences of Cav being so talented – for himself, for his sport and for his country. But while it was an honour and privilege to race with him, I can't forget that with so much pressure to perform over the years, particularly after 2016 when he stopped winning so much, the strain began to tell. The other issue was one of the more unexpected challenges that being so naturally gifted presented to me personally – like my not being able to train with him.

This all happened when I was trying to work more closely with him after he joined the MTN-Qhubeka team (by then Dimension Data) in 2016. But Cavendish is so talented that, at the time we'd try to hook up for training rides, he had no need for a consistent pattern: if he felt good he'd go really hard. Then if he was feeling tired as a result the next day, he could shut things down. Unlike some riders who'd take time to figure out what worked for them and who'd need to be within a few per cent of their best in order to keep their job, Mark is such an outstanding rider, that doesn't form part of his game plan. As I got older I realized he needed a training group and environment, someone to meet with and have fun, but rather than simply realizing I could enjoy my time with him – which I did – my attitude was very different and probably way too intense. I wanted to spend time maximizing my potential then get home to rest and eat properly and be with my family.

Another advantage of being a cycling genius was he could vary his training plans at the drop of a hat, so if you asked him, rather than the specific 'Twenty minutes on the flat and four ten-minute climbs,' I'd come out with, he'd say, 'Anywhere between two and six hours.' I never had the skills or the potential to have that much room for interpretation in a single training ride.

It was also interesting, but challenging, to have to handle somebody who could be so fiercely competitive in training. Cav wanted to be the best everywhere – downhill, uphill and on the flat, so at times it felt like we were racing everywhere. And apart from the 'racing in training' with Cav, training is always an adventure. I have fond memories of wading across rivers with our bikes above our heads or riding across fields because we'd gone too far in the wrong direction to retrace. My training was basically methodical and I wanted to simulate an element of the race, like the pattern of nutrition. But Cav – he liked to be off the cuff.

This difference in training objectives was also due to Cav being in demand and racing a hell of a lot more than me. So perhaps all he needed was to tick over in between, while I was chasing form and looking for ways to improve. As a result, I was perhaps too intense for what Mark needed at the time, while he'd get frustrated because I wasn't doing what he wanted. But it finally got to the point where I thought,

'I can't be doing with this.' Although I enjoyed the adventures, if you've got to do four hours' training, you just want to do the four hours and get on with your life, not go hiking through streams. Neither of our ideas about training were ultimately better or worse, they were just too different to function together.

We kept in touch even though the idea of training together faded away, but one thing I didn't realize was how much pressure he was under to produce results from the team. I'd experienced it myself at times, because there were points in 2018 when a very senior figure in team management would just shout at me on the phone for an hour at a time. But that in turn maybe caused people to behave way out of character because they didn't know how to deal with it. My way of dealing with it was to acknowledge that person wasn't behaving in a productive way, accept it and crack on with doing my best. I'd just block out the pressure and keep my head down, but maybe Cav handled it differently.

Either way, and for whatever reason during his time at Dimension Data, it became much harder for him to perform. This wasn't something that happened overnight. In 2016, Cavendish had a brilliant year, and we all more or less rubbed along even if the atmosphere inside the team had changed. But since 2016, a lot of the time he was ill and out of form, or injured, and up until this summer his winning tally dropped terribly.

We all try to make as few mistakes as possible, and one side of me thinks that Cav had the power to create the environment he needed in the team – and didn't. But ultimately we can all influence the atmosphere in a team and, as a team, we failed to do that. This makes me think that rather than Cav, who was getting all the pressure, the biggest problem was further up the ladder.

It didn't help me that some of the heat he was receiving for not getting results was deflected on to me, which I felt was unfair because I was capable of winning at the highest level. Instead of being allowed to do that, it felt as if I was ostracized for not being a good lead-out man. I was almost used as a scapegoat. But regardless of what happened to me, I only ever wanted to see the best Cav, winning again.

During one of his difficult seasons, I even had a conversation with members of his group: 'Ah, fucking hell, how do we get Cav back on track?' And in some ways I think maybe we all failed him, maybe off the bike more than on it.

Sometimes I reached out and really tried to help Cav, but we're so different, it was hard. I'm not saying what he did in areas like training was right or wrong, and neither was how I approached it – it was just different. We clashed at times because I wasn't scared to disagree with him, while a lot of people in Dimension Data were just the opposite, which was also damaging for the squad in the long run.

Thankfully, that time is over and having come back from where he was, in such a difficult, dark place, to win those stages is an amazing story. It's so amazing I find it hard to fully express what he'd done in words. That happens when you hit on stats that tell you he's won thirty-four stages, which is twelve more than an entire cycling nation as big as Colombia.

So where does he go from here? I know he was a bit doubtful after the Tour de France finished this year if he wanted to come back. But I'm sure he will. Firstly, if you are in this position now and you didn't stop before, why would you stop now? Second, and this is being honest, there's the financial angle and he should get a very good contract out of this. Thirdly, he's still got that Eddy Merckx stage record to break. And of course it matters to him. He's so competitive, he'll half wheel you riding down the road, for goodness' sake – everything matters for Cav.

Whatever they may say about Eddy Merckx and his winning all different kinds of stages like summit finishes and time trials whereas Mark has 'only' won bunch sprints, no matter how you look at it, thirty-five Tour de France stages versus thirty-four Tour de France stages is thirty-five Tour stages versus thirty-four Tour stages. And he only needs to get one. For sure he can do it.

Chapter 12

The Right Direction

When you're in a team pursuit, you break down the racing strategy into a series of phases. Phase one is handling the start, and that's when you ride really full on to get up to speed. Personally, I would think very hard about my body: how much I needed strong arms, for example, because they give you stability to be sure the bike is directed towards exactly where you want it. Above all though, I would focus on aggression, how I needed to storm out of the gate. Then there's phase two, once the line's formed and you're following your team-mate's back wheel. This is when you're more relaxed yet still, somehow, fully concentrated. Breathing steadily helps you keep that balance between the two, but there were little tricks too that assisted: as we'd be going at top speed by then, I would also roll my fingers over the handlebars to make sure it didn't feel to me that I was hanging on to the bike for dear life! Phase three is when you're on the front, but it's mostly not flat out until the last two turns, it's a measured kind of aggression. And phase four, you've swung off and you're thinking about how you get back into the line again, and the process starts all over again...

But that was then, back in the days when I was part of the GB team pursuit squad. In the spring and summer of 2016, the high point of my career when I won in every World Tour stage race I started, it's true all the steps I took were as part of a team too. But in a sense I was out there alone: the steps I took that year were just for me.

That was how I felt on the inside, though. Externally, after winning the Tour stage in 2015, the pressure had risen notably too. Faced by those circumstances of heightened expectations, there are athletes who, having previously achieved something important, never really come back up to that level. It's almost like what they once managed to do doesn't help them, it haunts them. Sometimes the added new pressure got to me, but I'd try not to engage with those kinds of thoughts. Mostly I'd embrace it, and use it to crack on.

The key thing was I'd accepted inside that that level of success at the 2015 Tour might never come again even if I was in the best shape of my life. But what I wanted to do all the same was make sure everything I could do was spot on and ready, just to give myself the best chance of succeeding again. Just in case.

*

I didn't know the specific roads we used on the Tirreno–Adriatico stage I won, my first victory of 2016. But it was typically lumpy terrain of the kind I knew well and on top of that it was another one of those 200+ kilometre stages the Tirreno organizers seem to love: so, in practical terms, that meant six hours in the saddle and a lot of altitude gain without there ever being more than three or four classified climbs, none longer than 8 kilometres. On this day we went up eastwards and north from the Tirreno coast, inland and to the foot of the Apennines to Foligno, a beautiful old Renaissance town with a huge river carving its way through the centre, stone-flagged streets and lots of stunning, conserved ancient buildings. For the race itself, such a hard day acted as a whittling down process until there were maybe forty or fifty riders left fighting for the stage. I wasn't complaining, though. This was exactly the kind of stage that I enjoyed and which increased my opportunities because if you attacked from a good way out, the sprinters' teams wouldn't have enough strength in numbers to pull you back. And that was assuming some sprinters had managed to stay at the head of the race in that tough kind of terrain anyway.

This time there were quite a few fast men up there in the front group, including the reigning world champion of the time, Peter Sagan, who'd been with me at Mende in France the previous year. The finale really started for me when our director Roger Hammond had come through on the race radio, telling us the last climb was about 20 kilometres to go, after which it was downhill and then mainly flat to the finish. Three of us Qhubeka riders were in the front group alongside Sagan: myself, Edvald Boasson Hagen – who's also a fast finisher – and an Eritrean lad, Natnael 'Natu' Berhane. So if there being a reduced group in the peloton sets the scene for me, part one of how I actually won that day began when

I told Natu we'd better start policing the moves on the front and keeping the pace high.

There were three tactics in particular for me to apply at that point. First I'd make the most of every inch of the last climb before the finish to put the hurt on the other guys. Then on the downhill I'd hurl myself out of it, just when everybody was going slow as they came off the climb. That way a) I'd stay out of trouble if there was a crash somewhere in the pack and b) I could string the group out and c) if there was a slight wind, I'd try to put the power down even more in exactly the right places and perhaps squeeze some riders out the back. With so little road space to draft they'd have to do some time, as we'd say, 'in the gutter', which is never good for morale. Or for winning.

Once we'd got through all that on the climb and began following moves again, the second, final part of the win 'process' was actually physically less of a challenge. It started at the point when I'd chased down two Italian rivals, Matteo Montaguti and Salvatore Puccio. When they'd asked me to ride with them, I'd refused because we had Edvald behind and our stage strategy was to try to get him to win. So my job in the break was purely that of 'policeman', to make sure the break couldn't consolidate by shadowing those ahead.

Neither of the Italians were particularly happy about this, but they couldn't do anything to stop me either, and they knew that if they waited, then it would inevitably be a sprint. Then with 4 kilometres to go, just as another three riders came across, I stomped away, and as soon as I'd got 100 metres I knew the stage was done. When I was pouring out

470 or 500 watts of power in my aero position, I knew it'd be impossible for anybody to catch me.

As for the actual last attack itself, and how it happened, it goes in bits. First your thought process in those sorts of situations is, 'We're doing the stage for Edvald,' but at the same time I'm also thinking, 'Hang on, these guys are pulling me along and I'm pretty dangerous with 4 or 5 kilometres to go if they keep on riding like this.' Then when the other three riders join our little group, it's a moment, a sensation. Your mindset changes. You're there for Edvald, but you have to be flexible and dynamic and realize that the pendulum is switching direction because the more I'm getting a free ride to the finish, the more this pendulum is swinging over towards me.

I'm not riding against my team-mate. It's quite the opposite. I'm just using the strength of the team to play my card. So when the moment finally comes for me to go for it, it's just the moment when they hesitate slightly, on a bit of an uphill, right before a corner, where the riders not on the front will have less time to react before taking the bend themselves. That's all I need because there has to be an element of surprise. For one thing I know Puccio's probably got a more powerful acceleration than me, and without that surprise and on a flatter piece of road, he's always going to be able to get on my wheel. But with that uphill, you don't need that acceleration as much as you need a bit more sustained power. So, thanks to that combination, as the pendulum keeps swinging over towards me and my feeling that I can win from this situation, my mind's looking for a launch pad. You need that element of surprise because if they're looking the other way or slowing for a second, there's a kind of concertina effect where you and your rivals have got momentum in opposite directions. Their momentum is pulling them backwards, but yours is heading forwards. Then if you add in the slight climb and the corner, it's *arrivederci*.

Another factor is how hard I decide I'm going to accelerate. Sometimes, like at the British Nationals the following year, I was holding back for a long time until the climb became steeper and then I put my power down on the hardest part of the ascent. But when it was more of a false flat like this one, it's a case of all or nothing: you go right up to full power, get your speed and go really hard out of the corner and then once that speed is so high, get tucked into that aero position. And then they can't catch you.

*

Probably the three biggest differences between 2016 and other years were that I was never sick, never injured and I had a great race programme. Also, for the second year running, I had a team that was quite supportive of what I was doing – at long last. There was a bit of a discussion about whether Tirreno–Adriatico needed to be my first race, but I told them I just needed two days to get some race rhythm and that was that.

In 2015 I'd been sick in the spring when Perla was born, but from then on, I'd been in good shape. So I had a long run-up to the Tour, and within that it felt like deep, deep condition could be built. I never really rested that much in winter, but I'd never let it go out that far either. So my November was solid, December was solid, January and

February too. There were months and months of unbroken good work to build on.

I hadn't adapted my training programme; I simply continued doing what I'd been doing since I left Sky. But that absence of injuries and illnesses gained me more consistency and, put in its most straightforward form, I got better at refining the process.

On top of which I had amazing morale. In 2015 there hadn't just been the Tour win in Mende as well, there had been the whole season, beating Valverde on my first day with the team, taking top ten in every race I did, getting in that Dauphiné break and only getting caught a few kilometres from the line because Froome, the race leader, wanted the time bonus for GC. It had all worked out really well.

So my confidence was really high to the point where I felt like I was a level above a lot of the other riders and under the right circumstances I could always have a chance of a win. It was not just that I could, either, but that I would.

I also used those opportunities available in the race to create the right kind of circumstances. Very few riders can individually change the outcome of a race, but I felt that at my best I would certainly influence the way it developed. In its most extreme form, it was almost like I was just waiting in each race for the right moment to come. Then I would unleash the fury.

*

I am really proud of my Basque beret that I got as a prize for winning a stage of the Vuelta al País Vasco (later known as La Itzulia) in April 2016, because those one-week spring bike races meant, and mean, the world to me. I don't think people appreciate how hard it is to win one of those stages, which is a shame because as races go, they are 100 per cent the genuine article.

Outside the Grand Tours, they're some of the hardest events that exist, and you could even say they are the ultimate confirmation of your strength as a racer. For a rider like me that weighs 74 kilos, even more so.

My País Vasco win came on a slightly shorter stage than Tirreno–Adriatico, 193.5 kilometres as opposed to 216 kilometres in Italy. So that was a similar five hours in the saddle, but it was a much harder, more intense effort too, particularly as it had rained hard early on. In this race, with big crowds of fans at the starts and finishes of the small towns País Vasco usually visited, and also on the tops of the key climbs, but a lot of empty woodland and fields in between, there are two typical stage formats. One type has a key moment that forces a selection – be it a hard climb or a tricky downhill. The other consists of a series of short, punchy climbs where the group keeps on getting whittled down each time the road steepens, then ends in a flat or slight uphill. And that second type was the kind of stage that I won.

Often in a race like that with a lot of rugged countryside, the descents and how they're tackled end up being more important than the climbs – as long as you're climbing well enough to get through them. The key thing is that each time you look round, the group of guys that have made it through is smaller.

If I'm honest, that day I won, in the final hour or so I wasn't in a good position in the peloton, but I kept on passing more and more people nonetheless. Then with around 10 or 15 kilometres left to race, we were going alongside a river on rolling roads deep in the Navarran countryside, and I started looking round and thinking, 'If I get my timing right, I can't lose.'

I wasn't the only one thinking that. My team-mate Serge Pauwels came up and said, 'Hey, Stevo, pick the right moment.' It was a small thing, but a few words at a time like that from a team-mate can be all you need for there to be a difference. There were little groups of riders attacking and going up the road, almost as if it was all in slow motion, but I knew I had an extra gear that day and that at any minute I could move across.

I don't want to sound boastful, but once a race had been cut down to a small group of racers, my key advantage was that I could use positions that were super-aerodynamic. At the same time I was probably one of the heavier riders out there, so my absolute power output was higher. With that combination, if I did want to get a little gap, or needed to close a gap on somebody else, that was my strength, particularly for five- to ten-minute efforts. I also fine-tuned those areas in training through constant repetition. It was all about feeling the limits you had, measuring them, finding them and holding on to them.

So in a race like this particular stage of the Basque Country was turning out to be, the key thing was waiting and then waiting some more until you knew you were at the right distance, then making sure if a dangerous group got away I was part of it. Seven kilometres was usually a long way out, and five kilometres was about right, because if you left it until any later, normally the speed's so high it's difficult to get a gap. However, on this occasion, I left it to the point where I couldn't really wait any longer, and where on paper I wouldn't have much chance of winning: only a kilometre to go.

We were on an uphill, just like in Tirreno too, and the front move had just stretched out to its maximum length without breaking apart then crammed itself into the tiniest space possible – a slingshot moment, we call it – and there was already an attack up the road. A Cofidis guy had gone clear and another person was following. But I felt like I could get up to twice their speed, simply by freewheeling then tucking myself just behind the second rider's back wheel. Then they attacked and brought me up to the Cofidis guy, so I just went again. Full gas and blasting away on that slight uphill finish, which meant the final part was all about timing, good aerodynamics and a lot of power for what was essentially a 'smash and grab' victory.

Again, though, for all it was a last-minute dash for the line, I'd do a lot of in-race thinking before we got there. I'd try to work out, above all, about what was best for the team. In this particular context, with me and Serge left on the front in a nearly flat finish, I knew I was the best option. So once that was clear, I felt like I had complete freedom to find my own path to the win.

It was always a question of winning alone, basically because I couldn't win in a sprint or in a time trial or on a summit finish. That meant I had to find the best place to attack so I could do that. On this occasion, it came very late, because so many other riders were trying to go clear. But for whatever reasons they couldn't see that attacking on a flat stage 5 kilometres out means a seven-minute effort and it's just not possible to go at 50 km/h for that distance on your own. You had to make the calculations. In my case, I'd also have the feeling that I had nothing to lose. I wasn't a favourite, so I'd think about it logically, calculate where the best moment could be depending on the race dynamics, but remember all the time: why not have a try? And that would be that.

I'd also have a clear idea of which of my rivals would do what. For a long time in my career, I knew almost every key rider, their strengths and weaknesses, and what strategies particular teams tended to use. By doing that, as well as by knowing each director's favoured strategy, then the way a race plays out tends to become much easier to predict. But it takes time, racing and hours and hours of watching of bike races on TV.

As a result of that knowledge, I'd very rarely have to talk or open up negotiations of any kind during breaks. Normally, in my breaks, I'd be sure I was there with riders with the same mentality, who already appreciated how hard it was going to be, and that if you didn't commit it wasn't ever going to happen.

One of the few occasions I did speak out in a break was on a second-week move in the 2016 Tour, coming out of Andorra. I was going well and I'd got over the top of the day's big climb, the Envalira, in fourth place. But Sylvain Chavanel, another rival, was sitting on the back without collaborating at all, and he was following me wherever I went in the break. It was like he was my shadow. I said to Sylvain that if he wanted to race like that, I didn't care because I'd already got my stage win. It got to the point that I wasn't going to go out of my way to make him lose. But one thing was certain – rather than staying calm, I was annoyed with Chavanel, and for sure I wasn't going to let him win.

My strategy, as a result, ended up being completely wrong: I should have been more ruthless, attacked on the finale and seen what happened. But my team-mate Edvald was in the move, and when I dropped back, and half the group promptly sat on my back wheel, led by Chavanel, I thought I was helping Edvald out.

My last card was a vague hope that Chavanel would try to close the gap after he'd realized what I was doing, and then we'd have been even on energy levels. But he didn't do that, so being annoyed with him ultimately cost me a chance of the stage. And a rival, Michael Matthews, won the stage too – not Eddy, who took third.

*

Another consequence of studying races wasn't just that I knew who was a good climber or descender; as racers I'd study their behaviour and see what their performance would likely turn out to be. For one thing, I'd always pay attention to how much they were eating and drinking and see if they weren't fuelling correctly. Obviously, you wouldn't know what was in their bottle, but you could get a sense if the guy wasn't drinking, or if he was slowing and going for a gel in a moment where they normally wouldn't, then you'd know they were close to cracking.

It's not that I want to brag, but there weren't many riders I'd look at and think what an amazing breakaway rider they were. My biggest weakness came when I very occasionally made mistakes on my own account, like when I got frustrated with Chavanel in the 2016 Tour. Overall you have to bear in mind, though, that one breakaway rider is rarely similar to another. You've each got a very different path towards that success. What's the same is the determination to make the most of yourself.

One of the best of my generation is the Belgian Thomas De Gendt. I once read that his main motivation for getting in breakaways and trying to win is that he wants to see how deep he can go in terms of pain and suffering. But while I have huge respect for him, my attitude was different – for me it was all about racing with my brain, maximizing the performance and saving as much energy as possible in my legs for as long as possible. I could live with somebody being stronger or faster, but I didn't like the idea of being outsmarted.

Possibly one of the few areas Thomas and I had in common was that we would study the route of a stage beforehand in massive detail. In my case, the crucial element was a hard start, because that made it so much easier to get in the break. But then you'd do the next few sections step by step: getting in the breakaway, staying in the breakaway, formulating some sort of tactic, and then, when you've already made your decision about how you're going to go about winning, waiting for the right moment, having that momentum when the road favours you. You just feel it, and go.

But you're also trying to get an outside perspective on what's happening, watching your rivals even if you can't affect other teams and what other riders are planning or doing. Say one of them attacks down a valley road at 65 kilometres an hour – you have to work it out and think, how long do you honestly think you can ride at that speed? Then if you are strong and other riders aren't, you start to tweak them a bit on the climbs, wear them down even more and soften them up. Or you push them as hard as you can on the downhill so that they've got to take a little bit longer to close that gap again, even if it's only ten or fifteen seconds. But then sometimes you don't want to do that, because the gap is coming down between the break and the bunch and you need that person to help you. So all day long, you keep chipping away at your rivals or using them to your advantage, whichever works best for you. It's like it's a game, and it's bloody good fun.

Other riders apart from De Gendt whom I admired as breakaway artists included Alessandro De Marchi. Alessandro is a better climber than me, but if there was a stage where I could limit my losses on the uphills and then re-bridge back across, then I'd have the advantage on him. Greg Van Avermaet is another great rider in the breaks and so much more, although he wasn't a particularly aerodynamic racer. What was to their credit was whereas I had moulded myself to be a breakaway specialist, they had other skills – De Marchi the climbing stages, Greg the Classics – whereas I didn't do much else.

I didn't ever really rely too much on my directors to teach me how to handle my breaks. Brian and I reached a point where he'd just say, 'You know what you've got to do, do what you need to,' and it never went any further than that.

Volpi was good, which I didn't fully appreciate at the time, because he'd try to break down the race into segments, suggest when was best to attack and when not. He wasn't always right, but the way he thought about it was useful.

Probably the one who taught me the most was Max. I spent a lot of time with him and it was like a mentoring relationship. For one thing, he was great at telling stories that would simultaneously give you something to remember and something to learn: 'I was with [Gilberto] Simoni when he won the Giro. I'd tell him, "Hey, Simoni, don't pull, I'll pull, then after the climb we're gonna go." And then I said, "Hey, Simoni, relax!" If he wasn't with me he wouldn't win the Giro.' But probably the best thing that Max taught me was that you had to commit once you've made a decision, because otherwise it wouldn't happen. There are often so many variables that you can become indecisive. But as he'd put it in that Vuelta stage I won, 'Fucking go, don't look back!' And even though I still looked back a lot, that attitude of making a choice and sticking to it 100 per cent was exactly the one I had to have. It might be the wrong decision, but we can always learn from that and improve the process of it all.

What also helped me to hone my talent for breakaways was that in two of my teams – Landbouwkrediet and Barloworld – part of their strategy was not focusing on controlling the race at all. Rather we'd get in the break to gain visibility in a race (in a nutshell, when small teams get in on moves to ensure they appear on TV), and in Barloworld's case, hopefully using the break to get results. Those thoughts were always there, then in Discovery and Sky, it was the opposite: often they wanted to control the race and make sure the right break went. That made me see the initial part of the race from two very different, opposed, perspectives – and work out how best to outmanoeuvre the opposition.

People have asked me if I use board games to improve my racing strategies, but I was only ever into my cycling to the point where I realize that I spent a very large part of my life thinking about bikes, bikes and bikes. I'm not sure if that was so healthy, but it did mean I was thorough.

In terms of equipment, probably 2015 was the best combination of material – the bikes with a chrome finish and Enve wheels which I had at the Tour were ideal, for which I have to thank our manager Brian Smith. On top of that I had a special skinsuit, which for sure helped me do well when riding along over a long distance, like when I won on the Aspin stage of the Tour, and when Van Avermaet won the Olympics that year, he was wearing the same one too. I'd even gone into exploring which chain options were the best and I was one of the first to have chains coated in a special friction-reducing lubricant – well known for its white colour – and bigger pulleys on the chain, again to cut down on the friction. For some reason I wasn't allowed them in 2016 but that was the one setback compared to 2015.

So more than one particular factor, by 2016 almost everything was honed to the finest point it could be. My position on my road bike had reached a point where it wasn't a million miles from how I looked on my TT bike. (That's all to do with the Coefficient of Drag times Front Air Surface or CDA, to be technical about it.) I was very smooth in terms of riding and didn't need to get out of the saddle much, and my equipment was, within sponsor limitations, as good as it could be... if you put all that together, whenever I got to a start line, I knew it was as good as it was ever going to get.

*

If there was one time that I felt I almost blew my chances for a stage win because I didn't fully appreciate how well I was going before I started, it was in the 2016 Critérium du Dauphiné.

Held in and around the Alps, there's a similar atmosphere in some ways to the Vuelta al País Vasco (or Itzulia as it's now called) at the Dauphiné, in that there aren't that many people, except at the starts and finishes. But you know how hard it is to win, and how prestigious those wins are, and as the Tour is coming up so soon, a win in the Dauphiné always has a deeper meaning. The people on the side of the road sense it, and you sense it: it's the last official test before the Tour.

We'd started a 9-kilometre climb mid-stage and I'd got in a break, but the others were trying to do what I often did – get a little bit further ahead and split things up so everybody suffers behind trying to catch them. Bizarrely enough, that wasn't such a bad thing for me, because if I'd gone off by myself up the road ahead of the rest, they'd have combined behind to catch me and it would have been game over. This way, with guys ahead of me, I could use them as stepping stones, jumping from rider to rider, and I'd be reducing the strength of the chase group at the same time.

About two thirds of the way into the stage, which was hilly throughout, we got on to the first of two long, first category climbs. I decided to ride it at a medium pace, and going pretty hard, at threshold level, on the steeper parts, so that way I'd weed out the weeds but not spend too much energy in the process.

There was still quite a lot of interest behind, as there often is in the final day of a stage race, because it's the last opportunity to win. It hadn't been a great break, with minimal collaboration, and although we'd got four or five minutes on the main pack before things started splitting apart, we'd needed to commit and it hadn't happened.

That's why I'd opted to try to get rid of these people, and I did my mixture of fast and steady up the climb, but by the top it had worked out too well. I'd ridden them all off my wheel, which wasn't the plan at all. There were still 60-odd kilometres to go and now I was out there alone at the head of the race and with a target on my back.

When we dropped back down to the foot of the climb into a short section through a broad valley, Oli Cookson, our sports director, drove up and gave me a bottle. But I was so cross I flung it to the ground, shouting at him, 'For fuck's sake, where are the muppets?' I really didn't want to be out there, on my own, with a whole wolf pack of riders chasing behind and when I was in the zone with my race head on, I wasn't as patient as usual. But it didn't matter how I felt: none of the muppets who'd been chasing me behind appeared capable of bridging across. I was stuck out on my own. So I was chewing over what I could do – wait for the muppets or continue – and eventually I opted for the second. I decided that I'd take it on a medium pace and see what happened. And somehow, the gap between me and the guys chasing kept on going up and up.

At that point, when I realized I had a chance, I thought about the remainder of the stage – and literally broke it up into phases as you would in a TT – in terms of how I'd use up my energy between there and the finish. My strategy was to put the power down when it was most important to keep a high pace, and when I was on easier terrain – on the downhills or on the flatter bits – the less power I would be willing to spend to achieve an increase in speed. That's because if you put out a hefty 300 watts of power when it's easy going, you don't actually gain so much in terms of velocity – you'll be pushing up your speed from 55 km/h to 57 km/h. Plus you have momentum, so you're getting speed for free anyway. However, on the points where I went slower because the course was harder or more uphill (and there's much less momentum), the same 300 watts power I was willing to invest, say, would push my pace up from, say, 20 km/h to 25 km/h. That's a slightly bigger km/h gain. So you're covering more ground for the same energy, and it's a better investment as a result. Inversely, the drop-off in ground covered if you choose not to use up so much energy on hard climbs is greater, and the harder it is to keep your distance from the guys chasing behind.

However, when the road is constantly up and down like it was on that Dauphiné stage, there is a fine balance and quite a skill involved in getting that power investment right, especially as it's the first time I've seen these roads, so I didn't know what was coming up. But I managed to get it right, and that certainly helped me stay away.

With my advantage on the pack looking good, I also had to start crafting my tactics for the last two climbs of the day, one a much harder first category, and then a short third-category ascent to the finish itself. I tried to visualize them both as one single climb, because I knew the downhill off the first category should, in theory, give me enough time to recover for the final ascent. And I tried to keep the same tactic going of maintaining a medium pace on the easier parts, and then going much harder on the steeper sections.

By that point there were a lot of attacks going on behind but it wasn't so worrying because each attack would be followed by a lull in pace, and the speed varying so much allowed me to keep the gaps open. Even so, I'd gone so deep after that first long climb that I was suffering a lot, and I was so concerned I might end up cramping that even with a four-minute gap, I didn't let myself begin to think I'd won until the last couple of kilometres.

I had just gone past Luke Rowe's wife, Cath, standing there on the side of the road with a friend close to the finish. It was unexpected and nice to get a shout of support, and at that point, I began thinking it was possible I'd win. And finally, it happened. It was one of those 'wow' victories because it had been such a long distance on my own, and they were chasing hard behind and couldn't catch me. Rather than them gaining time on me, I was gaining time on them. So, as was always the case for everybody when they did a good Dauphiné, it gave me a huge amount of confidence going forward into the Tour as well.

I'd had to win that stage by really forcing myself on the physical front with a 60-kilometre breakaway, but probably the key thing was not kidding myself that I could control all the factors and accepting that the situation was at no point ideal. I'd thought through what I could, from my own strategy to how my rivals were handling the stage, remembering that they hadn't been collaborating well behind. So I just tried to anticipate when they might chase and when they wouldn't and work out from there how the race could play out in my favour. Beyond pre-empting events as much as I could, I opted to take it step by step, by being flexible and accepting that in such a challenging scenario a lot was going to remain beyond my control: making as much of my luck as I could, then rolling the dice with the rest.

*

By the time I did the Tour de France in 2016, one problem I had was that everybody wanted to be in the break with me and I had a target on my back. But at the same time no team wanted me to be in the break.

Earlier in my career it was really easy to go into the kind of breakaways that go up the road on the flat stages where there are five teams who want a bunch sprint to happen and they let four guys from wildcard teams – the ones who don't automatically qualify from the Tour – ride up the road. The wildcard teams get visibility, but it's a virtual given that it's always going to come down to a bunch sprint, so the sprinters get their chance and everybody's happy. But after I'd won so many races, teams didn't want me even to be in those breaks, with the barest minimum chance of succeeding, which then limited my stage options to the harder, hillier stages where it was much harder for the sprinters' teams to control. But what happened then was riders who were able to get in those tougher breaks would follow you around.

In a situation like that when you're on everybody's radar, conventional wisdom says you should keep a low profile for as long as possible, narrow things down and hone in on a couple of days when you can be sure you'll have a really good chance of winning. But life lesson number one for winning from breaks, or for that matter for succeeding in any kind of field when you don't have any kind of God-given advantage, is that you should think outside the box as a matter of course. So I forced myself out of my comfort zone, mentally raised the stakes as high as I could and got ridiculously ambitious. In fact, rather than the five Tour stages in 2015, say, I'd identified as possible for me to have a crack at winning, in 2016 I marked down no less than nine.

Before you start thinking that I thought I could win nine stages of a possible twenty-one in the Tour, I didn't. Even some cycling legends like Eddy Merckx had only won eight at most in a single year. It was partly that I worked through all the scenarios that could play out in each one, and then I'd worked out how I fitted into each. The big difference with other years was that by that point in my career I was way more confident: in less than two years I'd won breaks from all sorts of different scenarios, be it hilltop finishes, attacks in the last kilometre, long-distance moves... All I wanted to do in the Tour 2016 was empty the tank on one day of those nine. If I won as a result, I won. And if I lost, I lost.

I wasn't daunted by the Tour any more. By that stage in my career it was business: I was there to win. I had been a bit concerned about my condition for the Tour because I had gone so deep in the Dauphiné, I was completely exhausted afterwards, and I had a pain in my legs that was so bad that I had to spend two or three days in bed. But after the Dauphiné, I then did a really good 'recovery week' of just riding on the bike with no specific work, and only did a little bit of structured training before the Tour. Then when our team got the yellow jersey with Mark Cavendish in the first days of the race, I did a lot of work at the head of the bunch pacesetting for Mark and the squad, and it was just what I needed. On stage two I remember I had a big, hard day of riding. Thanks to all the power I set down and a few efforts getting up small climbs or pulling back breaks and so on, I got my motor used to running at full again. Plus that whole day, I was riding for the team in the best way I could which is what mattered too. So mentally, I was in the perfect place.

The physical side of building for the breakaways wasn't all about effort. If I was thinking I'd get in a break the next day, the night before I'd make it a 'treat night' and allow myself a dessert (which generally I wouldn't ever eat) at supper. Something like an ice cream would build up my glycogen stores a bit and I'd found that if I had treats that were planned, not all the time, they'd work more effectively. But it's a fine line because if you eat too much then your legs are heavy, but if you get it right, you've got a bit more fuel at the end.

Then there was kit. Up until the Tour I'd been using a fairly normal pair of shorts and jersey, and the jersey in particular wasn't lightweight, it didn't 'breathe' well. I wanted something better, so using an awful lot of diplomacy and negotiating with the team both up front and on the QT, I managed to get myself a prototype race suit. This is like a skinsuit you'd use on the track, but for a race, so it's got pockets for your food and so on.

I didn't have time to go to wind tunnels and get an exact figure for its wind resistance before the Tour, but even by looking at it, you could see it had less drag because it fitted so much better. It was definitely more 'breathable', like being inside a teabag.

It helped add to the psychological benefit of standing on the line when you know you have gone to that extra degree of everything: I've got that chain with special coating, my wheels are sorted, my bike's on the limit, I've got my suit, the best helmet possible for me. I've done all the training I can, I'm as lean as I can be. All I've got to do now is fucking go and execute. And enjoy it.

(In those circumstances, you can also glance around at the opposition as they're waiting at that start line and say to yourself, 'That guy's not got this. That guy's not got that. That guy's not as aero as me.' Put it all together and the name of this scenario is 'the halo effect' and mentally, it's a heck of a powerful weapon to have.)

That was the good news. The bad news was when, having raised the stakes so much higher with all those different possible stages for moves in my head, I got into a break on the first real opportunity of the nine I'd envisaged. It was on stage seven and I found there were twenty-eight other riders in it – a huge, unwieldy kind of move.

Generally, to boost my own chances, I prefer much tougher terrain at the start of a stage because that way only the best riders get in the break. But instead we'd had a flat start so this massive move had developed and within that we had around fifteen really good riders. Guys like Fabian Cancellara and Tony Martin, both of them former World Time Trial Champions. Or like Vincenzo Nibali, a former Tour de France winner who'd just taken his second Giro d'Italia. On top of that almost all of them had a string of team-mates in the break too.

So if somebody had asked me if I could win a stage with a lot of flattish terrain and an ascent and descent of a single Pyrenean climb, the Aspin, as the main challenge, with that kind of opposition, I'd honestly have said, 'No.' In fact, I dropped back to the team car at one point and told them it was going to be very difficult to do anything.

But then I begin to work out what I can do to whittle down the opposition to at least get a fighting chance. Ideally, by the time we get to the Aspin I'll be a little bit ahead of this group, but can I ride off on the front by myself? I don't think so. So I'll have to wait for the others to start attacking, which they eventually do, and then be sure I get myself across to one of the smaller groups in exactly the right way. The best strategy is letting the moves go, not panicking, and then timing my bridging across to each group at the exact moment before they're so far ahead that it's become impossible to reach them. That moment or distance between you and the group is more situational than physical. There are so many variables: how you're feeling physically, the road, the wind, the number of riders... You have to feel it: you have a kind of intuition about how the race is panning out, about if the break ahead is collaborating or not, meaning the gap's rising faster or more slowly, about what the combination of riders in the move could mean... It's that moment where you feel in yourself 'it's just about bridgeable for me.' That's not something your director in the car can ever tell you or I can write or talk about, but getting that right is up to each rider. It's your responsibility to do that, pay attention to the situation and not be robotic.

It's a fine balance, but when it comes to bridging across, I know it's an all-or-nothing effort: it means I have to go flat out to reach each group, but on the plus side, I'll be going so fast and hard because of my characteristics – my aerodynamic position and so on – that only the strongest riders also chasing can follow. It's a whittling down process that consists of jumping at full pelt from one mobile stepping stone to another ahead of you, and then another, and then another. And on stage seven of the 2016 Tour, as the day warms up into a full summer's day of heat, my counter-attack goes so well that each time I make that jump, there's nobody following me at all.

By the time I get across the front group of attackers around 10 kilometres to the foot of the final climb, it's only got three other riders in it: a Canadian rider, Antoine Duchesne, Matti Breschel, a Danish guy, and a lightly built Spanish guy from Cofidis called Dani Navarro. So the odds have got a lot better, even if it's not over yet. Not by a long shot.

First I get my breath back, because I've literally gone to my limit and that's not easy because we're moving very fast, slightly downhill on a broad, well-surfaced valley road at maybe 50 or 60 kilometres an hour. There are not many people watching from the roadsides, maybe because they're all waiting further on for the big battle between us on the mountain itself. And then I'm thinking, 'OK, it's advantage

Steve now, because the guys behind are going to have to work hard to get across to me. And if I attack, these guys will maybe catch me halfway up the climb and all I've got to do is hang in there and I can perhaps win the sprint, or at least play around a bit, wait for an opportunity in the final kilometre to "go long" and launch my attack from a distance.'

In those moments, you always try to maintain the fluidity of a break at as high a point as possible by encouraging the move to keep going as a unit. That's because you want to harness the power of the strongest guys to your best advantage, and if you don't smooth things out as best you can and they go too hard, then they can kill the group. Once someone stops contributing because it's not a fluid break working as a unit, that's when someone else says I'm not going to help either, and it all breaks down.

In this case, it's definitely energy worth spending because we had that good-sized gap on the Nibali group. I've got that famous cycling phrase in my head of 'do as little as the guy that's doing the least', which is fine because it's all pretty smoothly divided between the four at first.

But with time that changes and the three other guys in the break effectively become two. I know Breschel is getting to be out of it, because he's shirking a bit and whenever I ask him to come through to the front and help keep the pace high he keeps on telling me to relax. But I'd fire back, 'Relax, no – let's go.' I know when people are in Breschel's situation, you just try to encourage them, because whatever contribution they can make, it always helps you a little. So that's what I try to get Matti to do for a while. Then, hopefully, I'll be gone.

But then all at once the game changes again and for some reason the two others abruptly stop collaborating at all as well. At the same time the team car radios through that the remnants of the break of twenty-nine are splitting further behind and starting to try to come across. This is all bad news. It's not just that life has gone out of the break, but really dangerous guys, like Nibali, who I know is in good shape because he's won the Giro and he's using the Tour to build for the Olympics, are making a move.

It's a crunch moment. So before Nibali gets there, I think, 'Right, this has to happen now and I'm attacking now.' It's not just what's happened in the break. I also know that anybody who reaches us right now from behind will be in the red coming across to us, and they won't be able to follow me.

So when the other three go round one side of a traffic island, I go round the other and attack as I do so. By the time they've seen me and realized I'm away, they can't get back on my wheel; it's too late. And they know it too. I have a friend who worked as a soigneur in Navarro's team and he tells me afterwards the directors had been telling Navarro over the radio that 'whatever else you do, stay on Cummings' wheel; always stay with Cummings.' Which explains why, when I do get away, all they can hear over the radio in the team car behind is Navarro screaming at the top of his voice, 'Puta madre, puta madre' – for fuck's sake, for fuck's sake – cos he knows that's me gone. And that's his chance of winning gone too.

So I'm alone now, off the front, and when I get to the Aspin climb, the last big challenge, the good news is it's similar to the last big climb when I was off the front in the Dauphiné. Sure, it's 12 kilometres long, and that's daunting for anybody to ride solo, but it's a great last climb for me, not too steep, mostly between 5 and 6 per cent and pretty steady all the way up. On the downside, normally 10 kilometres of non-stop climbing, rather than 12, is my limit before I crack. But then I think to myself, 'Ah, come on, throw the crowd in – that'll give you a bit of extra motivation. OK, I'll try it.'

I'm not sure I'll make it. I just keep thinking I'd get up as far as I could, powering out 400 watts mostly, 90–100 revs a minute, and see where that gets me. I'm not feeling as good as I did in the Dauphiné climb though, where I'd have continued to drive on without thinking like that at all. I'm also concerned that I might be overheating given how warm the day is, but then I quash those worries by telling myself the further I get up the climb, the cooler it'll get so the better I'll be.

And the gap I have on the chase group stays, somehow, between a minute and seventy seconds and I make it to the summit alone. But that's only 'alone' in one sense. Right at the bottom of the climb there were loads of people on the roadsides because the access is easier, but then the numbers thinned out dramatically. However, as I get higher up the climb, it's like there's a crescendo of people watching, more and more and more and you can sense the anticipation, the buzz in the crowds, because you're the first guy they see in the race and they've been waiting for this moment all day. The noise is deafening with the cheers and the helicopters and cars but I don't hear much noise, because like anybody in those circumstances would be I'm in the zone. I'm concentrating on the effort, constantly gauging it all the way up, asking myself, 'Does the gradient level off? How far to the top? Can you still hold this?' I'm constantly reminding myself, 'Your threshold's 400 watts so when it gets a bit steeper, do a bit more, 420, when it drops off, do a bit less.' Constantly balancing. 'Twenty minutes to go now to the top... 5 kilometres, now it's fifteen minutes, how long's that going to take?' Constantly thinking, 'I can do this,' or 'I need to knock this back.' Constantly measuring, measuring, measuring. And the atmosphere and the crowds spur you on but it doesn't just make you hang on to the limit of what you can do physically that bit longer. It makes your hair stand on end because it's the dream, to be out there in the Tour de France, ahead of the field and alone. It's poetry in motion. It's fantastic.

At the top, in the last couple of hundred metres, I go as hard as I can to get over the top of it with momentum to try to keep ahead, even though I also remember thinking, 'Heck, there's still another 8 kilometres to go and I don't know what's coming up. I've only got a minute. It's going to be touch and go this time.'

Fortunately, the last part, the descent off the climb down to the finish town, is not too technical. My director Rolf Aldag does a fantastic job helping me, guiding me down by telling me over the radio what's coming up. He's got VeloViewer so it's, 'Sharp left, easy right, full gas, three k straight, two sharp corners...' whatever's next. It's only human to doubt your chances though and all the way down there's a voice that keeps popping into my mind saying, 'Nibali's chasing behind; he's a great descender and a minute's not that much.' But another part of me, the part that doesn't want to question my chances, is just thinking about what I've got to do:

'Relax when you're going into the corners; you've got a good aero position so make sure you come out of the corners really aggressively.'

There are always two voices in your head at times like that, both yacking on at the same time, one saying, 'Ah, you're going to look like a dickhead here. You won all those races this year and it might have been a fluke what you did in the Tour last year; all this is going to be pretty pointless unless you win.' But then another's saying, 'Ah, you've already won, done well, go out and just perform.' And that second voice is the one I'm listening to, because I know that my doubts go back to a fear of failure and my believing in my chances comes back to how I've overcome that fear. Yet again, it's all about forgetting the outcomes and thinking about the process, just as it was in the 2012 Vuelta, just as it was in the 2015 Tour, just as it's been in every stage I've won in 2016.

So I get there, and the last part of the stage, when I know I'm going to win, is amazing, because the last kilometre's straight, and there are a lot of people cheering – you can hear the noise coming towards you. I'm lucky, maybe, because I know some British riders get booed in France, but I always had a good reception there. And when you ride into that applause it's the best feeling there can be.

In fact, that's what it's all about. You've worked for this, and it's finally here. As I ride to the line I'm thinking a lot about my wife and my daughter and family and I kissed both wrists in the last kilometre, something I'd never really done before, to say thanks to everyone who supported me. (Why the wrists? Because from back in the Vuelta I had good luck wristbands that my wife and other people, family and friends, had got me.) And one last detail: just before I reach the line I don't have to remember to do up my jersey for the victory salute, as the team always likes you to do when you win to show off the sponsor's name, because I'm wearing that race suit you can't unzip anyway. One thing less to think about...

The second Tour stage win is so many things, carries so many feelings in the wake of crossing the final line. It's a confirmation because some people have said that one Tour stage win's a fluke. So there's happiness, there's relief, it's a moment of serenity, a moment to savour. Satisfaction is the key because I think to be fair, it's a pretty stylish win. Then there's all the effort I've gone to, the little details, from the race suit and the friction and the chain to the training and the food, everything that I've done, and when it all comes together, it's an incredibly good feeling. It's a moment to move on from because ultimately you have to move as you can't live in it. I don't want those things to define me, I want to carry on and do other stuff. But even so, of all my wins, and I don't have hundreds of them, this is the best one.

*

I was really motivated to do well in the Tour of Britain that autumn, partly because I felt like I'd never really shown the British public the best of myself on home soil. I'd been gutted when I'd finished second in 2008 but had lost by only five seconds. The race had ended in Liverpool too, and I was trying to do the sprints for the time bonuses so I could sneak ahead overall at the last minute, but a sprinter of the calibre of Alessandro Petacchi was after the points jersey, so I was operating way out of my league. But in 2016, after all my success abroad that year, the Tour of Britain was my chance of having a 'will the real Steve Cummings please stand up' moment in the UK.

Britain is, in any case, a really hard race to win, because the course that often has no time trial and which invariably contains all those medium mountain and hilly stages makes it very unpredictable. So to have the overall as an objective would never really have made sense and I wasn't ever going to be the strongest on the sprints or in the climbs either. But in September 2016 somehow I became considered one of the favourites, right when I just wanted to leave it all out there in the coolest way possible anyway.

Apart from having good form, how I did that was by looking very hard at the course map and its past. Often you look at the Tour of Britain's history and there's a key stage here or there that isn't always expected to be the 'GC' day, but that's where the entire race ends up being decided. For some reason, for the last few years before I won it, there had often been a break on stage two. This was seemingly invariably a hard stage, and it'd weed out some of the GC riders and bring in a few new names in the process.

So I identified that stage, which went into the Lake District, as the one to get in the break and by playing my cards right by the end of the day's racing I found myself out in front with a Belgian guy, Julien Vermote. It hadn't been straightforward getting into that situation: on one climb, appropriately called The Struggle, I had got dropped by a group of top riders including Irish star Dan Martin and two World Time Trial Champions, Tom Dumoulin and Rohan Dennis. Over the top it was foggy and the downhill was tricky, but somehow I descended it pretty well and caught up with the group again shortly afterwards.

It wasn't ideal because Dennis had got away and he was the strongest guy there. But thanks to it being such hilly terrain he'd bitten off more than he could chew. Then when we caught him I realized this was a good moment to go on the attack myself, finally bridging across to Julien Vermote, the lone survivor of the early break.

It was looking good, but I knew that I'd have to be careful too, because I needed him to take the stage win and get the lead. If I'd have taken the top spot overall that day, I'd have lost the race.

The reason for this was that at Dimension Data in Britain I had Cav, Bernie Eisel, Mark Renshaw, Johan van Zyl and Jay Thomson as team-mates. In other words a non-climbing line-up that meant whenever we went over anything as hilly as a bridge, I'd find myself quickly isolated and had I taken it, I would have lost the lead for sure. On the plus side they were brilliant at positioning me in key moments; Cav even did a Poggio-style lead-out for me one day into Hardknott Pass, which nearly killed me.

I told Vermote he could have the stage win if he collaborated a bit with me. That way I'd get him to take over as leader and his team, Quick-Step, would have to control the race for a few stages before we got to the final climb of one key day, the Haytor ascent on Dartmoor, where I was pretty certain I'd drop him. After that there'd only be a split stage left to control and Cav and the rest of the team would have no problem handling the opposition. Game over.

So Vermote took the stage and the lead, and the race duly unfolded as planned as far as Haytor. I knew what Haytor was like, so I wasn't too worried about it before or during the stage. But then I couldn't believe my luck, because Tony Martin, a rival team worker, opted to keep things under control by keeping a driving pace at the front of the pack for almost half the ascent, which meant the race was playing out at the steady rhythm I could manage best. Vermote cracked and fell behind, as predicted, and all I had to do was limit my losses to the out-and-out time triallists of this world like Rohan Dennis and Tom Dumoulin. Which I did, taking the lead, and three days later, the biggest stage race victory of my career was in the bag.

It was fantastic for that reason alone, but also for the last day being in London. The crowds at the finish were immense and a lot of my family and friends had come to watch too. There were familiar faces everywhere you looked and they'd all come to cheer, which was wonderful. I also remember Bradley and other guys from other teams who weren't going to do anything on that last stage trying to help me out, which was a nice feeling. I'd been riding the crest of a wave all through the season abroad, and now I'd done it at home too. For a short period, it felt like 'You're the man, aren't you?'

*

Each of the wins I took in 2016 was very different, and each of them happened in very different scenarios: from a small group, a break in the last kilometre, a long distance break and a breakaway over a big mountain climb. But the similarities were that they were all World Tour events, and they all demanded a world-class performance. Then as the cherry on the cake, there was the Tour of Britain too.

Other riders have got a world-class sprint or a world-class power-to-weight ratio. In my case, what I was world class at was my speed on the flat at a given power. One fundamental part of that, as I said, was being very aerodynamic and another was absolute power output.

But it doesn't just happen on the day. These wins have deep roots. What I learned in Italy was that you've got to keep on thinking about the bike. So when you go hiking, say, and you're always thinking about the bike, you're trying to track your knees perfectly, thinking about good technique, and about your legs turning like pistons but hitting the ground from exactly the right angle. Then slowly, when you do get out of the wood, you follow that up by starting off with slow cadence work – walking and going to the gym – then doing strength training and weight training on the bike. And then after that, building that up to turning the pedals at 100 rpm.

Whereas some people think it's all about zones when you're training, there's also the technical aspect, which fuses with an aesthetic aspect. If you go back to dreams and aspirations, I always admired both style and performance on the bike. Because I learned that there's a colossal difference in terms of power between turning out 300 watts output when your legs are turning in a way which has efficiency and style, and turning out 300 watts when it's a struggle and it looks ugly into the bargain. In the former case, you can see when somebody has done their homework, literally, and when they haven't. I know it all sounds a little bit Rocky Balboa-esque. But it works.

On top of that there was training, where my strength was that I could really go deep for long periods, months or years, often to the point where it was harder than efforts in racing, even when I've won. Normally, on a training ride you'd have done all your interval work at full gas but leaving room for a little bit more, but every now and then you'd leave it all out there.

The best example of the opposite extreme, where the racing hurt more than the training, was the Dauphiné stage in 2016. I wouldn't go that deep in training because it'd take too long to recover. What was so hard about the Dauphiné was that I had a high average power for four hours, like a slow kill of working between 300 and 500 watts. Time-wise it isn't so long, but in training you'd normally only do that level of intensity for two or three hours, and in other races like the Vuelta al País Vasco, you'd be going above 500 watts, but for a much shorter period.

So rather than using the strategy of hurting myself in a race to win, normally I would be very motivated and very organized. For one thing, I knew why it was important to do each session in training and I could relate it to the race scenarios. But above all I trained on how to go to my absolute maximum in terms of power output. I'd be thinking to myself: go full on, get it out there and if you're dropped, you're dropped. A lot of riders don't do that, so then when they need to find their absolute maximum, they don't know where it is. But by practising that constantly, you'd maximize yourself. It's not a question of how much you can stand, because you're not thinking about the pain – that comes afterwards: it's all about being as self-aware of your physical limits as possible. That mindset of getting everything out is critical to avoid going through the motions. Some riders will say to themselves, 'You know what, I'll ride easy with my mates today,' and everything ends up getting compromised.

With me there wasn't much room for compromise, which was a strength but also my biggest weakness, as the teams could find me difficult. Even so, ever since I'd worked with Steve Peters, I'd been obsessed with getting it all out.

As I got older, I got more comfortable with being like that. I wanted to maximize every day of training, every pedal stroke and make sure that when I finished, I could shrug my shoulders and say, 'That's it, I left it all out there.'

For sure you can look back now and say, 'Could you have done better here or there?' I know I made a lot of mistakes, but they were my mistakes and they provided a platform for me to learn and improve. So because of the way I did it, the answer to that question would be 'I did everything that I thought was right and I did it 100 per cent.' And that's all there was to it.

Chapter 13

A Race Against Time

A s soon as I hit the ground I knew this crash was a bad one. It was April 2017 in the Tour of the Basque Country, where we were coming into Bilbao on a main road, pretty fast, and there was a pinch point and they crashed in front. The road was not fully closed, so there was oncoming traffic and I was next to my team-mate Lachlan Morton. So I went left, both to avoid the crash and to avoid causing him to crash too. But eventually I ran out of road, and I couldn't avoiding hitting the riders already on the ground, which catapulted me into the air and a green traffic bollard broke my fall. I took all of the impact on my left shoulder.

The full diagnosis at the hospital later on was a fractured sternum, scapula and collarbone, but at first I was in denial, telling the race medics who attended the crash I was OK, that I was still able to walk and I wanted to walk, even though I was clearly not fine. Such was my state, I was telling them to put the other three who were injured in the pile-up on the stretchers, not me.

I stayed calm as long as possible. The other three injured guys were screaming like death was staring them in the face, so I sat on the floor in the ambulance to give them more room. When we got to the hospital, though, they were seen to first and were discharged quickly because it turned out they had minor injuries. But I got told I had to stay in overnight, and then when I tried to walk again, I couldn't. I stopped in the middle of a corridor where I had to sit down on the floor and then they got me into bed. I called my wife to say I was OK, and that was when I cried. I don't normally cry much. But I was so, so sad because I'd known that a race win or a good performance had been in the pipeline. Everything had been there, everything had felt good. I hadn't had the result yet, but that's cycling too, especially when you rely on winning from breakaways – you can put in the performance and you can finish 100th, of course, but you can also finish first. That's the way it is.

It wasn't just in Bilbao that I cried. I started to cry more in the last part of my career in general because of the challenges it represented for my family. My wife had only a small support network around her in Italy and I knew it wasn't easy for her at home looking after Perla. The last thing they needed was having to look after me as well. I found it difficult not being able to help my daughter and wife when I was injured. I guess what made that bearable was knowing that being a bike rider gave them a good platform for life.

That day, despite the diagnosis being bad, I started thinking it through and somewhere very early in that process I hit on one crucial point. 'My legs are good, so all is good, don't worry.' As with any kind of grieving, I had had to cry and get it out, but by that point in my career, I had worked it through so frequently that that period lasted minutes. Then you'd realize, 'It's not useful to be in this frame of mind.' And all of a sudden, it'd be like I'd pushed reset, the switch had flicked and something was gone.

So once you've accepted it, you start to deal with it. In this case, I went through the list of what was broken, and after that it was a question of taking things day by day, and what did I need to do.

But if the overall perspective and goal is getting back on terms as quickly as possible, how do you do that? The bottom line is eat well, sleep well, stay positive and don't feel sorry for yourself. While you have to be smart, and not overdo it, at the end of the day you have to be a hard bastard on yourself too, and when you find solutions, recognize that everything you have to do has to be done. You can't skip parts of the process.

So after this, the worst accident of my career up to then and in what became my toughest comeback, I went step by step. Then, as now, it's always all about finding the best solution to bring through as much fitness as you can, under the circumstances, to the other side of recovery. And I really mean as much as possible, to the point where back in the Vuelta al País Vasco crash case, that 'carrying fitness' process initially involved me being strapped to the ceiling every time I had a training ride on the rollers.

It was my good friend and coach at the time, Jon Baker, who had the idea of putting TheraBands around my chest, semi-suspending me from the ceiling to take the weight off my shoulder because ten days after the crash one side of

241

my body couldn't handle any kind of weight; it hurt far too much. With the TheraBands, the pressure was more balanced and I could, at least, ride on the rollers. When we did that, it wasn't just a physical relief, it was mental as well, because it meant I knew I could ride. And that meant I knew I'd be all right, because I had a clear idea of what I could still do.

On the bike itself, it was step by step: first with twenty minutes' training, then thirty minutes, then an hour and then two hours. And if at that point, say, things weren't OK, then I'd ease back to an hour again. However, the team management were not so optimistic, and the vibe I got was 'forget the Tour'. I never understood why the management would send such negative vibes to a rider; it wasn't a useful approach. But whatever they said, I just thought to myself, 'OK, we'll see.'

I may like to think of myself as a hard bastard but the truth is this time I knew I was right on the limit and even to get back into a position where I could race again was going to be extremely difficult.

On top of which the crash coincided with a lot of changes in the Dimension Data medical team. We lost much of the South African element, something I regretted, as I'd liked the African side of the team, and they'd replaced it with a new German medical contingent. As I've written, the new team medic's idea was that whenever there was a serious injury they'd send us to this hospital in Germany which operated very quickly and efficiently. But although logistically and financially these decisions were surely sound, particularly as I'd heard bad things about the Bilbao hospital, at the time I didn't know about the background to what had been decided. On top of that uncertainty, for me in the short term the switch in policy meant two flights and then a two-hour train journey alone to the middle of Cologne, and then a taxi ride... all with only one effective arm and struggling to get the small backpack, which was all I could manage to carry, over my shoulder, in turn held in place by two ribs, which were all that remained unbroken. The team doctor helped me put my bag on my shoulder when I left to get on the plane, and that was it.

Anyway, having had the operation, I began shifting for myself, starting with walking around Cologne for a few days, even if it was very, very slowly. From my point of view, I needed to sweat a little and get the medicine out of my system. And the one thing I wasn't going to let myself do was sit on the bed and feel sorry for myself. So first thing the morning after the surgery, apart from walking around Cologne at a snail's pace, I went straight to the rehab gym and started out on the exercise bike – much to the surprise of the physio, who was not just surprised to see someone there so early, but so soon after surgery he was not expecting that someone to be me!

Just when my rehab was way ahead of schedule, one day in Tuscany I got worried about the kids falling over on a wet floor, so I got up to move a mat and promptly slipped over myself. I really did go down hard; it winded me and hurt a lot. Nicky said we should go directly to hospital but I played it down because the kids were having a good time and also, if I'm honest, because if I'd done myself more damage I really didn't want to know. So I insisted on staying at home and that I was OK, and as such I soldiered on on the home trainer and the gym despite a significant amount of pain.

I couldn't help feeling very surprised though about how much my range of movement had become limited. So eventually I went for another scan and it turned out that in my second fall I'd extended the fracture of the scapula right into the joint. This made the surface of the joint uneven, meaning had it been left as it was I would have required an entire shoulder replacement in two years at most, because the scapula had started to heal in the wrong place.

This was quite serious now, because I needed to find the best surgeon to re-break the bone and plate the rear part of the scapula back together. I was paying for all this surgery myself, and it wasn't cheap. So I travelled back to the UK and was recommended a Doctor Potter and his anaesthetist, who was called Snape. You couldn't have made their names up...

Anyway, rather than heading for Hogwarts Dungeons on the day of the surgery, I woke up at 4 a.m. and drove across to Sheffield for the operation. It was a longer than expected operation and involved losing a lot of blood, but Potter did an amazing job. On the downside, I was seriously weakened by it all, and when I tried to ride the bike a day or two later, convinced that a little sweat would get all the most unpleasant of the medicines out of my system and stimulate the healing process, it nearly finished me off. I think it took me ten days before I could try again and I had to take a maximum permitted painkiller dose for ten days and then slowly reduce it, just to be able to get out of bed.

Things were tough at that point, I have to admit. But on the plus side, I was pretty good mentally. (You might sum my attitude up as 'shit happens'.) However, another issue developed: because of the crashes I'd had, and all the time off the bike, I'd gained weight.

If I wanted to keep the dream alive of getting to the Tour that year – as I still hoped – I didn't have time to lose that weight over a longer, more sustained period. I didn't like very strict diet programmes, on top of which I'd also had the boomerang experience of the fruit diet at Sky. But to have the best chance of a quick return, desperate times called for desperate measures. One way or another, it had to happen.

*

So what did I do? If you wanted to sum it up, I was training on a programme of huge power outputs and massive calorie deficiency by limiting it fuel-wise. But it was really, really hard to manage.

In the final countdown to the Tour, I trained in three-day training blocks. I'd do four hours on day one, then three the next, then often push that up to six or seven hours as the Tour got closer. Much of my training would be based around me having a circuit of around 4000 metres of vertical climbing, which included a tough ascent of the Passo San Pellegrino in Tuscany. We'd do the climb at about 400 watts, a fairly high power output considering the work I'd done by the time I hit the bottom of the ascent. Between the other climbs I'd be doing a medium power output of around 370 watts, averaging a high pace of 45 km/h for at least half an hour, and then on top of that, I'd start the biggest climb of the day.

Day two of the three-day blocks would be the fastest paced of all, and I'd take two bottles of Beta Fuel, which allows you to maximize your carbohydrate intake without messing up your guts too much. (I also needed to train my system to handle the fuel it needed to perform optimally.) Then on the last day, although I'd eat during most of the training, I'd stop eating in the last hour. So in effect I'd be fuelling like I was in a race, training my body and fuelling my system to churn through a huge amount of calories. At home I'd have a vegetable shake with a bit of protein and amino acids that a biochemist designed for me and then after all of that, I wouldn't eat until dinner. All in all, I'd turn around 6000 calories while on the bike, but the first time you'd eat properly, other than bike food, would be around 7.30 in the evening – a salad and a steak and then bed. Then the next day would be a rest day, you'd have some carbohydrate, and start to filter back in the fuel so you'd have some energy for the next day's training.

In a nutshell, I did everything I could to try to come back, because I knew I could. The biggest question was when and if I was in time. If I was progressing on the physical front, I found communication with the team challenging. I just used my legs to talk and pressed 'send' on the computer every day, because I needed the management to see the power files, but that was it. I focused on the things I could control, like process and preparation, and tuned out any white noise that wasn't helpful.

If the countdown to the 2017 Tour was proving to be a real roller coaster, ever since I'd won the Tour de France stage in 2016 it had been one battle after another. From 2016 onwards, the mentality of the team began to change and we'd ended up in a command and control environment. I'd experienced this in the past, and it wasn't conducive to the best performance, either individually or collectively. I immediately raised my concerns, backed up by numbers, and my communication skills weren't bad by then. But my approach seemed to cause offence and my evidence-based opinion didn't fit the narrative. Eventually, I felt that I was branded a maverick, which perhaps had an element of truth, but I was a reasonable maverick who'd performed pretty well since day one of my time with MTN-Qhubeka and Dimension Data. I knew in my mind that discipline equalled freedom and if I wanted freedom I'd have to earn it. But I was convinced I should let my legs do the talking.

At the time, though, communication was close to breaking down and what messages I was getting in any case were inconsistent and confusing, so I continued focusing on getting better, either building towards the Tour or whatever the next race would be.

Early on, given the speed at which I was recovering, some of the management realized that 'Hang on a minute, he's still able to do what he normally can even if he is on the turbo and with all these injuries. So his fitness must be fine.'

I had told them that I would be 100 per cent capable of fighting for a Tour stage – something I actually did when I got there – and that I could race myself back into top condition in the first ten days. But they didn't agree. So we reached a situation of stalemate.

I remember chatting with Doug Ryder about the psychological aspect and told him that while I knew I would be scared, everybody felt that at times and I had coping mechanisms for the crashes in place. The mechanisms were accepting those crashes might happen again at any time. I knew cycling was a dangerous sport – that's the game – but the trick was to try to limit the risk and find the balance between risk and reward. Given the circumstances the ideal role would have been to use me first in a helping position for the team and to lead out Cav in the appropriate stages. I was more than willing to do that role: it would have been a privilege and a pleasure. In addition I felt I had another string to my bow: having won two stages in previous Tours, realistically I felt, and perhaps more importantly the numbers suggested, that I was ready to hunt again.

*

I was out training on one of my first sessions back on the road when the phone rang. By this point I'd just done three hours, a pretty hard session, and although my arm and balance had felt rough early on, overall everything was on track. I knew there'd been a management meeting though, so I was waiting for a verdict. But when they told me I'd have to do the Nationals to 'prove to us you're fit and can ride in the bunch', I had to laugh – and agreed.

Apart from anything else, they were giving me seventy-two hours' notice to drop everything and get to the Nationals on the Isle of Man for what was to become a performance test. Not ideal. But I wasn't going to let it put me off.

I went home, organized everything I could at the drop of a hat, together with Nicky who was (and is) excellent at these sorts of activities, be it sorting out food, bikes, accommodation or hire cars. We had no time to waste and in this case the best place to stay was a none too glamorous room above a Thai restaurant. We had looked on the internet to see if we could get people delivering us fresh food from local cafes, but in the end we didn't eat that stuff. Rather, the Thai place had all-you-could-eat rice included on its menu, and they took a shine to me too, perhaps because I only ever asked for rice and chicken unlike their usual fussier clientele. We just tried to make everything as good as we could, but it certainly wasn't the classiest place to be doing all the background work for an achievement that would make me very proud for multiple reasons.

In previous years I'd had the option of staying in the same hotel as Team Sky and the GB National team but I never did do that. I wasn't interested in getting involved in combines with them in the race for one thing. For another I didn't enjoy being around people that, under normal circumstances, I liked a lot, but I also knew that when I put my leg over the bike, I'd want to crush them. This year, more than ever.

*

So with all this in the background, as well as the toughest comeback of my career culminating in a fair amount of all-you-can-eat chicken and rice, I made my way to the start of the UK Nationals Time Trial. My performance turned out to be an accurate reflection of my form. It also got me a gold medal.

It wasn't my best ride ever, but it was good enough to win. So I was more relaxed afterwards and it was a huge boost for my morale for the road race. I knew I could feel confident, as I'd demonstrated to the team that I was really close to my best. However, on the team bus, at the meeting before the road race started, things changed yet again. What quickly emerged was perhaps the real reason why the Dimension Data management wanted me at the Nationals, and it wasn't that they wanted me to show I could ride in a peloton or show race fitness. They wanted me there as a team worker for Cav. He was convinced that he could get over the main climb of the race and be in the thick of it at the end of the day.

In my case, I was just being open, because I did want to do what was best for the team. I was fine with the idea of Cav being up there in the final, and of course I'd try to help him. But my reaction to Cav was to say, 'Great, but there's only me, you and [another team-mate] Scott Thwaites here. With two of us working for you, we can't control the race. So, get yourself through the race well and if you're there on the finishing circuit we'll try to control it.'

When we got going it didn't turn out to be easy racing because, as usual in the Nationals, there were three or four Skys in the front. I remember one of them, Tao Geoghegan Hart, who later won the Giro d'Italia in 2020, seemed to be glued to my back wheel wherever I went. It feels quite flattering now, given how good a rider he's become. But back then, it was fucking annoying, even if we were quite far behind so that made it more normal and, to be fair to him, I was his last ticket out to get across to the break. On top of which a rival like Pete Kennaugh was a better climber than me, and he went on the attack at the foot of the main ascent.

Cav was dropped in the crosswinds from a front group on the top of the mountain and that was a make-or-break moment. I shouted at Scott to keep it going because he was struggling too, and finally we made it to the front group as they hit the finishing circuit – and we all hit a brief stalemate.

There weren't any really hard parts on that circuit for the two strongest guys, me and Pete, to try to drop each other, and on top of that there were lots of amateur racers also taking part who had no idea of strategy and who kept attacking with 50 kilometres to go, when I wondered if they could keep going at 40 km/h for so long. The whole 'on' and 'off' style of racing that characterized the race was not ideal, because it's so hard to recreate in training, but that day I coped well with it.

Even so, I was getting increasingly fed up of guys attacking from so far out because it seemed like a junior race. But finally, when yet another move fizzled out, and we got the usual concertina effect as the peloton jammed together, I went for it myself. Even if it wasn't a great place in terms of terrain, in terms of momentum it worked perfectly.

I tried to lull the people that were following me into a false sense of security by appearing to be riding at full tilt and so it always looked bridgeable when in fact I was going at 80 or 85 per cent. Pete was the only one who tried to close me down. But I wasn't too worried, as when he regained contact, I went up to full whack for the last 200 metres of a climb on the steepest part. He was there for 40 to 50 metres but then popped and I was alone. And that was all I needed: a ten-second margin ahead of everybody over the top.

On the downhill to the finish, I was happily smiling to myself because I was back to a situation where I was on my own, I was sure they weren't going to catch me and I was able to enjoy it all. And I got to the finish alone, the first rider to win the Nationals Time Trial and the Road Race in the same year in over a decade. It was a good performance for sure, my first race back after the injuries, and if you took away the injuries the performance was even better. I was delighted to be National Champion, but deep down what I really cared about was the Tour and that was where I wanted to be. If I'd had a choice, I'd have gambled and gone into the Tour directly, without riding the Nationals, as the optimal preparation.

I remember my director coming up in the team car behind me in the last few hundred metres before we won and I grabbed his hand in a victory salute – bam! I wasn't being funny or a cunt or trying to tell him I told you so about what they had decided. I wanted the team to be together. But I never felt that we fully understood each other.

*

The rest of 2017 had two more special moments, one because I won and one which even though I didn't, I still treasure to this day.

I'd kept on top of things and at the Tour of Tuscany that year, I had what proved to be my final victory in a professional road race. At the time I didn't know that, obviously: I was simply glad, and relieved, that I had had a win in the British National Champion's jersey in what was a pretty good race with some more than pretty good riders.

The victory came on the opening stage and it was against one Tour de France winner, Vincenzo Nibali, and another rider who, as it turned out, also went on to win the same race: Egan Bernal. At the time Bernal was still racing with his first pro squad, the Italian Androni team, and he shot over a climb late in the day at a pace that you wouldn't believe. Nibali was after him in a flash and we'd had quite a fight for the best position going on to the climb, and I was slipping back through riders as we went up it. But it narrowed near the top, and just as things were really slowing down, I managed to dig deep and get past them all, going flat out. After a long chase across a plateau for Nibali, Bernal and a Belgian rider, I bridged as the descent began. But that was when the talking started – and I had more problems to deal with.

Cav was in the race and we were supposed to be riding for him, so with that in mind I was rolling through each time I was due to go on the front, but only doing just enough to ensure the group stayed fluid. Above all, I didn't want to piss Cav off. But then Nibali told me I should start collaborating properly with the rest of the group. I answered that I wasn't entirely sure that could happen as I had Cav behind. Nibali said that was fair enough, but 'you can win in this situation and anyway, I've got Colbrelli [Sonny is a very decent sprinter and Vincenzo's team-mate] in the group behind too.' To which I replied, 'That is a bit different as you are *il capo* [the boss]' and 'Cav's the capo in our team'. To be honest, and despite the discussion, I didn't know if Cav was close behind or the third group on the road. However, I waited for a while before collaborating, but a bit further on, when I felt the break had passed that threshold of 'now we can win', I began pulling at the front too and the four of us reached the finish together.

I did a good sprint too. Bernal was probably faster, but I got close to the barriers and took the lead position. Then I opened up a little bit, so there'd be a bit of a gap – or what looked like a gap – and Bernal tried to come through. But then I squeezed back towards the barriers – gently – so he couldn't pass. And I won.

My former team-mate Philippe Gilbert was killing himself laughing afterwards, saying I had screwed Bernal over, and it's true what I did was certainly a slightly subtle way of dealing with the opposition. But a very minor drift in line like mine is a normal, permitted tactic.

It wasn't a major win by any means, but it was one on home soil in Tuscany and it gave me a chance to round off what had been a very roller-coaster year. Above all, after such a difficult first half of the season, I'd come through on a practical level in a way I'd never have expected.

*

The breakaway I treasured, even though it ended in defeat, came on the Tour when I got away on the Port de Balès. It was liberating for me, particularly getting away on such a long climb and the same one I'd crashed so badly on a few years before. We started climbing the Balès in the breakaway but by the time we'd reached the top I'd dropped Thomas De Gendt, the strongest of the other guys in the move, and was going solo. I had recollections of me lying in the gutter there in 2012, and it was the first time I'd ever gone alone over the top of a Hors Categorie climb, so it felt fantastic, five years on, to have put that memory behind me in such a special way.

If I had taken that win, in the National Champion's jersey and on the fiftieth anniversary of the death of British cycling legend Tom Simpson – something I knew about before I broke away – it'd have been beyond special. I wanted to showcase the jersey well, and even if I was caught a relatively long way from the finish, I gave it my all. I also know that if I had managed to get over the summit of the Peyresourde instead of being caught 5 kilometres from the top then I could have won. In terms of pure power, that was one of my best rides ever, so I went away with a huge sense of satisfaction, more than after the Nationals. That breakaway summed up something important for me – that I preferred to focus on performance, because the results were a by-product of that and they can be a false way of interpreting your rides. What you can't ignore is if you're producing twenty minutes of your highest ever power, or if you do a climb and manage to stay in a group that you wouldn't do normally. These are the key indicators, and that day, they were all good.

I did try again in that year's Tour, but my overall sensations were that the peak form lasted ten days and then had dropped off a little bit by then. I'm pretty sure, and this is ironic, that I could have done better, or been more sure about when I would have good form, if I hadn't had to do the Nationals. (The Nationals were a bit like Amstel Gold for me that year, in that the Amstel is a race where there are lots of short, sharp accelerations over short ascents and that kind of climbing takes time for my body to assimilate.)

Either way it was a shame the group chased me down that day on the Tour but it wasn't to be. That's often the nature of the breakaway – it's how teams react behind that is key to its chances of survival. When they caught me there weren't many riders left in the bunch, so I just stopped, got off the bike for a moment and chatted to a fan. Perhaps I should have fought for twentieth or thirtieth but so late in my career and even after such an incredibly tough recovery process just to get to the Tour, for me it was still all or nothing. And staying true to that still mattered.

Chapter 14

Back to My Roots

I rode the Vuelta a España in 2018. Ben King won two stages for the team and I'd help wherever I could. At first I wasn't really in very good shape, but I was getting better, as always happened when I wasn't ill or injured. However, that was on the bike. Off the bike, my main memories of all 3000 or more kilometres and three weeks in Spain that August and September are that I was reading books and studying. My body was there in the Vuelta. My head was far away.

It had gone well in 2017, considering how bad things had been in the spring, and I had no sense that I was going off the boil in general. But the challenging situation between the Dimension Data heads of staff and the riders continued into the following years.

I realized more and more clearly that one reaction I could have to this situation was to study to understand performance, management, team culture – all that stuff. Because it's easy to say, 'This isn't any good,' particularly when you're younger and you look at things from a more selfish point of view. But as I got older I started looking for different ways of resolving problems, trying to find thought-out solutions that had solidly researched logical arguments to back them up, developing a 360-degree view on situations and, equally importantly, trying to discover the best ways of introducing those solutions to teams. I thought this side of the sport was both intriguing and relevant.

So as I read my way through the '18 Vuelta, I was soaking up all sorts of stuff, mainly focusing on high performance-related books from different sectors of life like *Tribe of Mentors*, *Extreme Ownership*, *The Culture Code*, *The Talent Lab*... but the one I got the most out of was *Tools of Titans* by Tim Ferriss.

Having read them all, I did feel that, even if there were alternatives I hadn't thought of, I had dealt with the issues I'd had as well as I could. But I remained hungry for knowledge and understanding too, about how different sectors of the sport worked and transferable skills between them, how to improve my communication skills and deal with challenging situations and, within that, how to deal with people who weren't fair and how to handle situations that weren't right.

A lot of the stuff I'd done with Steve Peters had nailed these dilemmas and issues in a simple, concise way and I loved them for that. The more I read, the more it added value to the work I had done with him. For me the most essential element of his many key learnings was 'accept that this is what you've got to deal with. You don't have to like it, but you do have to know how to handle it, and how to move on from it.'

I got even greater perspective on this whole situation in Dimension Data in 2018–19 by what happened to me after my career ended, when I joined Ineos Grenadiers – my former team that had previously been sponsored by Sky – as part of the staff at the end of 2020. Being inside Ineos Grenadiers, I could appreciate better that what had gone right and wrong two years earlier at Di Data had boiled down to a failure in people management, and a collective lack of communication.

For one thing, I've never seen a team with so little internal friction as Ineos Grenadiers. It's not like everyone always agrees, but there's a permanent sense circulating in the squad that the team is more powerful than the individual. At the same time we spend a lot of time on working out how the individual and their goals can fit within that greater scheme of things.

Secondly, when Ineos Grenadiers make a decision, they always work back from it, considering every aspect of what that decision implies. When it comes to acting on those decisions, team boss Dave Brailsford is firm and fair, but ruthless with it. That's something I'd realized all the way back in my team pursuit days, but having studied business ethics at university I understand it much better, as I can see Brailsford's sole underlying purpose is to make sure the team performs. He wants to look after individuals, of course, but if it comes to a point where looking after individuals is affecting the team's performance, eventually the team's at risk. He's got the knack of managing that balance down to a pretty fine art. And I can appreciate now that that fine art of people management was very much missing in Dimension Data in 2018–19.

The massive differences between the Dimension Data of 2015 and 2016 and the years that followed were partly because there had been a lot of personnel changes. Above all, Brian Smith had left. For me, personally, this was bad news, because he was the guy I had talked to most in the team, and he was the guy for whom if you committed and made sacrifices and did your best, then he'd reciprocate, doing all he could from his side to support you.

With Brian gone, many of the team's key ideas going forward were born out of the remaining management's long careers as pros. Rather than favour innovation or at least discussion of possible different approaches, an area I'd been working on from reading up and studying all those different management techniques, some of the remaining top members of staff didn't seem to appreciate that just because something's worked one year, it doesn't mean it's going to work the next.

It has to be said that when traditional approaches work, I'm all in favour. For example, the way cycling's calendar is designed brings you almost naturally into top shape for the summer. However, the calendar is changing again now: we have more and more non-European riders; the race schedule is far more international and less Eurocentric than it used to be; there is a great deal more emphasis on the World Tour races; and finally altitude camps and riders doing less racing in general have all had an impact. But while you don't need to try to make square wheels round as happened at Sky ten years before, you do need to be open to new ideas and things you can tweak and look to improve. So it's very challenging when you suggest something and, before it's even considered, the answer's no.

I remained positive within a tough situation. Using that Steve Peters philosophy about accepting what you have to deal with, I encouraged my team-mates to appreciate that the management were doing their best to make good decisions. That was even if some of the decisions made by the management didn't make sense from a riders' perspective, and what the management were now asking of the riders wasn't realistic.

The main problem was that any team in bike racing has to switch riders around for races, but that year at Dimension Data it reached an extreme. Race programmes were literally changing every five minutes. So people were hovering at around 90 per cent of their potential, going through the motions because they didn't know if things would or wouldn't change.

Secondly, I'm not a team manager but I know if you have too many objectives, you spread yourself too thinly and, in my opinion, Dimension Data had so many different goals they started making short-term decisions that clashed and conflicted with each other.

For example, one team goal was to maintain a lead-out group for Cav, with a group of people dedicated fully to supporting him. Then we had another group dedicated to stage hunting that were also fully prepared to support Cav. That combination initially worked really well in 2016 because Cav was in good shape and we were used best; for example, my best role on the sprint stages was doing the spadework early on and the regulating of the breaks. But the crossover grew far less effective and team goals started to conflict when Cav wasn't in good shape – for whatever reason – in 2017 and 2018, or when riders like me were asked to do specialist roles that I wasn't good at, like being there for Cav in the closing kilometres. Beyond that, there were times when riders who might have been good in breaks and won at World Tour level – like me – as well as providing early support for Cav, were substituted.

Yet another element in the conflicting mix was the team's objective of developing young African riders. I had a conversation with management in 2015 where I said if the team wanted to do that, perhaps it shouldn't go into the World Tour as the level was so high and you needed to be fully ready to handle that. As it was we did go into the World Tour, and as a team it felt like we were overwhelmed. All that decision did was put pressure on the rest of the team, and, as a result, rather than being proactive we were all getting too reactive, and when races came thick and fast it became a real challenge. Performance-wise, that step up put the team under pressure. However, there were also economic aspects that I knew nothing about that would have to have been considered when deciding to move up to the World Tour. So I remained open-minded, even if I felt criticism levelled at individuals didn't help anybody. But then and now there's no bitterness on my part about this: it was what it was.

On top of that, in 2015, we had been the underdogs, on an upward curve. By the time it got to 2017 or 2018, we had a higher budget and higher expectations, but we were pretty useless. One reason was that in 2015, 2016 and 2017, if you looked beneath the surface glitter a little, very few of our riders had been getting top results, and if they weren't operating at their full potential, as happened in 2018, it developed into a huge problem.

If you wanted an example of how badly things were disintegrating on a personal level as a combined result of all of these developments, you could do worse than look at the race programme Dimension Data had designed for me in 2018.

In an ideal world, of course, I'd sort out what I wanted to do, basically going from race to race with a little time for training in between, and 2016 was the perfect example of how to do it right. But then early in 2018, the team management began freaking out about World Tour points because we'd come last in the World Tour ranking in 2017. So they wanted me to do the Abu Dhabi Tour, the predecessor of what is now the UAE Tour, with a view to trying to get a good result overall.

I said that was not at all practical, given the top ten in that race is invariably made up of talented climbers, and I couldn't beat them on an ascent as hard as the race's final ascent, Jebel Hafeet. There was also the issue of handling crosswinds, always an issue in the UAE, and that wasn't my strongest suit either.

To which their answer was, if you can do what you did in the Tour de France on medium mountain stages, you can do that in the UAE Tour. I disagreed, but they didn't care, or they didn't understand.

Given the lack of insight and empathy on their part, the tense discussion would go round and round; I suspect they'd get pressure from higher up the chain of command, he'd shout at them and, in turn, they'd shout at me. I wasn't being awkward. I was not the only person who had this issue and in this specific case there was a clear reason for me not being able to do Abu Dhabi. But they didn't want a human, they wanted a robot.

So I went, on the condition they didn't hold me account-able and it was fucking terrible – I finished 129th. It had been

super-hot all week and I had been using so little power, sometimes as little as 150 watts, that I was actually losing condition.
I didn't mind, in one sense, that it didn't go well, because we
had tried. But then, having made me go, the management
turned it round and insisted that it was my fault.

If Abu Dhabi was bad, then management and I had another
disagreement. After the success of 2016, doing well in Liège–
Bastogne–Liège was a dream for me, and something that had
been for a while. But I was asked in no uncertain terms did I
really think I could win it? I said if you wound the clock back,
no one had thought I could win a stage of the Tour either and
no one had thought I could win in Tirreno, or País Vasco, so
why not try to take the next step in other races? People could
think I was crazy but I really didn't care, and maybe it was
a step too far. But if I didn't keep striving for more I would
drift, and performing in Liège was something that made me
jump out of bed in the morning.

There was a similar heated debate about the Giro d'Italia:
I had dreamt of winning a stage in the Giro in the National
Champion's jersey. That was a big motivation when I thought
about it. However, the team told me that I could not go to
the Giro as their Giro strategy was focused on the GC and
stages were not a target. I disagreed. I was happy to support a
GC challenge knowing that there were likely to be opportunities to go for stages and still being able to do my work to help
sustain a GC challenge.

It could have been an incredible year given my motivation and condition, but instead the whole spring had been
wasted. It had got to the point where I felt I was no longer
welcome whenever I got on the team bus, and I felt that I was

considered as a filler by the management – 2016 could not have felt further away.

*

My interest in trying to look at the way management looked at riders, not vice versa, and trying to improve the philosophies behind race strategies had already sharpened considerably during the 2016 Olympics. Initially, I'd not been selected, and I couldn't understand why I wasn't on the list since I'd won a stage in every World Tour race I'd taken part in. I'd won more consistently than a lot of sprinters, and if you looked at my power files the numbers coming through were world-class level. Even with all the other considerations like tactics and roles, it still didn't make sense. I realized that it had to be 100 per cent all in for the team, but the tactics and execution of deploying what forces we had as effectively as we could did make me feel concerned about how that might play out.

For a long time anyway, the team selection committee were adamant they wanted Pete Kennaugh and Ian Stannard instead of me. Initially, as I've pointed out, I didn't like the overly rigid tactics and selection they seemed to be applying, but thought it was better just to accept it and move on. But then they changed their minds after my Tour stage win and said that I was going.

Rather than get too upset, I started to view the race as another opportunity for me to look at the way things were being organized and try to work out if it was the best approach. In the case of the Olympics, I would have liked to have pushed for a number of supported riders in the team, with Adam Yates included rather than it just being Geraint and Froome. You can't be so limiting on what people do and their roles. But that idea was hard to get across, particularly given Froome had just won the Tour; the two key guys in the line-up – Froome and Geraint – were both Sky; so was Ian Stannard, the third team-mate, and so was the GB coach.

In the opposite corner there was just me and Adam Yates, riding with the Australian team Mitchelton-Scott. So at dinner I'd tell him, 'Always say yes if you get an opportunity; don't ride against them. But get in the breaks and act like a policeman so you can think about winning it too.'

As for the road race itself, the initial idea was that Stannard was supposed to be controlling the first segment of the race and I was supposed to be looking after the second. But then his bike broke and I ended up being responsible for both. Because there was no race radio we had to decide on the road what to do and I changed the team's strategy there and then. At the time GB and Sky were so closely connected that they had a clear style of racing, which was pulling on the front and controlling the race and perhaps rightly so given their Tour de France success. However, I think there are more intelligent ways to approaching one-day races, particularly when we didn't have the favourite. Rather than try to control the race all the way through, late on I started driving hard in a way that brought the pack to the foot of the climb at full speed and Geraint used that as a foundation to go for it. It looked like a really good move, and it's fair to argue he could have got a medal or at least fought for one. But as it was he crashed on the downhill section.

From a personal point of view, I didn't get a result, but it was a good performance and looking back I wouldn't change too much. What's more, if you see that a rider like Greg Van Avermaet won the Olympics, maybe under the right circumstances I could have been up there too. It would have been a very long shot, that's for sure, but under the circumstances, in a race that's so difficult to control because you've only got four riders and a leader per nation, the essential lesson is that you have to take a different approach to that of controlling it full stop.

The idea of having one leader and all working for him is something that I support when we have the clear favourite. However, when we don't I prefer to take a different approach and try to pre-empt whatever the other contenders are planning. I think this can work out better for the team providing the ground rules are clearly discussed and defined a long time before the race. If we are as a nation going to try to win big one-day events, I believe this approach can benefit everyone.

*

Fast-forward two years and I was in a team-created predicament that wasn't about a single event like the Olympics, it was about my entire racing season and trade team. I was still trying to find the way ahead in terms of organization and strategy and navigate team politics as best I could.

I looked forward to getting to the Dauphiné and the Tour, even though I suspected there could be some parts of the team that did not want me there. However, after a straightforward start to the Dauphiné, I had an allergy attack similar to one I'd already had in Romandie. I'm sure I could have finished, even if I felt like I was breathing through a straw and was gasping for air, but again, rather than simply soldier on, I wanted to find out why. The team, meanwhile, were simply furious, and suggestions that I only cared about the Tour flew around. I just felt I was being treated as a scapegoat for their bigger issues.

I flew to London to see a specialist, paying out of my own pocket as had been the case for the majority of my career. He was 100 per cent sure I would be fine for the Tour and certainly training in Tuscany proceeded normally for the rest of the month. I was ready to go, but I wasn't selected, for reasons that were never made clear to me. Sure, there had been discussions about my health, but on the medical side of things I felt fine and my training numbers made it clear I was close to top shape.

If there had been some kind of underlying strategy here, I'd have understood that. But for someone, other than a doctor, to say I was not healthy enough to race was ludicrous, particularly when the medical team had said the opposite.

The opinion of some parts of the management was not evidence-based. We didn't have many riders capable of winning stages in the tour, so to leave at home a healthy one who was willing to support the team when required was difficult to understand. Even if I did accept it, it made no sense. And I would go away and try to improve and be better.

Underlying all this, of course, were two issues. First was my struggling in the overly autocratic environment that now dominated in Dimension Data because I wasn't the kind of rider to whom you could say, 'Go here and do this job,' just like that. I needed a lot of work and a long build-up to be good. At the same time, there was my wanting to challenge myself a bit more, do things like go to the Giro. But I was finding that as the team had changed, my opportunities to do that were quickly diminishing.

Before, I'd had a free rein in races, not to do completely what I wanted. From the start of my career, I was more than prepared to work for anybody in the team but it had to make sense and be logical, not just be pissing in the wind or being sold some bullshit. I also needed autonomy, drive and a high level of ownership of where I was heading. Without that I could do as they requested, but I wasn't the same animal. To potentially sacrifice my chances in those circumstances when I knew I could win in a few days, that was fucking difficult. Because in a way I felt I'd earned an opportunity and if I didn't have my opportunity, I'd always be thinking, 'Fucking hell, that was my dream, and you're taking my dream away.' I was never going to be on the line with that halo effect; there would always be that bit missing. That was why it worked so well initially at Dimension Data, but when that freedom of manoeuvre was taken away, it didn't work at all.

So instead of the 2018 Tour de France, I went to the Tour of Austria, a race which runs at the same time. I had a simple mindset: have fun and enjoy spending time with a different group of riders. But I didn't just race for pleasure as my form was at a level similar to when I was winning in World Tour races. I got in a break on stage three where I had made it off the front and was alone with 3 kilometres to go, and had over half a minute's advantage. They wouldn't have caught me, but my gears went into crash mode and I couldn't unblock them. So I got off the bike, furious, and threw it against the wall.

That gesture of mine infuriated the management, particularly because they were having a very poor Tour de France – nobody was even close to winning and then Cav went home after ten days. But there was no chance of me getting any more results in Austria either because on stage four or five a lot of riders went down on a fast descent, including me. I was right at the front of the bunch, but I'd hit a guard rail and went straight to hospital with a suspected broken leg. Fortunately, that wasn't the case, but I had to rest, due to severe bruising, to the point where the bone itself had been affected, and my whole leg had turned black after it had absorbed the shock. Needless to say, I couldn't ride my bike. But at this point, after such a terrible first half to the season and with the team behaving the way they did, my only thought was, 'Fuck this, I've got my family to look after as well.' So we went camping.

*

The team hummed and hawed a lot about sending me to the Vuelta that autumn, but finally the decision was made to send me with a view to me getting in condition for the following year. From my perspective, halfway through 2018, I took a hard look in the mirror and pushed the reset button, started to build for 2019 and began reading too. That was partly as escapism, as I said, partly to learn more about team culture and self-help and partly because, to put it bluntly, I didn't want to hear any bullshit from the team during the Vuelta and reading helped me block it out.

Clearly, something went right because physically my performances, my power output and, for most of the time, my weight was the same as other years. But as 2019 got under way, my motivation in the first half of the season still wasn't great. The senior management team once again lacked any real harmony. And in my own case, I was missing that feeling of having an extra push on the pedals, getting that tunnel vision of focus, the feeling of wanting to jump out of bed in the morning and getting straight down to things.

It didn't help that I broke my collarbone again at the Vuelta al País Vasco. This was – and I hold my hands up and admit this – one of the few crashes that was largely my fault. There was a big stone in the road I didn't see, not for any particular reason, just by chance, and I ran into it, fortunately at 25 kilometres an hour when I was going uphill. I was just glad that nobody else fell off because of me.

But things were OK before the Basque Country, and they picked up notably in a race in Norway where at one point we had the job of defending Eddie's position in the overall classification. But when I rode the Critérium du Dauphiné, the same allergy issue I'd had there the year before cropped up again, only this time it was worsened by stress. It was also symptomatic of how badly things were going with the team that when I quit the race, I was adamant I would do it on my own terms and in my own way.

*

While I've had quite a few issues with senior management in my time, I've always got on really well with the masseurs and mechanics in the squad. Often I'd leave my room and go and talk with them, the normal, grounded people in a team, just so I could have a normal conversation. One of the guys in Dimension Data, Gunther Landrie, was particularly friendly and he understood me well. He said that both he and his daughter had that bit of a free spirit in them too. So rather than do what the team wanted me to do to get home, which was fly all the way to Paris from eastern France and then back down again to Italy, when I told Gunther that I just wanted to get out and away from the race as quickly as possible, he offered to drive me to the bus station in Lyon.

I found myself standing in some dark, dangerous corner of Lyon queuing for the overnight bus to Milan, which cost me all of £12 one way, but then when I got to Italy, there was no room on the train down to Florence. So I jumped over the barriers, got on the train anyway and sat in the bar all the way. By the time I would have been in Paris, I was sitting in Florence railway station eating a brioche. Then I went out on my bike and it felt so good to be there and have got there in my own way. But I still had to handle the rest of the season.

Yet again there was a raging debate within the team over whether I'd be OK for the Tour. Some guys, like Gino Van Oudenhove, our sports director in the Norway race, were scratching their heads because he thought it didn't make sense that I could have been so good there and then so terrible in the Dauphiné. But as I put it to them, there has to be a season for allergies, but when there isn't one, I'm OK, which is why I've never had these issues in the Tour. Even so, I was surprised when the team finally selected me ten days before, which is not ideal for the biggest annual sporting event in the world, and I thought they'd put me in the Vuelta so my weight wasn't where it could have been for July. I was 2 kilos over, which seriously affected my chances. But for all it wasn't ideal, applying the Steve Peters lesson at thirty-eight, I saw it as maybe being my last possible opportunity to ride the Tour, so I had to accept it for what it was, and I also hoped I could improve through it.

As I did improve, it actually led me to think that perhaps I should continue to race for another year, if I could find the right kind of environment. Rather than thinking I wasn't good any more, I came to the conclusion that the engine was still working well and maybe all I needed was some fine-tuning.

The Tour itself though was a mixed bag of experiences as the entire team went down with a sickness bug after about ten days, and I was so ill and empty that there were two stages where I came close to not starting. One day I was sitting in the bathroom at 2 a.m. sweating and vomiting, thinking I wouldn't be able to get to the bus in the morning, never mind start the stage. The management were under pressure as we were struggling for results, but I was determined not to let external influences affect things and try to bring positivity to the group – I might not be in the best shape weight-wise but other riders might be – and not get drawn into being overly disappointed and frustrated if the results didn't come. I get that they wanted a result, but if you want a result, you have to plan meticulously together and believe in what you're doing, not fucking tell a rider he's doing the Tour ten days beforehand and not expect things that aren't realistic. So I managed to finish it. Knowing I might well not be back, and having come to terms with that, I even took some time to

273

look at what the race was and try to appreciate the whole experience of doing it.

Having showed my face at the team's final race party (but only because I felt it was an obligation), we shot off for some more camping, down in southern France. But I had a plan: to rest up, mentally perhaps more than physically, and use what I gained in the Tour to give everything that I could in what I was aware could be my last few races.

The team sent me to the Arctic Race, a multi-day event in Scandinavia where, at long last, my form was steadily improving. I got close to winning on one stage, but they caught me with about 300 metres to go. I was tenth overall, as well as leading the King of the Mountains competition for which I was awarded, of all things, a giant stuffed salmon. By the time I lined up for the Tour of Britain, I felt like I was in the best shape I had been for a good while. I had that feeling of calm which only manifested itself when I felt like I had another, invisible, gear on my bike, so effective that when others seemed to be going flat out I had the time and power to decide what to do. On top of which my weight was good, which is a performance benefit but it's also very much a psychological advantage too.

But then the crash that effectively ended my career left me wondering about what could have been.

*

It almost goes without saying that I wasn't going to re-sign with Dimension Data for 2020, so I had two choices: try to go somewhere else or stop. But while that was a reason to try to do well, in the Tour of Britain, where I finally had the condition, the bike and the motivation I'd been looking for all year, most of all I was trying to do myself justice. I wanted to make the most of it, especially for my family.

The first few stages confirmed what I knew. It was very much a normal bike race, and there were some nervous and chaotic fights for position, which I didn't get overly drawn into. My shape was great and I had the legs to get me to the front when it mattered. I started to feel as I had done when I was doing well, like I always had another gear. To the day I retired, I didn't feel I'd lost any power compared to the best points of my career. It's so hard to measure and it might have been perception or the people I had around me in the team, but I began to feel as if maybe, just maybe, I wasn't recovering quite the same. But then any scientific evidence didn't support that feeling; it was maybe just the people around me saying, 'Ooh, you're getting old.' And you get that as you get older, people saying, 'How long is he going to go on for?' But that's bullshit. Physically, I could have gone on, but mentally I was tired and I sensed my family were close to exhaustion.

Either way, the night before I crashed I didn't sleep well and I was getting quite emotional, because I'd had a lot of messages of support the previous evening. That intensified the next morning, because for the first time since I'd done the Tour of Britain, the stage started in Birkenhead Park on the Wirral where my racing career had begun and the day's racing went all round the area I knew the best. I'd also had an email from the Tour of Britain organizer six months before, saying that they were doing this Wirral stage in the 2019 race and it'd be great if I was there. But actually to be there was so strange and so special, to be on the drive down the A41 in the team bus, going back to my cycling roots in the very same park where I'd begun after the journey I'd had through the sport. I was so grateful for the opportunities I'd had, but it also does go through your mind at times like that, 'What would I have been or done if I hadn't been a bike rider?' I don't think a great deal, to be honest. I'd probably have been in all sorts of trouble... I don't know exactly how you'd define the emotion that I felt, because it was so odd. But there was a lot of emotion in there.

So all my family were there, all the bike riders I knew and all my friends and my parents too, and you could see they were proud. Then when the stage started, we rode past where we live now, we rode past where I used to live, and we rode out along my training roads, every metre of the way. There had been signs and graffiti supporting me everywhere; some friends had been out the night before in a high-vis jacket painting Stevo on all the roads with leftover gloss paint – you can still see it in some places even now. But a kilometre and a half after riding past my family, Perla and her schoolmates on one particular corner, I crashed. Really badly.

Some guys had been fighting for position – it was a bit windy – but there was a crash in front of me and I couldn't react in time. The guy in front of me went down, I rode into his back, went straight over him and landed on my head, really hard.

I got over to my bike and Gino the team director said I should give it a try. But when a crash was really bad, regardless of what it looked like to another person – and I literally didn't have a cut on me this time, my head had taken all the impact – I always knew. My rule of thumb was if I didn't get up and run for my bike straight away, then something was definitely, seriously wrong.

The ambulance guy was trying not to move me, but I got up and lay on the grass, rather than stay lying on the road. Then we went to A & E at the Arrowe Park Hospital, and I remember lying in the ambulance and asking the driver why he wasn't going the quickest way. I knew where I was without looking, even if I had no idea what was happening to my body. The Arrowe Park doctor was insistent, again, that I didn't move at all, and the next day I was transferred to another hospital, Walton.

It turned out I had broken my back, four vertebrae in the upper part of the spine, which is dangerous, because there's always a chance the fractures could increase because of the weight of your head. Yet at first, because the ward specializing in spinal injuries was closed, I had been sent to the brain surgery unit. I was surrounded by people who'd been in hospital for a year, with massive breaches in their heads, and I felt out of place because there were people with way more serious injuries who should have got the doctors' full attention. On top of that, in my mind I was telling myself I was fine (and that's the optimistic part of me) even though I wasn't. So I kept on telling the specialist that if he said I needed three months, six weeks would be more than enough for me as I was a bike rider and bike riders were special!

The brace they put on me regardless was very intrusive, running from my hips to my chin. It was the kind of thing that apart from being very uncomfortable produces an instant stare when people first see it. (I remember going to buy some milk and the lad behind the counter instantly saying, 'Fook, lad, what the fook happened to you?') As soon as I got the neck brace, though, I was up and walking round the ward, talking to all the people I could find and probably pissing them off in the process with my insistence on conversation. By then Cav – and this was a really nice gesture, and typical Cav – had been in touch and through his manager he got me tickets to go to the Liverpool match. There was much humming and hawing among the medical staff over whether I should be allowed out, but eventually I convinced them. I knew it wasn't ideal but I also knew I was sending a clear message to my family, Mum and Nicky that I had to be OK, if I was going to watch a match. So I went in a black cab over to Anfield.

The taxi driver was an Everton fan and was shocked to say the least that I was heading there with a neck brace – or as he put it, 'You're not fooking going to the match? Typical fookin' mad red cunt.' But that was how my Tour of Britain week ended, me sitting at a Liverpool game with my best mate in a neck brace, a bit uncomfortable because we had halfway line seats so I had to turn from my hips as my upper body was fixed in one position, not to mention stand up and stretch at any opportunity I could.

The situation was obviously rubbish because I hadn't managed to show my true form, on my home stage in particular. But after fifteen years as a pro, I'd come to learn that that's life – the beauty isn't in reaching the summit, it's in picking yourself up each time you fall. That said, had I not crashed I'm sure I would have done something, maybe won a stage alone – or died trying to do so.

And in the long term? I was just at that point in my career where it was a question of accept it and move on because there was no point in crying about it. To put it simply, shit happens. So I tried to take it as an opportunity to catch up on my business and sports management studies. I was very serious about that: it got to the point where I plonked the computer on top of a load of shoeboxes and, if I sat up straight and kept my neck in a stable position, and typed with my forearms raised up to face level, it was level with my eyes. I was equally determined to get back on my bike after the brace had finally come off, but I quickly realized I'd have to give it more than just a few days. That was my default reaction, get back on the bike as soon as possible, but this time I couldn't. And that scared me.

Essentially, I started to put it all into perspective and realized how serious an injury it was. The consultant told me that he'd seen patients with similar injuries who were paralysed from the waist down, which could be me if I didn't manage it properly.

It was then that I didn't really care if I continued racing or not, although Spanish team Movistar were briefly one possibility for 2020. Their boss Eusebio Unzué said he loved the way I won but regrettably he'd have to turn me down because of my age. But I wasn't pushing that search forward with huge enthusiasm.

A part of me was thinking, 'You're motivated to go on in the right role, and you could do a team job as well, so give it another year.' But I was ready to stop too. I knew that at some point I was bound to start going off the boil as age kicked in. I was getting fed up with the way I seemed to break one bone or another, something that didn't happen when I fell off when I was younger. It was getting harder and harder for me to have the key element that I needed to succeed, which was consistency, because, at the risk of saying the obvious, a broken bone has far more effects on your racing than a cut on the arm or knee. And after the Tour of Britain, with all the life-changing consequences those broken vertebrae might have had, a part of me was definitely thinking, 'OK, you've had fifteen years as a pro and you've got out all right in the end.'

I was also thinking about my family and what they needed, in terms of finances. One thing we'd always done well was limit our spending during my career, so we had savings and weren't worrying immediately where our income was coming from – which was a huge blessing, because I know some pros don't have that luxury. Ultimately, when it came to weighing up whether to go on for one more year or not, I was just glad that my family were OK.

My dad, Dave, always says that ending my career there on the Wirral, so near to home, closed off the circle in the right way, even if it was with a crash. I don't know if I'd go as far as that, but in a way it made it easier to think that was the way it was meant to be. I was meant to finish at home with my family. Either way, I wasn't the kind of guy who wanted a fuss over retiring. But to be there with my family when my career finished – that was a huge plus, there at the end of it all.

Chapter 15

Bottles, Britain and a New Beginning

P lease, don't come for a bottle. Oh no, I think he is coming for a bottle. He is. A rider was approaching me to take what would likely be his last drink of the stage. To make matters worse, it was a rider I may have upset the previous day: I had put my foot in it, though I still believe my intentions had been spot on and my message had been sound. Tensions run high at the Tour de France, and the tipping point is never far away. With the benefit of hindsight, my timing had been poor – the rider may well have still been angry with me. I could not afford to drop this bottle.

Stage eleven – I was standing at the foot of Mont Ventoux, with no shade, little wind, scorching sun and blazing heat. I'd been there for maybe forty minutes, trying to use my body as shade to keep the drinks cool for when the riders came. I'd done my best. I was concerned about two things: 1. Dropping a bottle with my sweaty hands, and 2. The bottles were probably not as cold as a rider may have liked given the weather and how intense the stage had been, in fact how intense the Tour had been.

'Process Steve, think about the process' – boom, I nailed it – he got the bottle – no sweat (no pun intended) – another one away. All good. I was used to and enjoyed taking account-ability for myself as a rider. Now riders were relying on me to deliver. OK, it was only a bottle. A small task used as an example of how important it is to stay calm and be reliable. The point is that as a member of staff, my worst fear was letting a rider down. If I let that happen, my mind would play tricks on me: 'Oh my God, if so and so doesn't get this bottle, he won't win the Tour, and I will be responsible.' Of course, this wasn't rational, and I knew my responsibility: just get the bottle away.

*

Some years before, I could never have imagined myself working for a cycling team after I'd stopped racing. But the process of doing that actually started before I'd retired. I was with G somewhere after I'd broken my back in the Tour of Britain and we were talking about the Worlds. About a week later he called me and told me to call Fran Millar, who was one of the top management names in Ineos Grenadiers at the time. Fran said she'd been talking to G and he'd said I had explained race tactics very well, and he also talked about how I'd had some other good ideas too. We discussed how I might fit into the team, particularly as I knew I was likely going to retire, but then soon afterwards there were some big changes at Ineos Grenadiers. Fran left, former members of the staff like Rod Ellingworth and Dan Hunt came back in, and it all went quiet for a while until I got a call from Dave Brailsford in November 2020 asking if I wanted to work for the team.

The last part of me coming on board with Ineos Grenadiers all happened quite fast, especially after April 2021 when Covid restrictions were eased and we could travel to races again more easily. My first race with Ineos Grenadiers was the Itzulia Basque Country, or the Vuelta al País Vasco as it was called when I won a stage there back in 2016. 'Just go there, and watch and learn,' had been the instruction. So that took me to the stage one time trial (TT) – I was in the race car following Adam Yates and talking him through the TT on the race radio.

It was a real baptism of fire, although I had a great teacher in Xabi Zandio. Xabi immediately helped me feel better when he shared his experience of his first day as a sports director or DS. Xabi had begun at the Tour of California, where he was driving the second in-race car. On stage one, team rider Danny van Poppel was having a bad day and had been dropped, so Xabi's racing instincts took over and he tried to pace van Poppel back on behind the car. Unfortunately, a commissaire – a race official – saw this and kicked Xabi, the mechanic and the second race car out of the race. Xabi spent the rest of the Tour of California handing out bottles from the side of the road. To me, moments like Xabi laughing about this showed a significant human side to Ineos Grenadiers, a team at times perceived externally as overly robotic, and those moments helped me relax as I started out in the team.

*

I was employed by Ineos Grenadiers as a development sports director (DS) / coach. The role was pretty open because the team wanted me to learn about as many aspects as possible. I was short on experience as a member of staff. But I wanted to enjoy the challenge of learning about the other side of the sport.

I was very grateful for the opportunity to be working with a team of people who had helped revolutionize cycling, including Dave of course, but also trainers like Tim Kerrison who had brought the coaching game to a new level. I knew there were people on my course at university who would have given their right arm to be able to do something like that. In any case, the race programme originally proposed by Ineos Grenadiers was quite different to the programme I had ended up doing. I'd thought that I was going to be very much in the background in my first year, doing races that were possibly less significant for the team. As it was after La Itzulia, I went to the Volta ao Algarve in Portugal, and then to the Tour de Romandie, where G and Richie Porte, two of the team's biggest names, finished first and second overall.

One of the highlights in Romandie came when I followed G in the last time trial. It was quite a technical course, and the conditions weren't ideal – it was raining on and off. G was running second on GC and needed a good ride. And he smashed it. I remember the final 5 kilometres of that time trial best of all. There was a fast technical descent into the town – white lines and manhole covers everywhere. But I could feel the progress: compared to my first day in the race car, where I was much more nervous, at Romandie I could fully concentrate on being as calm as possible.

Romandie stood out not just for the result but also for the experience we had on stage three, at a point where we had the top three riders on GC. Rohan Dennis was leading, G was second and Richie was third, and Dave Brailsford was also at the race, which always keeps us on our toes.

I was driving the team's second in-race car, and Xabi Zandio was driving the team's first in-race car. Everything was calm and the race situation was under control. Suddenly, Xabi's voice came on the staff radio, saying 'Steve, we have a puncture, we need you to come and pick me up.'

No problem – in theory. I drove up as fast as I could and saw race car one stopped, with the team doctor standing in the rain on the side of the road. I stopped, Xabi jumped in and we were off again – no problem. The stage was on a circuit, with two climbs per lap, narrow and quite technical to handle in places – especially in a car. On top of that I was used to driving a Polo at home and I was driving a massive Mercedes, so to me it felt like a tank with a jet-powered engine! But within 5 kilometres of picking Xabi up, disaster had struck. Pssssssst. I had punctured race car two, on a narrow section of road on a climb with riders being dropped and passing by the car as they fell back. I'd clipped the foot of a barrier on the side of the road, and the tyre was completely flat.

Now we had a problem – we've got the first three on GC and two punctured race cars. Luckily, we were on a climb which meant we could keep driving and formulate a plan. We called the Ineos Grenadiers bus driver who was at the finish, around 12 kilometres from where we were, telling him, 'Prepare a spare wheel, we're coming.' During the climb, it was no problem to stay behind the peloton, even if the top was approaching fast. I drove as quickly as I dared. However, we lost contact with the peloton on the downhill so Xabi would hang out of the window, Ace Ventura-style, every so often to check the condition of the tyre. 'Steve, maybe a little more gas.' Bits of rubber started flying off. 'Maybe a little less, Steve...' Finally, I had to slow down and watch the race disappear into the distance. Eventually, we got to the finish and the bus driver changed the wheel as quickly as he could. The tyre was completely destroyed. We were back in the game but by now far behind. Whilst the wheel was being changed, I had checked the map and found a shortcut, cutting out a section of the race. Meanwhile, back in the race, a masseur was following the lead group in a Vito van.

Back in the car, we floored it, taking a shortcut down a narrow farm road, which seemed to take forever given the circumstances. The end of the road was closed and a policeman was there – we talked to him and he moved the barrier. We literally waited one minute and the breakaway passed. Four minutes later the peloton passed, and we jumped back into position behind the commissaire's car. All OK. Twenty minutes later and we passed the place where Xabi had had the initial puncture. The doctor was waiting there, handing out bottles. The poor guy was soaked through from the heavy rainfall, glasses steamed up, and he looked confused. The mechanic had changed the wheel on that car, so I jumped out and into race car one (which became race car two). The doctor jumped in and we were all back to normal (except in different vehicles!).

This incident illustrates the (sometimes extremely) technical side of driving a race car behind the peloton, which

I guess you must learn by watching and doing. However, driving the car is actually only one tiny aspect of being a DS. You could tell that by what happened at the team directors' next performance meeting, I wasn't sure what to expect or how much it would be discussed. But actually, nothing was really said – we gave the staff full credit for how they reacted, and we tried to keep that part of the meeting brief and focused on the riders' performance.

Above all in a DS job, I was learning that effective communication is essential – and the biggest challenge. A DS has to deal with everyone: riders, senior management and staff members. In the Tour, for example, my role was to be in the recon car, the one that drives about 30 kilometres ahead of the riders and feeds back key information that may affect the race. But post-race, every day I had a few riders to talk to, to gather their feedback and provide their thoughts to feed into the tactic for the next day.

Without rider buy-in, it will always be a challenge to deliver the best performance. Emotions can be high at the Tour, and time always seems to be against you. Days are long, with early starts and late meetings, and I would find myself lying awake thinking through the night, writing my thoughts down.

However, I really enjoyed the challenges that we faced. It was exceptional for me to return to the Tour de France as it was the one event I really missed when I retired. For me, the buzz around the Tour is unique. The emotions, good and bad, give it a special meaning. I enjoyed seeing the race from another angle, with a new team and system that had evolved considerably since I left the squad years before.

The obvious highlight for Ineos Grenadiers was seeing Richard Carapaz stand on the final podium, in third place – the first rider from Ecuador ever to do so.

At times, Ineos Grenadiers are victims of their success, having won twelve out of thirty-six Grand Tours in which they have taken part. Most of the riders on the squad were used to being part of successful Grand Tour teams. They had huge expectations and put pressure on themselves to win. Getting Carapaz on to the podium as our stand-out 2021 Tour achievement was perhaps not deemed a success by all, given the previous heights the team had reached. But I think our 2021 Tour was underrated. There were elements of brilliance, Carapaz being the centre of many of those moments. One really good example would be on stage three, which had a chaotic final 10 kilometres down narrow country roads only a car's width in places. But Carapaz was able to harness the strength and experience of the team to stay out of trouble and gain time on most of the main GC rivals.

Eventually, in any case, the GC result was fair. The best rider won and Carapaz – whom I admire as a racer, but also for his humility – was the third best rider in the race. Some of our riders suffered. By their own standards, they did not perform as they'd hoped. Finding the right words at the right time to talk this through with them is a challenge, perhaps an art. Finding the balance between optimism and realism can be complex to communicate in such a pressured environment. But together we have to find it.

*

When I started work with Ineos Grenadiers, I didn't think I would be anywhere near the Tour de France. It wasn't in the plan. Although I enjoyed it and learned a lot, I would have liked to have had a more meaningful impact. For one thing, I had missed the journey many of the riders had been on leading up to the Tour, races like the Dauphiné, Paris–Nice and so on.

One key lesson I learned at the Tour was about the team's overall strategy. Ineos Grenadiers were used to defending a leader's jersey and/or racing with the favourite and/or controlling the race. That meant they were highly experienced and competent at shutting a race down and managing that situation over three weeks. But sometimes, as was the case in the 2021 Tour, suddenly that kind of plan needs to evolve, as the strongest bike rider was no longer in Ineos Grenadiers. That's a process which I could appreciate takes time.

The 2021 Tour de France was intense, and afterwards I was tired. I had been juggling writing this book, a university degree in business and sports management, starting a master's degree in coaching and mentoring, family life and the demands of learning to be a DS.

My final race was the Tour of Britain, a tough race to manage, tactically and logistically. I was second DS to Brett Lancaster, meaning he made the final decisions on the road. I drove the second race car and off the race itself I was in charge of boring stuff such as writing daily plans. These included everything from mealtimes, the times suitcases needed to be transported (most days we changed hotels), distance and times between starts/finishes and hotels, how to organize extra feeds along the route, working out the plan for moving staff from point to point, who is driving what vehicle and to where... It was a seemingly endless list, but that's logistics in any race for any team. For one thing, there are always extra bits that suddenly crop up. Just on the subject of food, say, my tasks involved overseeing the negotiations between several sets of hotel kitchen staff and our chef over whether he was allowed in the kitchen or whether we'd have to resort to Plan B and sort him out an Airbnb to cook our meals if he couldn't. (How far is the Airbnb from the hotel? What kind of Airbnb exactly do we want? and so on and so on.)

Thanks to a great group of staff workers we were able to do a good job. Guys like Carl, the chef there for Ineos Grenadiers, were brilliant at improvising food or handling these delicate kitchen situations. The bit I kept messing up in the Tour of Britain amid my various duties was remembering to pay hotel bills. Time after time I'd be on the bus trying to do something else and the phone would ring and Rod would be asking me who it was. 'Erm, nobody important, Rod!'

Once again, I could appreciate how much the team had moved on since my time at Sky – Ineos Grenadiers' former incarnation as a squad – a decade before. Take the case of food again: when I first joined the squad in 2010, they'd hired a really nice chef from a First Division football team. It turned out he was great at doing a Sunday roast, puddings and hospitality, but he was absolutely out of his depth at doing anything else the team needed. I don't know what Carl's Sunday roasts are like, but I do know he's very good at whipping up a basic rider food like pasta on a hob if need be. And that's what you need.

So many things too, a decade on, show just how much ground there has to be covered for a team like Ineos Grenadiers these days. It's got down to even the most minor of details, like, for example, the pressure to find a good parking space for the team bus on TT days. Factors affecting this decision on a parking space even include the position of the sun, so you're sure the riders will be in the shade when they're warming up on their rollers outside the team bus. Then the ideal distance between the team truck and the bus has been worked out to be three or four metres... No stone, in other words, is left unturned.

For the team time trial (TTT) in the Tour of Britain, we didn't get a designated finish area for all the team vehicles to be there in place for the riders as we'd wanted, and we didn't have quite enough staff to get that sorted out. It wasn't for the lack of trying. I'd started dealing with it all two weeks before, calling up the organizer, asking him where we'd be parked after the TTT. However, it's not just Ineos Grenadiers who are interested in this, and not only in races like the Tour of Britain where we'll chase so hard for exactly the right spot.

In many races a group of teams will ignore the organizers' usual instructions not to get to the parking spots before the permitted opening time. Instead, we all start leaving the hotels fifteen minutes earlier than planned after rumours begin to go off that some rival teams are trying to jump the gun. The stakes get higher and higher, and the teams end up blocking off roads halfway across a city in a mini-traffic jam... Put simply, the lengths we (and other teams) go to to get that best parking spot are intense, so much so that sometimes it brings a smile to my face. But the race itself, the tactics and talking to the riders is what I really enjoy, and that was as true at the Tour of Britain as anywhere else.

Working with Brett on the Tour of Britain was (and is) rewarding; we'd discuss tactical options and he'd check over the daily plans. The peloton at the Tour of Britain had its own race-specific challenges – as each race does – because it was very varied. There were some of the best riders in the world there, including the one who is possibly the current best rider in the world too: Wout van Aert or, as we'd call him, WVA, racing with the Jumbo-Visma squad. Then we also had locally based UK teams who do not have the economic or logistical resources of World Tour teams, meaning media visibility in itself, even without winning, is often deemed a success by them. Further ingredients in the Tour of Britain mix included smaller teams of six riders, constant changes of route direction, variable weather... It all added to the uncertainty and the challenge of controlling the race, although when it comes to the event itself, the sum total of all these variables made for great viewing for the spectators.

On top of all this, Britain often has a lot of transfers, before and after stages, which meant we really had to be organized to maximize rider recovery and we also needed a particularly good vibe on the bus. Riders' morale was critical in a race like this, particularly in events like the mid-race team time trial, which (hopefully) offered a key opportunity to take time out of the other squads.

Once we knew who was racing, I thought WVA could potentially win every stage, and that given there were time bonuses on the finish line, it was going to be quite a challenge tactically to win GC. On the plus side, our Tour of Britain team was strong, ranging from two former world champions, Kwiatkowski and Rohan Dennis, to experienced racers such as Richie Porte and guys with local knowledge like Britain's Owain Doull. Then there were young, up-and-coming racers such as Carlos Rodriguez and one of Ineos Grenadiers' breakthrough talents in 2021, Britain's Ethan Hayter.

Ethan is in his early twenties, and we did not know how he would fare against riders of the calibre of WVA so his initial role was to keep as close contact as he could to the other favourites. Based upon previous results we suspected WVA was faster than Hayter so clearly we would need to gain time somewhere in order to try to win the GC. With that in mind, we aimed to use the other guys to follow and anticipate from a distance if the opportunity was there to go for a win. We would not contribute to the chase if a break got away, as we felt we would help WVA take time bonuses on offer at the end of each stage. But we hoped we could weaken his team, Jumbo-Visma, for the TTT and perhaps, although that's easier said than done, even isolate him. We would make our moves late in the stage, which would give us a better chance of giving Ethan the best run to the line.

Jumbo-Visma had terrible luck and lost two riders in the first two days, meaning stage 3, the TTT, they started two men down. The Grenadiers, on the other hand, won the TTT by seventeen seconds and put Ethan in the lead. The whole experience was deeply satisfying as it really was a collaborative team effort. The team staff had worked long and hard to put everything into place and the execution was spot on. But it had been a long process – refining the strategy had begun weeks earlier with the performance team studying the

TTT in a smaller working group consisting of two DS's and four coaches/sport scientists. The scientists brought the facts (or science) to the table, one big question being the order of the riders in the TTT to ensure it was the most aerodynamic combination. Then together we refined the tactics that we delivered to the riders in the lead-up to the race. At the end of the day, it's about revisiting the basics, providing maximum clarity for the riders and ensuring that the team's performance was as smooth as possible. (If you were wondering, the team bus parking space also worked out as well...)

However, WVA won the next day, stage four, on the uphill finish to the Great Orme, regaining the lead he'd taken early on in the race by just two seconds on Ethan. We didn't panic and stuck to our strategy. If Jumbo-Visma wanted the time bonuses, they would have to ride hard on each stage to keep the breaks in control. Otherwise, we would let the break go to the finish and take the time bonus. Things nudged back towards being in our favour when Ethan took a surprising win on stage five. Jumbo-Visma had controlled the race, and we waited until the finale. Then the boys guided Ethan to the right place, and he was able to take the victory in a wet and chaotic run into Warrington and get back into the top spot overall. Another good day.

Eventually, the deciding phase of the Tour of Britain came down to the last stage of all, into Aberdeen. And unfortunately for us, WVA won the stage, taking the time bonus and moving back into first place ahead of Ethan, this time for good. WVA's final victory margin was only six seconds. At the time, given margins had been so close and how hard we'd fought, it felt like we had lost. But taking a perspective, you realize that the best rider won – he won four stages and towed his team around the TTT. We had done really well to win two stages, and second for Ethan on GC was a fair reflection of the race.

From a personal point of view, I had enjoyed the puzzle of the race, balancing risk versus reward. Whatever the race, the strategy you have needs to be well thought out, it needs to make sense, and critically you need to have the riders' buy-in. If you can create a shared team strategy, in that case, it is easy to adapt on the road if you continue to base tactical decisions around what you've agreed.

*

When I started work with Ineos Grenadiers, it was the beginning of a journey, both for me and the team, of finding out where I could have an impact and help them improve. I have learned a lot while getting to understand how the team works, and to see the sport from a different side has been fascinating. As a rider, particularly when I was younger, I was impatient and at times you could say the desire to perform killed me. I was motivated by being the best version of me. I needed my own opportunity to shine. At times I was disillusioned by team-mates/leaders whom I could not trust. Eventually, when I focused on all the things I could control, was able to take ownership and not be frustrated by external factors, I could enjoy performing optimally.

How does that help me now? Well, I think those traits are transferable. It's true I still have a lot to learn and, like everybody, I have limitations and weaknesses. But I believe my learning now is targeted in the right areas, and generally I enjoy the process.

Writing this book and retiring has forced me to look back on my career in detail, which I've found a kind of therapy and learning experience as well. Of course, I made mistakes, and I wasn't the perfect bike racer that's for sure. Results aside though, I'm proud of the fact that I took ownership; I learned to accept situations that were not fair, and I coped with what was thrown at me and continued to move forward.

So what did I learn? So how did I deal with situations? I'm not saying I did it perfectly or even well, and the list isn't definitive – how could it be? – but I did have coping mechanisms that I picked up along the journey.

In the next section I've tried to summarize and share those coping mechanisms or helpful habits. It's worth noting that some of them intersect.

At times, in any case, when I struggle I find it useful to reflect and remind myself in English or Italian – pull yourself together, man, come on, *mai mollare* – never give up, *andiamo* – get moving. Or as I used to say to myself right at the point when, after doing all the calculations, the preparation and the build-up, I was launching myself into a break: Fuck it. Just go!

Nine Lessons

Fear (of failure)

1. If faced with a challenge or situation that is impossible to resolve, accept it for what it is and move on. Concentrate on the process that drives you towards the outcome.
2. Commit and give 100 per cent in every aspect you have identified in your plan.
3. Accept the circumstances in which you're working. Is perfection realistic? At times you may not be able to produce your best work. However, you can still give your best under those circumstances, and 95 per cent of your best may be enough to get the job done.

Acceptance

1. If faced with a challenge or situation that is impossible to resolve, accept it for what it is and move on. Accept it and move on. You don't have to like it, but at times we have to accept it. The quicker we can reach acceptance, the more time we have to move forward.
2. Search for the positives and find the opportunity.

Resilience/dealing with adversity

1. Accept the problem. Communicate with those who can support you – this may speed up the process.
2. Define what you can control.
3. Focus on the small gains to regain momentum.
4. Overcome challenges through effective collaboration with the right team of people. Evolve – utilize technology and be open to change.
5. Recharge, don't endure – find ways to evolve.

Empowerment

1. Define what motivates you – dream big.
2. Instant gratification rarely applies to achieving our dreams.
3. Be accountable and be responsible for your journey – take ownership of your learning and your performance.

Visualization

1. Disregard – do not engage thought with negative technical and tactical experiences.
2. Focus on the experiences and the examples of when you have done things well. Visualize what motivates you and visualize the smaller steps you need to get there.

Ownership

1. Take absolute ownership.
2. No excuses or complaints.

3. Find the solutions to solve the problem.
4. How do you communicate effectively with team-mates/ colleagues/boss/staff?

Gratitude

1. Adopt an attitude of appreciation.
2. Celebrate the small wins.

Plan/Execute/Review

1. Identify the requirements to achieve your objective. What are the key pillars, the key areas to concentrate on?
2. Understand the how and why. Commit and execute.
3. Review. What went well? What went wrong? How can we improve?
4. Don't get lost in the plan; be flexible. Ensure you do the basics better than the rest.

Leadership/team culture

1. Be credible, i.e. know what you're talking about and if you don't know find out.
2. Be reliable; be consistent.
3. Build relationships. That will help you to be more credible and more reliable, because there will be times when you make mistakes, and you'll get through better if someone's got your back.

Palmarès

STEVE CUMMINGS

Date of Birth: 19 March 1981
Place of birth: Clatterbridge, UK
Turned professional: 2005
Retired: 2019

1999: ROAD – AMATEUR

Eddie Soens, National Junior Road Race

2005: LANDBOUWKREDIET-COLNAGO

Selected Placings:

GP de Villers-Cotterêts: 6th
British National Championships (RR): 2nd
Tour de l'Avenir: Stage 8 – 3rd
World Championships (RR): DNF

2006: LANDBOUWKREDIET-COLNAGO

Selected Placings:

Étoile de Bessèges: Stage 3 – 3rd
Trofeo Laigueglia: 2nd
Commonwealth Games (RR): 4th
British National Championships: 7th
Tour de Luxembourg: Stage 1 – 7th

2007: DISCOVERY CHANNEL

Selected Placings:

Milano–Sanremo: DNF
Ronde van Vlaanderen: DNF
Paris–Roubaix: DNF
Giro d'Italia: 110th
Giro di Lombardia: 97th

2008: BARLOWORLD-BIANCHI

WINS:

Giro della Provincia di Reggio Calabria: Stage 2
Coppa Bernocchi

Selected Placings:

Giro della Provincia di Reggio Calabria: 2nd overall; Stage
   3 – 5th
Volta ao Alentejo: Stage 3 (TT) – 9th
Liège–Bastogne–Liège: 95th
Giro d'Italia: 96th overall; Stage 19 – 4th; Stage 21 (TT) – 8th
Brixia Tour: Stage 1b (TT) – 9th
Tour of Denmark: 2nd overall; Stage 3 – 6th; Stage 5 (TT)
   – 2nd
Olympic Games (RR): DNF
Olympic Games (TT): 11th
Tour of Britain: 2nd overall; Stage 3 – 7th; Stage 4 – 7th
World Championships (TT): 25th
World Championships (RR): DNF
Giro di Lombardia: 73rd

2009: BARLOWORLD-BIANCHI

WINS:

Cape Argus Giro del Capo Challenge (Race 3)

Selected Placings:

Trofeo Laigueglia: 7th
Ronde van Vlaanderen: 76th
Liège–Bastogne–Liège: DNF
Giro della Provincia di Reggio Calabria: 5th
Coppa Bernocchi: 4th
World Championships (RR): 52nd

2010: TEAM SKY

Selected Placings:

Grand Prix d'Ouverture La Marseillaise: 4th
Liège–Bastogne–Liège: 22nd
Giro d'Italia: 55th overall; Stage 17 – 5th
Tour de France: 151st overall
Giro di Lombardia: DNF

2011: TEAM SKY

WINS:

Volta ao Algarve: Stage 3

Selected Placings:

Tour Méditerranéen: 9th overall; Stage 5 – 7th
Liège–Bastogne–Liège: 37th
Tour de Pologne: 9th overall
British National Championships (TT): 2nd
Tour of Britain: 2nd overall
World Championships (RR): DNF
Tour of Beijing: 4th overall; Stage 1 – 5th

2012: BMC RACING TEAM

WINS:

Vuelta a España: Stage 13
Tour of Beijing: Stage 5

Selected Placings:

Tour de France: 95th overall
World Championships (RR): 70th
Giro di Lombardia: DNF

2013: BMC RACING TEAM

Selected Placings:

Liège–Bastogne–Liège: DNF
Giro d'Italia: 149th
USA Pro Challenge: Stage 5 – 4th
World Championships (RR): DNF

2014: BMC RACING TEAM

WINS:

Tour Méditerranéen: overall; Stage 4 (TT)

Selected Placings:

Dubai Tour: 2nd overall; Stage 1 – 2nd
Circuit Cycliste Sarthe: 8th overall; Stage 4 – 7th
Liège–Bastogne–Liège: DNF
Commonwealth Games (TT): 7th
Tour de Pologne: Stage 7 – 3rd
Eneco Tour: Stage 3 (TT) – 6th
Tour Poitou-Charentes: 4th overall; Stage 4 – 4th
Tour of Britain: Stage 5 – 3rd
World Championships (RR): DNF

2015: MTN-QHUBEKA

WINS:

Trofeo Andratx
Tour de France: Stage 14

Selected Placings:

Tirreno–Adriatico: 6th overall; Stage 1 (TT) – 8th; Stage 7
  (TT) – 8th
Settimana Internazionale Coppi e Bartali: Stage 1b (TT) – 3rd
Circuit Cycliste Sarthe: 6th overall; Stage 3 (TT) – 7th; Stage
  4 – 6th
Milano–Sanremo: 157th
Liège–Bastogne–Liège: 26th
Tour de France: 86th overall; Stage 1 (TT) – 10th
Vuelta a España: 102nd overall; Stage 17 (TT) – 9th
World Championships (TT): 14th
World Championships (RR): 31st

2016: TEAM DIMENSION DATA (Formerly MTN-Qhubeka)

WINS:

Tirreno–Adriatico: Stage 4
Vuelta al País Vasco: Stage 3
Critérium du Dauphiné: Stage 7
Tour de France: Stage 7
Tour of Britain: overall

Selected Placings:

Milano–Sanremo: 77th
Liège–Bastogne–Liège: 19th
Tour de France: 140th overall; Stage 13 (TT) – 10th
Olympic Games (RR): DNF

Tour of Britain: Stage 2 – 2nd; Stage 6 – 8th; Stage 7A (TT) – 4th
World Championships (TT): 25th
World Championships (RR): DNF

2017: TEAM DIMENSION DATA

WINS:

British National Championships (TT)
British National Championships (RR)
Giro della Toscana – Memorial Alfredo Martini: Stage 1

Selected Placings:

Tirreno–Adriatico: Stage 1 – 9th; Stage 7 – 4th
Milano–Sanremo: 38th
Tour de France: 141st
Giro di Lombardia: DNF

2018: TEAM DIMENSION DATA

Selected Placings:

Milano–Sanremo: 73rd
Liège–Bastogne–Liège: 82nd
Vuelta a España: 124th overall
Giro di Lombardia: 85th

2019: TEAM DIMENSION DATA

Selected Placings:

Volta ao Algarve: Stage 5 – 5th
Milano–Sanremo: 57th
Hammer Stavanger: Stage 3 – 8th
British National Championships (TT): 3rd
Tour de France: 129th
Arctic Race of Norway: 10th overall

TRACK:

WINS:

<u>2001</u>
National Championships Team Pursuit

<u>2005</u>
World Championships Team Pursuit
National Championships Team Pursuit

<u>2006</u>
Commonwealth Games Team Pursuit
National Championships Team Pursuit

<u>2007</u>
UCI Track World Cup (Sydney): Team Pursuit

Selected Placings:

<u>2004</u>
Olympic Games Team Pursuit: Silver

<u>2006</u>
Commonwealth Games Individual Pursuit: Bronze
World Championships Team Pursuit: Silver

Plate Section: Photography Credits

Page 1 – The countdown to the Olympic team pursuit final, Athens, Greece, 23 August 2004 (Photo by Clive Brunskill / Getty Images)

Page 2 – Landbouwkrediet 2006 (Bettiniphoto); Tuscany 2008 (Andy Jones)

Page 3 – With my mum and dad (Tony Kenwright / *Liverpool Daily Post* and *Echo*); With Sean Yates and my first victory as a pro (Graham Watson)

Page 4 – With Brad (Gary Main); Worlds, Copenhagen 2011 (Graham Watson); Vuelta, 2013 (Tim de Waele / Corbis via Getty Images)

Page 5 – Suffering in the Dolomites (Graham Watson)

Page 6 – Mandela Day, Tour de France, Stage 15, 2015 (AOP. Press / Corbis via Getty Images); Over the Aspin, 2016 (Tim de Waele / Corbis via Getty Images)

Page 7 – Tour de France, 2016 (Graham Watson); Winning the 2017 Road Nationals (Gary Main)

Page 8 – With Mark Cavendish (Mario Stiehl); with Brett Lancaster (Gary Main)

All other featured images courtesy of the author

Acknowledgements

To my Dad, Dave, thank you for encouraging us to participate in sport instead of hanging round street corners. Thank you for working flat out to provide us with many opportunities. Thanks for teaching me to ride a bike. I still remember early trips to bike shops, I loved the smell of bike shops, I still do, happy memories. Up the Reds – love you big fella.

To Nicky, you have ridden every metre with me, thank you for always making it fun, your relentless support and unconditional love. When climbing a mountain, the beauty is not in reaching the summit. The beauty is picking yourself up every time you fall on your way up. You always help me get back up. Perla – keep smiling kid! To the Owens family, my brothers Andy and Gray and their wives and my nieces and nephews, my aunties, our Al, our Nic and Uncle John.

To Jack and Marge McAllister: thank you for lending me my first road bike, your time spent with me and many others, educating us on how to love the bike. Keith and Carol Boardman: always an inspiration on and off the bike – thank you for always answering the phone and providing a place of calm in the often chaotic world of bike racing. Stan, Steve and June Moly: your passion for cycling is unrivalled. To Danny McDonut, Scone Head, ODB and Mark Baker, Steve Lloyd, The Sniper, Jamie 'J-cloth' Murphy, Stevie Light, Citizen

Cain, Mike and Pat Taylor (Don't bother ringing if you're not in the first three.), Mark Bell (the only real training partner I ever had – I miss you mate! x). The entire BNECC, and the rest of the local, nation and international cycling community – thank you for your support, bike-riding connects us all.

Thank you to Terry Dolan and the rest of the Dolan family – you're ace, your kindness continues to blow me away (it's a good job you don't hold your pint like you hold your handlebars. Are my carbon stabilizers ready yet?). To Graham Weigh and the lads at Deeside Cycles, sorry about the bearing that went through the microwave (it wasn't me). Quinny, Dave Parry and the lads at Bike Factory. Pete Woodworth, Chris Boardman, Sean Yates, Brad Wiggins, G, Cav, Luke, Swifty, Yogi, Adam, Pete K, Eddy BH, Songezo Jim, Matt White, Andrew McQuaid and Jamie Barlow.

To Sir Dave, Rod, Shane, Steve Peters, Roger Palfreeman, Simon Jones, Matt Parker, Paul Barratt Gary Beckett, Pete Smith, Johnny Ev's, Ernie, Col, Mark Ingham, Helen M, Alison J, Doug Dailey (thank you for coming to our club room when I was 13 years old – something I have always remembered), and everyone at British Cycling, UK Sport and the BOA. There are too many to mention.

To my Italian teachers and inspiration: Leonardo da Vinci, Max Sciandri, Valentina, Patricia, Danielle, and the kids. Alessandro, Audrey, Giancarlo, Sue, Matteo, Andrea, Alison, Massimo, Zac, Liz, Stefano, Jay and Amy, Nieri, and Gianni (*grazie sempre per aver aggiustato la mia bici mentre aspettavo*), Dario Cioni, Jo. *Tutta la famiglia al Cavallino Roso, 'il fischio'. La tua dedizione e gli standard elevati costanti stupiscono me e molti altri. Ho mangiato spesso da solo nel tuo ristorante, mi hai sempre fatto sentire parte della famiglia. Grazie per aver tagliato la mia bistecca quando non potevo. Emanuele e tutti al centro di riabilitazione di Pisa, grazie per avermi aggiustato ogni volta che mi sono rotto. forse ancora più importante grazie per aver condiviso il sorriso mentre ci preparavamo a tornare.*

To all my professional teams, the *capos*, the riders, and the staff who made me feel welcome. Landbouwkrediet, Discovery Channel, Barloworld, Sky, BMC, MTN/Qhubeka, Dimension Data and Ineos Grenadiers – thank you for the opportunity and support. Special thanks to Brian Smith, Doug Ryder and family, Carol, Anthony Fitzhenry, Jon B, Trev, Marc Paeme, Gunther, Diego, Alice, Elvio, Vincent, Alonso, Santi, Felix, Tex, Klas (my favourite Swede), Matt Rabin, Tiebe, and the support staff – you guys are the essence of pro cycling – thank you for the highest levels of professionalism and the laughs we shared together.

Thank you to the many innovators who are driving our sport forward. I would also like to apologize for all my inevitable errors in the course of my career. Any conflict involving me that occurred was mainly due to my seeking the truth. I accept and deal with conflict, it stimulates responsibility, it generates meaning so you can live in accordance with the truth.

Finally, Ed Faulkner and everyone at Allen & Unwin – thank you for publishing this book! Also James Spackman for all his hard work behind the scenes, Catherine Coley for her excellent editorial feedback early on, and Steve Farrand for his timely help with translations. Dear Alasdair – thank you for listening, writing (often re-writing – sorry dude!), refining and helping me make sense of this crazy adventure. Your dedication to creating this book has been immense, you went above and beyond.

Index

INDEX

315